"*The Innovation Mentality* stands out from the rest by its elegant simplicity to point out the obvious: We are no longer what we used to be. Enterprises that are focused on the past and the present will miss the future. Llopis knows where America's profitable future will be. He has lived it."

—Mike Fernandez, Chairman, MBF Healthcare Partners

"Llopis has identified a winning strategy for 21st century leadership: be forward thinking, embrace diversity of thought, and commit to strategically aligning the needs of your people, consumers and business."

—Robert W. Stone, President and CEO of City of Hope, a Cancer Research and Treatment Institution Dedicated to Innovation in Biomedical Research

"Llopis approaches business issues of diversity, leadership, and innovation from a fresh perspective and has crafted a book that is both inspirational and highly applicable. *The Innovation Mentality* is a must read for anyone who wants to leverage rapid demographic shifts in the workplace and marketplace to achieve personal and professional success."

—Taylor Flake, Vice President, Human Resources Global Groups at PepsiCo

"Our evolution and growth as a business is founded on an unwavering commitment to putting people, customers, and associates at the center of what we do. The six strategies in *The Innovation Mentality* elevate and strengthen our core values by reinforcing the importance of creating environments where authenticity is encouraged and deeply valued."

—Gisel Ruiz, Executive Vice President, International People Division at Walmart

"When it comes to our diverse, multigenerational workforce and customers, leaders have been solving for the wrong things far too long. *The Innovation Mentality* provides the wisdom to solve for the right things and guide companies of any size to seize one of the last remaining true bastions of growth opportunity."

—Fred Diaz, Vice President and General Manager, North America Trucks and Light Commercial Vehicles, Nissan North America, Inc.

"*The Innovation Mentality* clearly identifies how diversity of thought drives people and business to grow and evolve together. Llopis guides organizations to renew and reinvent how they lead to establish competitive advantage in today's fiercely competitive marketplaces."

—David L. Casey, Vice President, Workforce Strategies and Chief Diversity Officer at CVS Health

"We need time-sensitive and people-sensitive leadership strategies to drive growth in more diverse workplaces and marketplaces. Llopis' breakthrough methodology provides that and reminds us that leadership must have intimacy with both the people and the businesses that we lead and serve."

—Jorge Caballero, Senior Tax Partner at Deloitte Tax

"Llopis knows first hand that what moves people's minds and hearts is what moves business. In a world of accelerating and volatile change, any company that ignores the lessons of this book does so at their own peril."

—Robert C. Wolcott, Clinical Professor of Entrepreneurship and Innovation at the Kellogg School of Management at Northwestern University and Cofounder and Executive Director of the Kellogg Innovation Network

"Glenn Llopis tells it like it is: businesses are creating opportunity gaps rather than seizing the right opportunities for growth. This book not only tells us why but also shows how the workplace and marketplace must embrace the courage diversity of thought brings to rebuild an organizations' and leaders' mindset to seize previously unseen strategies for growth."

—Victor Crawford, COO at Aramark

"*The Innovation Mentality* captures exactly what is missing in business today: an investment in people, competency requirements, and an overall mindset that converges workforce and marketplace and places people at the center of our capital management and growth strategies."

—Nik Modi, Managing Director at RBC Capital Markets

"A new set of skills and strategies are required to be successful in the reinvented American economy. Glenn Llopis clearly maps out these strategies and teaches us how to operationalize them in a socially and ethically responsible manner. *The Innovation Mentality* is a must read for anyone looking to create true sustainable opportunity and growth."

—Adlai Wertman, David C. Bohnett Professor of Social Entrepreneurship, Marshall School of Business at University of Southern California

"*The Innovation Mentality* hits all the right notes when it comes to business growth. What makes Llopis' six strategies different is they're profoundly human. Leaders must have the courage to seize the demographic shift and make innovative thinking a core competency. Diversity of thought is a strategic imperative to building the future."

—Stephanie Neuvirth, Vice President, Talent Acquisition at Mars Petcare

THE INNOVATION MENTALITY

six strategies to disrupt the status quo and reinvent the way we work

Entrepreneur PRESS®

Glenn Llopis with Jim Eber

Entrepreneur Press, Publisher
Cover Design: Andrew Welyczko
Production and Composition: Eliot House Productions

Library of Congress Cataloging-in-Publication Data

Names: Llopis, Glenn, author. | Eber, Jim, author.
Title: The innovation mentality: six strategies to disrupt the status quo and reinvent the way we work / Glenn Llopis with Jim Eber.
Description: Irvine : Entrepreneur Press, 2017.
Identifiers: LCCN 2016040449| ISBN 978-1-59918-603-0 (hardback) | ISBN 1-59918-603-9 (hardback)
Subjects: LCSH: Leadership. | Creative ability in business. | Organizational change. | BISAC: BUSINESS & ECONOMICS / Leadership.
Classification: LCC HD57.7 .L5896 2017 | DDC 658.4/063—dc23
LC record available at https://lccn.loc.gov/2016040449

Printed in the United States of America

21 20 19 18 17 10 9 8 7 6 5 4 3 2 1

To my wife, Annette, and my daughter, Annabella Marie. Annabella: Your grandfather, Frank Llopis, will always be my hero but you are my inspiration to stay hungry enough to see, sow, grow, and share opportunities for the advancement of global enterprise and humanity.

CONTENTS

PART II
MASTERING THE SIX CHARACTERISTICS OF THE INNOVATION MENTALITY

ORIGIN STORY

BEYOND DIVERSITY

Long before the world knew the name Fidel Castro, my father, Frank Llopis, came to the U.S. from Cuba to attend high school at the Massanutten Military Academy in Woodstock, Virginia. His letters from his days as a student there are filled with stories of his seeking to understand the customs and cultures of his host country and to connect with the people. Dad was especially good at creating opportunities for others. In one of my favorite letters, he describes taking his passion for photography and turning it into a way to make friends and money. He noticed that many of his classmates enjoyed taking pictures, too, but they all had to walk three miles to develop the film and paid a high price per print. So, my father built a darkroom in his dorm and sold prints to the students for half the price and none of the walking. He soon found himself making lots of memories on paper and fast friendships in life.

Had the technology been available back then, I like to think my father would have given Mark Zuckerberg a run for his money. In fact, like Zuckerberg, my father ended up going in a different direction than the one college pointed him in. He graduated from Cornell University with a degree in chemical engineering in 1940 and returned to Cuba. But after a short stint as an engineer for Colgate-Palmolive-Peet and then running his own vinegar distillery, he decided to pursue his passion for music and became a famous Latin musician, TV, and radio personality in the 1950s. His quartet, Los Llopis, was the first to integrate the youthful beats of American rock 'n' roll and the liquid wail of a steel guitar into the rhythms and sounds of Cuba, originating Cuban crossover music. During this time, at the height of the famed Tropicana Nights, he also met my mother, Jenny, a prominent Cuban dancer and model. They toured together, and he became an international star, performing throughout South America, Latin America, Spain, and Mexico.

It was while my parents were performing in Buenos Aires in the late 1950s that they lost their country to Castro's revolution. Stuck in Argentina with no cash or line of credit, just each other to depend on, my Dad managed the crisis by selling recording contracts everywhere they were known in exchange for cash. Later, they moved to Mexico where my father made several gold records and, by the early 1960s, became one of the country's most popular performers. When political crisis started to brew in Mexico, the lessons my parents learned from their experiences served them well: They anticipated what was about to happen and got out before the political unrest and upheaval, heading north to the U.S. They became American citizens, and Dad played his final concert at the Hollywood Palladium before reinventing himself once again—this time pursuing his collegiate passion for chemical engineering at the Miller Brewing Company. During my teenage years, he was one of three chemists at the company who together formulated Miller Lite. (You can imagine how fun my high school years were!)

For all these stories, reasons, and more, my father is and will always be my hero. So, after I started my business career and found myself facing my own struggles to reconcile the rigid structures of corporate America with who I was, where I came from, and what I wanted from my career, I asked my father how he had successfully navigated his life's journey in the face of tremendous adversity. He shared stories about his immigrant journey and the values that allowed him to make the transition from Cuba to the U.S. These stories and their accompanying wisdom inspired me to look both inside myself and beyond my own career path to understand them on a deeper level. I started researching and discovered common threads that make immigrants masters of opportunity and reinvention, great leaders in the workplace, and devoted family and community members. The stories and my research eventually became the foundation for my first book, *Earning Serendipity* (2009).

Earning Serendipity introduced what I called the "immigrant perspective" on leadership and the four skills of "opportunity management": see, sow, grow, and share (Figure OS.1). These are the skills everyone needs in business and in life to "earn serendipity"—a term I created to represent opportunity mastery, innovation, and the advancement of humanity.

As I saw it then and still do, companies and their leaders who master these skills would create opportunities and good fortune, cultivate innovation, own their marketplaces, and sustain the significance of their successes. They would understand the power of the immigrant perspective for business, personal reinvention, their legacy, the spirit of giving, and the urgency of "Now!" Problem was, most companies and their leaders lacked balanced proficiency in seeing, growing, and sharing. In fact, American businesses had been proficient at only one of these skills since the turn of the 21st century: sowing. And I was concerned. Sowing without balance in the other three skills had created the economic equivalent of a

Seeing with Circular Vision
Search beyond the obvious to diversify opportunities and avoid being blindsided
Sowing Entrepreneurial Seeds
Plant seeds of opportunity in everyday activities
Growing Seeds of Greatest Potential
Recognize the most promising opportunities and give them full attention
Sharing the Harvest
Focus on meeting others' needs to multiply your momentum

Figure OS.1—The Four Skills of Opportunity Management

steamroller in our country—all execution and transaction, little nuance or perspective—and the steam from its overheated engine had created an overinflated economic bubble that was about to burst. But with growth so easy on paper, most companies and their leadership didn't care enough to listen to anyone who called the results into question. Easy-to-obtain lines of credit and paper profits had made many leaders self-satisfied and too lazy to do anything more than sow more of the same seeds—seeds I believed came from the fruit of poisonous trees. They had not only lost their hunger to compete but also forgotten how to innovate by seeing opportunities beyond the obvious to avoid being blindsided and growing more seeds with different potential to have more balanced growth.

Earning Serendipity sought to remedy all that. Unfortunately, when the book came out, the bubble had burst: The U.S. had just entered what would become known as the Great Recession. America's corporations and its leaders were not yet ready, willing, or able to accept the breadth and depth of my book's message. They were too busy scrambling to do anything—fast—just to hang on.

Fortunately, things have changed, albeit slowly. We continue to struggle with the legacy of the Great Recession and the rapid changes to our workplaces, markets, and demographics, but companies and their leaders have become more and more receptive and attuned to the need to earn serendipity and see, sow, grow, and share. They bought my book and its ideas and reached out to understand more about the concepts. "How do we do it?" they asked. "What do we do next to master the four skills of opportunity management and the immigrant perspective to better compete for talent and customers in today's fiercely competitive, fast-moving global marketplaces?" Good questions—ones *Earning Serendipity* did not answer. It showed what people needed to do but not how to do it. To help my clients, my readers, and me evolve to capitalize on the opportunities and leadership requirements the book opened us up to, we needed to understand how to operationalize them.

This set me on a journey to identify opportunity gaps and understand how leaders were closing them with greater speed and agility. So, to move forward, I went back: back to the research; back to the companies I created, worked with, and for; and back to my father and our family's experiences.

And by going back, I "discovered" the answer that was right in front of me: There is a kind of worker who is already wired to survive in difficult, fast-changing times like these, can lead fast-changing organizations, and seeks to find new areas for sustainable growth. A worker who:

- Takes on an entrepreneurial mindset
- Embraces risk as the new normal
- Creates a family environment
- Makes room for passion
- Creates a cultural and generational mosaic
- Does well by doing good

And that's the immigrant.

The Immigrant Perspective

The skills immigrants inherently possess from their pasts and what they have learned through the hard knocks they've experienced on their way here stand them in good stead for facing adversity and earning serendipity. Think about my family: After surviving the fallout from Castro's Cuba, the recessions my parents experienced in the U.S. were cakewalks. That's because they had learned never to get too comfortable with the resources they had. They understood uncertainty and change. They understood the power of their identity as founded in their cultural roots and the need for personal and professional reinvention. They always remembered in good times and in bad what was important, the work they needed to do, and where they came from. Is it any wonder why, according to the Partnership for a New American Economy, many of America's greatest brands—Apple, Google, AT&T, Budweiser, Colgate, eBay, General Electric, IBM, McDonald's—were founded by a first- or second-generation immigrant? Is it any wonder that, according to the National Foundation for

> *Recent immigrants to the U.S. have founded 40 percent of the current Fortune 500 companies and more than half of America's startup companies valued at $1 billion or more.*

American Policy, 44 of the 87 startup companies valued at more than $1 billion in 2015 (i.e., those tracked by *The Wall Street Journal* and Dow Jones VentureSource, like Uber, SpaceX, and Tesla, but yet to become publicly traded) have immigrant founders?

As I widened my scope of research into these and other companies and studied how immigrants not only embrace their cultural roots, heritage, and immigrant values but live them proudly every day and capitalize on them to succeed, I found some common themes: Immigrants approach the global market using a perspective that allowed them to see and seize new opportunities; lead and manage change; never give up; cultivate continuous innovation; promote a spirit of giving; and leave a legacy. I soon realized I had the answer my clients asked for, and I needed. How do you solve for the four skills of opportunity management—see, sow, grow, and share—that define the immigrant perspective? You use the six characteristics that define that perspective:

See

1. The Inspiration to See Opportunity in Everything
2. The Flexibility to Anticipate the Unexpected

Sow

3. The Freedom to Unleash Your Passionate Pursuits

Grow

4. The Room to Live with an Entrepreneurial Spirit

Share

5. The Trust to Work with a Generous Purpose
6. The Respect to Lead to Leave a Legacy

Once I had identified these six characteristics, I developed tools, speeches, ebooks, a proprietary methodology, and curricula to help leaders of businesses of all sizes embrace them and started writing for Forbes.com and *Harvard Business Review* to communicate them to a wide audience. Receptivity and acceptance of my new message was strong across industries and right up the alley of some of the biggest companies in the world as Fortune 100 companies like Walmart, CVS Health, PepsiCo, and Target brought me in to consult. What I did for these companies and their leaders worked *but* revealed a new problem: When they saw (and still see) the words "immigrant" and "Hispanic" in my materials, those companies had classified my work with their leadership and throughout the company as "diversity training," which minimized its long-term transformative power and enterprise-wide impact.

By and large, diversity-training programs are limited. They are most often developed to comply with corporate governance and self-regulation (often under the heading "Corporate Social Responsibility," or CSR) to increase the percentages of certain minorities in the overall employee pool and align them with the population percentage of minority groups in the country. As a result, in most workplaces, diversity-training programs are usually poorly funded tactical inclusion initiatives disconnected from broader, more substantial, and well-funded general leadership training programs—as if diversity and leadership strategies are unrelated. But at most companies, the two are more than disconnected. While many diversity-training programs are well meaning, they are misguided in their approaches and outdated in their ideas. They cater to the status quo. They assume existing and potential employees targeted by these programs must change to fit into the current workplace culture. They ask and answer one question: How can we acquire, train, and change diverse employees for them to succeed and thrive in our culture?

It is clear from my work with leaders and consumer groups, and from personal experience and years of research, that this question and the approach to answering it does nothing to value diverse populations as people—as employees or customers—or what their opinions, ideas, and ideals mean. The question implies that *employees* lack something and need to make it up to succeed and thrive. This also ensures those workers and customers are not feeling valued or finding success, because learning to value all people requires new ways of thinking.

Sure, my programs make companies more sensitive to the needs and differences of Hispanics and other "minority" groups as employees and customers to try to better serve their needs. I see those companies engaged with my senior leadership programs wanting to create more executive roles for these groups and connect with them as employees and customers on a deeper level. But because too many of my programs and others labeled as diversity training are disconnected from larger corporate leadership initiatives and company-wide programs within those hierarchies, companies squander their momentum when the training is over and I am gone. The work thus often stays marginalized within traditional corporate hierarchies. This happens even when companies have what is commonly called a "chief diversity officer" to carry the proverbial torch. If the work of that officer stays disconnected and the most senior leaders never engage that officer's work, then neither the mindsets of that company's broader leadership nor the culture will really change. Long-term success is still an anomaly, not to mention inauthentic. As a result, cultures at those companies are also unknowingly creating more tension with the people the company is trying to reach by answering them when they say, "Hey what about me?" by throwing them a bone (which quite frankly devalues both the person the bone is targeted to *and* the person throwing the bone). Every company wants to perform better in diversity and inclusion, but they are sure not making it easy for themselves when their approach unknowingly creates tension with the very people they are trying to attract.

What do I mean by this? Here is a small, but potent example: Consider the way CNN compartmentalized its questioning in the first 2015 Democratic Presidential Debate. Anderson Cooper, who is white, asked the white candidates every question, with three exceptions. Those three questions were posed by other journalists: Don Lemon, who is black, asked the candidates about "black lives matter"; Dana Bash, a woman, asked a question about family leave; and Juan Carlos Lopez from CNN en Español asked a question about immigrants. The point isn't whether these questions are important to these journalists personally or professionally (I imagine they are), but these were the only questions those other journalists asked. And it pays to note that Cooper, who is openly gay, did *not* ask a question about gay rights or gay marriage to avoid undermining his status as the nondiverse leader. You thought we were beyond this? Clearly not.

This is why diversity programs, even when they bring me in to consult senior executives, can only work to a point: They are about checking a box marked "compliance" rather than taking the first step in a series called "Evolution."

That's why diversity training, corporate social responsibility, employee resource groups (ERGs), and similar initiatives are usually viewed as *cost centers* (expenses) to comply with mandated diversity initiatives, rather than as *profit centers* (investments) to drive influence in the workplace and growth in the marketplace. This is why most chief diversity officers struggle from the margins of most businesses: They are tasked with mollifying groups labeled as "minority" rather than reinventing leadership across the company by incorporating their differences into current power structures and making them a centerpiece of any growth strategy. The result is further marginalization—false inclusion based on dialogues of racial, ethnic, and gender divisions—not alignment and unification under new ways that value individuality and differences across departments, the current powers that be, and everyone else from the middle of the organization on down. This is especially true for those ERGs that sprung up in American businesses during the 1990s. Sometimes called affinity groups, colleague resource groups, or employee networks, I hear all the time from leaders how their ERGs have become more than social clubs for people with disabilities, veterans, LGBT people, women, and "multicultural populations." They pat themselves on the back for the way their ERGs have "evolved" and help with things like recruiting, retention, and marketing. Then I'd meet people who actually *go* to these meetings and hear things like the woman at one Fortune 100 company who told me: "I go back to my desk after ERG meetings, and my manager will say, 'Why are you wasting your time? These things are not helping you. They are hurting you. They don't value the group to begin with. So every time they see you are part of that group and associating yourself with it, then they have more reason *not* to value you.' "

Tell me, how this is evolution?

We Need Evolution, Not Substitution

We need to promote the individual strengths of everyone our businesses touch, but we have to be willing and able to see the value in those strengths first. But we don't; we perpetuate the problems by creating silos for each "diverse" group and celebrate their differences the *wrong way*. If you do not create reciprocation, you cannot create progress, and without progress, there is no evolution. Companies may tell members of these groups that they are unique and different and how much they really want them to engage and invest in the opportunity, but they do not talk about how that connects and contributes to the bottom line, because they do not connect the discussion to their overall growth strategy. As a result, the only real engagement comes from people of diverse backgrounds, while c-suites just cut checks to feign support but don't engage themselves and perpetuate their confirmation bias that all the initiatives are compliance cost centers, not part of real strategies for growth. That, in turn, silos people even more. In other words, instead of evolving to embrace new ideas and mindsets and seeing how businesses are losing talent, market share, shareholder value, and innovation by becoming more diverse, the result is too often more sowing without seeing, not to mention growing and sharing. Just do the work, check the box, and move along. That's what got our country into the mess. *Earning Serendipity* tried to prevent execution and transaction without understanding the need for proficiency in the other three skills of opportunity management and all six characteristics of the immigrant perspective. I have also realized something I said in *Earning Serendipity* is even more essential to understand now:

WITHOUT STRATEGY,

CHANGE IS MERELY SUBSTITUTION,

NOT EVOLUTION.

America may be innovative in many things, but when it comes to understanding the entire marketplace and attracting and retaining "diverse" talent, too many businesses and leaders have stopped reinventing themselves and have instead remained complacent for decades, only to find themselves unprepared for real evolution. Real change requires leaders to understand how they can influence the evolution of their businesses, but much to my surprise, companies—even relatively young high-tech ones, often called the most innovative—have not evolved when it comes to talent because they are trapped in substitutional thinking. They may understand technological innovation, but they don't know how to evolve their thinking. As a result, they simply repackage and repeat the same approaches that have failed in the past and create tactical "diversity and inclusion" initiatives without strategy that fail to generate results.

Just ask Facebook and Google, two of the most dynamic companies in America. According to *The New York Times*, their 2014 efforts to improve workforce diversity using the traditional approaches of diversity programs showed no progress. When Facebook's diversity initiative started, Hispanic employees made up 4 percent of the workforce and black employees 2 percent. At Google, it was 3 percent and 2 percent, respectively. A year later, those numbers were . . . unchanged. That's pretty much reflective of the tech industry as a whole, from Apple down to the smallest startups. This holds true, even at the source of the money in Silicon Valley: The Information's 2015 Future List's analysis of 71 of the area's leading venture capital firms found that only 8 percent of the senior associates were women, fewer than 1 percent were black, and 1.3 percent were Hispanic. And don't think it is any better in traditional media: A 2015 *Publishers Weekly* survey found that 89 percent of the book publishing business remained white, despite efforts to make the industry more diverse. Discouraging and chilling, especially given there are more women than men in the U.S., nonwhite groups are rapidly approaching 50 percent of the U.S. population.

You might think companies like Facebook and Google would get this, because other areas of their businesses are so progressive. But most of them aren't and don't. On the one hand, progressive, growing, respected companies from across Silicon Valley, and indeed any industry, shouldn't have to waste their time attracting top diverse talent; they should have them lining up at the door so they can pick and choose who fits their bills.

On the other hand, if they have to go find these people, they are already recruiting in the wrong way, looking in the same places over and over for the same nondiverse recruits. How do those companies expect those efforts to change the conversation, let alone the numbers? Perhaps an even bigger question: Why do we have to open a new door to these populations in the first place? Why are the candidates not packaging themselves better and seeking these companies out?

There are exceptions, of course, even in Silicon Valley and high-tech companies. Slack, makers of cloud-based collaboration software, became a media darling when it sent four black female engineers to the podium to accept TechCrunch's 2016 award for fastest-growing startup. By Silicon Valley diversity standards, Slack's 2015 employment numbers were exceptional: 4.4 percent black employees, 7.8 percent black engineers, 43 percent female employees, 24 percent female engineers. I applaud Slack for its efforts to put diversity and inclusion at the center of its recruiting—how many businesses could do what Slack did with its engineers or any senior position *at all*? Pinterest won publicity from American Public Media's "Marketplace" for hiring a head of diversity to ensure all job descriptions use inclusive language that does not favor any group. The company also has a rule to interview (not favor) at least one woman and a candidate from an "underrepresented" group for every position. I applaud that too . . . to a point. I don't mind that these companies won attention for their efforts. Good publicity is an excellent recruiting tool, but why should we have to highlight these as exceptions? What happens after the recruiting process at Pinterest? Does diversity and inclusion (i.e., people) stay at the center of the entire business as a strategy for growth or just the pressure to hire more people of color? And do those numbers sound remarkable when you consider the makeup of the country as a whole or even California, where Slack is located and Latinos now outnumber whites? What happens when the culture does not reflect the conversation?

I am *not* saying Pinterest, Slack, and companies like them are not considering these questions. But too often, they aren't: Changes in the conversation are really just re-inscriptions of old diversity templates by another name and repacked affirmative action tactics that benefit few—and slowly. That's substitution, not evolution. That's about compliance not strategic, long-term growth. And it's happening in countless businesses and organizations nationwide. Consider the NFL's "Rooney Rule," which Pinterest cites as inspiration for its efforts. Created in 2002, it is the name for the league's policy that requires teams to interview (not favor) minority candidates for coaching and other senior positions. After some initial success, the league publicly called the results disappointing in 2012. Yet Pinterest chose to reinscribe the Rooney Rule on their efforts. This is not a problem specific to Pinterest, nor am I ascribing any malice to their efforts. I have great hope that its efforts will succeed long term where others have not. But it won't succeed there or at any company that substitutes and complies rather than evolves. Because their approaches are tactical, not strategic, the thinking is incomplete, and thus the initiatives don't go far enough and lack the clarity, understanding, and leadership influence and investment to reflect commitment. The intention is good but the problem goes back to something I ask constantly to organizations and companies I work with: What is the content and thinking around this diversity and inclusion activity? What is the framework? How did you come up with it? What are you solving for? Mostly I get blank stares. Why?

> *Diversity and inclusion initiatives are too often fringe activities focused on compliance, representation, and reputation management, not strategies for growth.*

As we shall see, the goal of diversity and inclusion should be to take a conversation that is divisive and often disheartening and move it from the fringe of the organization to the center so it becomes part of the organization's overall strategy. Put it this way: If you are saying diversity and inclusion initiatives will result in inclusion and diversity, you are already wrong. That's the prevailing mindset, but it shouldn't be just about diversity; it should also be about genuine inclusion and how that inclusion will result in growth for the organization. These initiatives should result in a stronger brand-value proposition. They should result in better serving our clients and all our employees as well as continuing to add value to our industry. What diversity and inclusion should allow us to be is evolutionary in our thinking and be courageous enough to steer away from like-mindedness.

> *What happens when we start to associate ourselves with people who aren't like-minded? Our thinking evolves.*

Simply put, when it comes to diversity, most companies are doing it the same wrong way: They put the way they are already thinking in the way of change—exactly the *opposite* of what made companies like Facebook and Google disruptive and successful in the first place. In other words, they didn't evolve; they substituted. They asked a version of that same question companies have been asking for a generation or more ("How can we acquire, train, and change diverse employees for them to succeed and thrive in our culture?") that devalues people and forces them to assimilate to the status quo. Maybe they don't use those exact words in their questions, but if words are the only difference and the meaning is the same, then that's still change by substitution, not evolution—and will remain that way no matter how much money they commit to their "diversity problem." Google alone has pledged hundreds of millions of dollars for "diversity initiatives." But the initiatives won't go far if Google fails to listen to its own advice once its new employees get in the door. In 2015, Google released an employee survey, called "Project Aristotle," through *The New York Times*. In Charles Duhigg's story, "What Google Learned from Its Quest to Build the Perfect Team," we learn that *all* people on every team just want to speak and be heard: "Project Aristotle is a reminder that when companies try to optimize everything, it's sometimes easy to forget that success is often built on experiences—like emotional interactions and complicated conversations and discussions of who we want to be and how our teammates make us feel—that can't really be optimized."

What companies like Google and Facebook, and indeed any company in any industry, need to do is listen and then have the courage to change the question. What they *should* be asking is, "How do *we* need to think differently and change to make our workplace one that actually embraces diversity in approach, culture, and the opportunity to cultivate new possibilities previously unseen?" *That's a question for a strategy based on evolved thinking.* But how can we do this in the workplace, let alone the marketplace, if we don't even know who, what, or how our diverse employees think, because there is no mandate to understand? Every business has or wants more diverse employees and customers. How do you integrate them, their voices, and their perspectives? You need a fresh mindset to do that.

You're more like-minded than you think. Organizations must embrace diversity of thought to truly discover new ways of doing things and successfully lead through change.

Unfortunately, we're using the wrong words to propel this mindset and move the conversation forward.

Words Get in the Way

Diversity—the word and the concept—is not only unhelpful but also extraordinarily confusing and divisive. There can be no doubt we are already a diverse or multicultural society, yet when it comes to inclusion in business and beyond, talking about diversity typically promotes and results in the exact opposite of inclusion: marginalization and victimization. Along with related words like "alien," "migrant," "refugee," and, indeed, "immigrants" (the very people who made our country and made it great), "diversity" is charged with prejudice and stereotypes. That's why the conversation about diversity has not evolved: It is a dialogue around loud voices of victims who have been stereotyped as a group, rather than focusing on their individual contributions. When we put words (e.g., Hispanic, Millennial, LGBT) in front of people, we think more about the words and less about the people. These words close our minds to embracing how people communicate differently, and we push those people and their differences to the margin, which is why we have those marginalized diversity trainings, corporate social responsibility programs, and ERGs—all of which have good intentions but are inherently flawed. They are not linked to evolution; they are linked to compliance and political correctness and are seemingly "doing the right thing" without much thought about what they are solving for, let alone who they are for, why we are doing it, or if what we are doing is actually right for "them"—or anyone.

As a result, diversity as defined in the workplace and marketplace is solving for the wrong things, and those silos between groups are widening. Here's an example of what I mean by that: A gentleman approached me after a keynote to state proudly that his company now had a "group of acculturated leaders. They have passed their cultural training, and now they are suited to deal with diverse populations."

"Look," I told him. "The intention behind what you are doing is phenomenal, but the fact that you are doing it is *not* good. You're further siloing the environment rather than bringing it closer together. If a person has passed the training, that's great. That person should encourage others to do the same, but we don't need to brand that. What is the value in branding it? All you are doing is creating more division because there are a lot of people who don't believe in this stuff to begin with. They may not tell you that, but they don't." These are acts of poor leadership that are making us weaker every day by enabling further disconnection and marginalization, and it will never end until *everyone* stops judging each other based on misguided stereotypes rather than the value in all our differences.

If leaders are not ready to unleash their diversity of thought to fully embrace the changing face of America, then how will they be prepared to lead effectively and manage change here and in a global marketplace and workplace?

We need to change the conversation and get *beyond diversity*. What we need to do is embrace *diversity of thought. We must all evolve to embrace this idea.*

Diversity of thought is about unification and embracing differences that when further explored support the values that unite us, not the words that divide us. Diversity of thought, not just of population, must touch our businesses and leaders every day and serve as their competitive advantages to stimulate new growth, attract new talent, and generate new marketplace opportunities. Diversity of thought is about inclusivity: Everyone listens to each other and values individual differences enough so everyone contributes and believes they can achieve. Our businesses, indeed our entire economy, should be about *people* first—they are the infrastructure to build on, not just money. That means *all* people, including you, no matter what group you identify with. This is what embracing diversity of thought allows us to do.

And if you think you already have, think again.

If the term "diversity" on any level continues to confuse and alienate leaders, adding the word "thought" can be more confusing, even for those who are inclined to support diverse thinking and yet struggle to say and do the right things. I participated in a leadership summit for a Fortune 50 company focused on building innovative teams. One of the executives mentioned the importance "diversity of thought" plays in developing teams and addressing the changing dynamics of the business, and only one executive in the room of 300 raised his hand and asked, "What does this mean to me? How does this translate to my role as a leader?" Is that because all the other leaders in the room knew the answer? Of course not. He was the only brave enough to ask. Because the answers to that executive's questions are . . . more questions. That's a big part of what diverse thinking forces you to do: Ask different and tougher questions. Asking these questions takes the wisdom to strengthen knowledge through question-asking and the courage to be vulnerable enough to admit you don't know the answers. This lack of wisdom, courage, and vulnerability is why only one leader in that summit asked what others that day and most leaders in boardrooms across the country never do.

Do we have the wisdom to evolve from substitutional thinking? Are we vulnerable enough to be courageous and courageous enough to be vulnerable?

Albert Einstein said that a kind of new thinking is "essential if mankind is to survive and move toward higher levels." But we don't need to be geniuses to implement diverse thinking in business, stay ahead of change, and evolve. We only need those three things seriously lacking and undervalued these days: wisdom, courage, and vulnerability. These three words will follow us throughout our leadership journey—and they will ultimately *define our path toward success and significance in our career and the legacy we leave behind*. We need real leadership that's courageous and wise enough to evolve, take action, and embrace the six characteristics of the innovation mentality. That's what my father did when he united American rock 'n' roll with the rhythm and sounds of Latin music to pioneer a signature crossover sound: He was wise enough to celebrate the value in the strengths of their individual sounds and brave enough to break free from what everyone else was doing to pursue a new direction. In other words, what my dad did as the originator of that crossover sound was reinventing music through diversity of thought, adding flavors no one had ever heard before to compete and grow. As he explained to me, he had been privileged to be educated from high school through college in America and saw the opportunity (the first characteristic of the immigrant perspective) to bring the country's music back to Cuba where it did not exist. He knew he took a risk by engaging with rock 'n' roll music—something that wasn't just different but banned from radio stations—but he also knew it added value in unexpected ways that audiences would appreciate (the second characteristic). As a result, his diversity of thought changed the music industry on a global scale, and his legacy resonates today because he created something sustainable (the sixth characteristic). In fact, my father's music is generating more revenue today than ever before.

That's what happens when you use diversity of thought and apply the six characteristics of the immigrant perspective. They are constructive disruption that breaks us free from old templates to shift and grow, rather than grow more complacent or get too comfortable in what we are doing. We need the courage diversity of thought gives us to rebuild all our businesses, organizations, and institutions on a foundation of shared values that support a cultural and generational mosaic of differences, not a melting pot of manufactured (and inauthentic) assimilation.

> *Be wise, vulnerable, and courageous enough to a shift your mindset from melting pot to mosaic.*

Why vulnerability? That's what a Fortune 10 executive asked me: "Doesn't vulnerability make me look weak? Doesn't it minimize my clout?" Yes, historically, being vulnerable as leader was viewed as a sign of weakness. But in today's business climate, the speed of change forces us as leaders to bring others into the fold much quicker. Let's face it, no one has all the answers—and when we think we do, the marketplace tells us otherwise. Leaders, regardless of hierarchy or rank, must be vulnerable enough to admit they don't always have the right answers and that what got us here won't get us there. Why can't we do this? Because we don't see power in things like transparency. We also don't understand the value in admitting we may not know everything—and how others both inside and outside the organization can help. We see power in resistance not relationships. This is not just a problem in American enterprise but increasingly America as a whole.

Diversity of thought fuels the wisdom to understand this. Are you courageous and wise enough to accept this? Those not afraid to be more vulnerable will take ownership of this mindset and leadership of this new normal. The speed of change in the marketplace requires us to share challenges we wouldn't have in the past and to be more transparent so others don't get blindsided and momentum is not disrupted. As such, being vulnerable is a sign of strength in 21st-century leadership. That's how we learn to see, sow, grow, and share, instead of just sowing and sowing the same seeds, never searching beyond the obvious and breaking free from the status quo. America is transitioning from a knowledge- to a wisdom-based economy. It's no longer just about what you know, but what you do with what you know. In the wisdom-based economy, it's about ethics, trust, empowerment, transparency; it's about opening your mind and valuing differences. When we are vulnerable enough to open our minds to other people's perspectives, we see the need for greater advancement and realize we don't have to be right all the time, just grateful that someone valued us.

As employees, diverse or multicultural populations *want* to use the six characteristics and help their companies evolve. As customers, they *want* to support brands that enable them to evolve and allow them to influence the brand's future. But to start doing this in business, leaders and the organizations they work for first need to stop: Stop blaming others for our problems. Stop fearing the market and other outside factors and adhering to "the way things have always been." Then, start again from the beginning and be wise enough to see the power of the difference that surrounds us, and be courageous and vulnerable enough to let it unite us.

And *anyone* can do this. This book is not about indicting nondiverse leaders; it's not about calling out their past problems and saying they have screwed up so bad, they can't be part of the future. *No one is irrelevant just because they have not embraced all these changes.* The innovation mentality is about a new mindset—for everyone. We all need to act, including diverse employees who have been waiting for change to come to them. We all must step up and start seeing the opportunities and take on an evolution mindset. Right now, most of us are simply substituting, and that simply reinforces homogeneity. Evolving means accelerating our ability to turn around as *people*—from being victims of unexpected change without preparation to enlightened leaders that embrace the six characteristics of the immigrant perspective:

1. The inspiration to see opportunity in everything
2. The flexibility to anticipate the unexpected
3. The freedom to unleash your passionate pursuits
4. The room to live with an entrepreneurial spirit
5. The trust to work with a generous purpose
6. The respect to lead to leave a legacy

We can all embrace these characteristics regardless of how long our families have been in this country or how we got here. Only 13 generations have passed in the U.S. since the Mayflower landed in 1620—13 generations to lose the diversity of thought that America's first immigrants embraced. We just need to be wise enough to understand this. Of course, in the inflamed rhetoric of our increasingly polarized and politicized culture, this wisdom is hardly a virtue. Most leaders are more interested in being right rather than being wise.

Thinking? That's a dirty word. Appreciating difference? Positively not. That's why so many of us, not just politicians and business leaders, surround themselves with people who think exactly like them. Sameness is a virtue, not wisdom—not diversity of thought. That's not making us smarter or wiser in any of our relationships—political, professional, or personal. That's not the path to valuing all people; that's valuing only people like us.

Are you becoming wise and allowing others to become wiser? Are you creating enough distinction to be original or allowing your evolutionary thinking to fuel the wisdom of others?

I get how this happens. Diverse thinking is not easy. If I had any doubts, I only had to look in the mirror. Turns out, I needed to get beyond diversity too. In talking about the six characteristics of the "immigrant perspective" with incredible people at some of the most dynamic and largest companies in the world, a proverbial lightbulb went on: The six characteristics define more than the immigrant perspective. It wasn't just the companies that were getting hung up on words like "immigrant," "minority," and "diversity." *I was too* and failed to really see how they had the power to divide. That realization forced me to rethink more than 25 years of work on the immigrant perspective—25 *years*! First, I had to reconsider the 20 years it took me to write *Earning Serendipity* and understand the four skills of see, sow, grow, and share (ten years for my father to tell me the stories and teach me the principles of my own immigrant values and history, and another 10 years to put perspective into practice so I could design and refine a methodology for teaching others). Then, I had to reassess the following five years it took me to develop the thinking and work around the six characteristics of the immigrant perspective. Trust me, it would have been much easier to turn out this "light" in my head, but I couldn't; the voice of my father was also in my head telling me to keep it on. Before he passed at the age of 97, my father told me, "If you focus on enriching your mind with meaningful knowledge each day, it will continue to grow stronger. If you put it to the test, it will grow wiser." This was the advice I needed to hear to broaden my thinking and have the wisdom and courage to do myself what I was asking of others. And this is where I have landed: The six characteristics of the immigrant perspective go beyond diversity. They are about the power of diverse thinking to create inclusive 21st-century leadership and a new mindset—a paradigm shift back to what we have lost and need to regain in business and in life for renewal, reinvention, and survival.

I call this mindset *the innovation mentality*, and it should serve as the core of any organization's growth strategy.

Think of it this way: The six characteristics of the immigrant perspective are an inversion of the way we typically view the American dream, focusing not only on seizing the opportunities America offers but how immigrant characteristics allow them to see, sow, grow, and share those opportunities to generate growth. The six characteristics are not about merely celebrating differences for the sake of compliance with corporate diversity mandates but about *evolving the way we do business.* The six characteristics of the innovation mentality are about using the power of what makes us different to create something new that impacts the business as a strategy for growth rather than minimizing or trying to assimilate those differences and dismissing them as cost centers for compliance.

The six characteristics are the foundation upon which we see, sow, grow, and share. They break through old templates and guide the ways leaders work and lead:

- They compel us to be vulnerable and give us the wisdom and courage—not to mention toughness, adaptability, patience, passion, and generosity—we need to survive and thrive in the tough, fast-changing terrain of business today.
- They are the path to self-awareness and understanding of the power of our authentic leadership identities and ability to serve people in the workplace and marketplace.
- They support transformation and change management, authenticity and agility, corporate social responsibility and sustainability.
- They are the principles for defining workplace culture, attracting and developing new talent, marketing to and engaging with consumers, and building strategic alliances internally, domestically, and internationally.
- They are a powerful ecosystem that forces us to accept that differences exist everywhere—throughout our companies and beyond—

to better value and connect with our people, customers, and clients, and dominate their marketplaces in the years to come.

How the six characteristics of the innovation mentality do this and how to operationalize and master them to enable leadership and business evolution in the 21st century is what this book is about.

PART I

EMBRACE THE SIX CHARACTERISTICS OF THE INNOVATION MENTALITY

CHAPTER 1

LEARN THE SIX CHARACTERISTICS OF THE INNOVATION MENTALITY

Dr. Ben Carson made waves as a black Republican Presidential candidate in 2015. But the fact that he is a black medical doctor is even more of an anomaly. Only about 5 percent of all doctors in the U.S. are black, while approximately 6 percent of the black population voted for Mitt Romney over Barack Obama in 2012. With Dr. Carson's retirement in 2013, those numbers on the medical side got even worse: According to the Association of American Medical Colleges, 515 black men entered medical school in 2014—27 *fewer* than went to medical school in 1978, the year after Dr. Carson got his medical degree. There can be no doubt that the need for more black male doctors and black doctors overall is profound. Blacks make up more than 13 percent of the American population. Having more doctors who look like you is important, not only for patient health (as numerous studies show all people are more likely to listen to and follow their doctors' directions if they identify and have a cultural affinity with them) but also for getting those patients to trust enough to go to the doctor in the first place. Still, Ivy League and most universities have struggled for decades to find solutions to the problem. Meanwhile, a relatively small institution, Xavier University in New Orleans, did.

See the Opportunities and You Start to Evolve

Never heard of that Xavier? Neither had I until I read a 2015 front-page story by Nikole Hannah-Jones in *The New York Times Magazine.* "A Prescription for More Black Doctors" tells a fascinating tale of the university. Despite having no national name recognition, tuition under $20,000, and a student body of only 3,000, Xavier "consistently produces more black students who apply to and then graduate from medical school than any other institution in the country." This is more than any Ivy League university, state schools ten times its size, or traditional black colleges with more prestigious names. According to Jones, "Xavier is also first in the nation in graduating black students with bachelor's degrees in biology and physics. It is among the top four institutions graduating black pharmacists. It is third in the nation in black graduates who go on to earn doctorates in science and engineering." Yet Xavier has no high-tech science buildings to rival those other institutions. In fact, it has only one small complex. It doesn't even attract the elite black students that the Ivies and other top universities do. In fact, Jones added, "Most of Xavier's students are the first in their families to attend college, and more than half come from lower-income homes."

When asked how all this happened, Dr. Norman C. Francis, the former president of the university who supervised this remarkable rise for nearly half a century replied, "We decided we could do something about it. And what we did, what our faculty did, was just plain common sense." This is not an understatement: Their solution was a system to address students' problems early and direct them toward help early, study groups led by the smartest students who had mastered the material, collaboration by the faculty to coordinate what and how they teach, and a blueprint "to help students navigate every step in the process of becoming desirable medical-school candidates" so students always know what they need to do to get into medical school. Sure sounds like common sense to me.

There can be no doubt that universities can be innovative, but they are also among the most traditional—change does not come easily or quickly to most of them. And while most universities are not-for-profit, they are businesses, and when one breaks free from tradition and template like Xavier it is worth asking: How did Xavier affect its change? They owned who they are and who they serve, and embraced diversity of thought, using the six characteristics of the innovation mentality (shown later in Figure 1.2 on page 10):

1. *Seeing an opportunity* for its students to be premed, despite the hurdles.
2. *Anticipating the unexpected* problems they would face.
3. *Unleashing the passionate pursuits* that all its students can bring to the sciences.
4. *Having an entrepreneurial spirit* to build relationships and maximize resources.
5. *Working with a generous purpose* of having other's best interests at heart.
6. Collaborating to *lead to leave a legacy* that affects the health of not only black Americans but all Americans these future doctors treat.

Here's what also makes Xavier even more extraordinary: Its legacy touches its community (more than half its students come from Louisiana) and has brought a more diverse black population into the medical pipeline. Here's what I mean: Reflecting on the "immigrant perspective" that informed the evolution of my thinking on the innovation mentality, it might not be surprising to hear that many black medical students in America today have more in common with Dale Okorodudu, Oviea Akpotaire, and Jeffrey Okonye. The three men were part of a follow-up story about Xavier on National Public Radio's *Weekend Edition Sunday* about the decline in the number of black male medical students. Akpotaire and Okonye put in long days working with patients at the veterans hospital in south Dallas as fourth-year medical students at the University of Texas Southwestern. Dr. Okorodudu is a third-year pulmonary and critical care fellow there. But as NPR reported, "A desire to care for others isn't the only thing that Okonye, Akpotaire, and Okorodudu have in common. All three have had doctors or nurses in their families. And all three are the children of immigrants from Nigeria. Okorodudu says that means the group of black men who are applying to medical school now is very different from the group in 1978. 'In 1978, those people we're looking at, a lot of them were probably black American males' whose families had been in this country for generations, he says. Today's black medical school students may be more recent immigrants from Nigeria or the Caribbean. 'So if we broke it down that way, that factoid is actually even more alarming.'"

Xavier University bucks this trend by using the six characteristics of the innovation mentality and the four skills of opportunity management—see, sow, grow, and share—to close opportunity gaps by maximizing all black students' potential and strengthening their identities in society. Xavier did more with its people and what it had to strategically activate all its students. In other words, it did what most companies don't do: moved diversity and inclusion to the center of the organization. It saw it as a strategy for growth. It took enough time to define their strategies as the basis for accountability, which is about people first—people who *care* on the deepest level about both the advancement of their careers and the community they serve as they strive to lead to leave a legacy and resow opportunities for themselves and others.

Who does the innovation mentality solve for? People whose differences we must listen to and are wise enough to value to multiply opportunities previously unseen.

And it all started with that first characteristic: seeing opportunity. Knowing this, however, only gets us so far. Problem is, those same people as well as their leaders have been conditioned only to see and be accountable for what others want them to see and be, rather than what they seek. As a rule, *people in the workplace like doing what they are told.* They are most comfortable when they are being told what do to and when they are incentivized to do that and only that. When assigned a task, given a special project, or asked to execute a plan, employees who take direction well will work to get the job done. That's what they are best at: knowing how to execute and deliver immediate, short-term results. That's why most employees, especially diverse ones, are not engaged and are scared to speak up, let alone evolve their thinking, because they see their nondiverse colleagues and leaders have become complacent and stuck in substitution mode. So, they keep sowing, sowing, sowing, and sowing like those around them and forget about seeing, sharing, or growing.

This is not just hyperbole or unsubstantiated generalization. It's based on data from my company's two proven qualitative and quantitative assessments: The "Workplace Serendipity Quiz" (an online quiz taken by more than 500,000 individuals since 2009) and the "Workplace Culture Assessment" my company uses to measure organizations through surveys of their leaders and managers. Taken together, they measure individuals' and organizations' ability to propel innovation and initiative in the four skills of opportunity management and the six characteristics of the innovation mentality:

- *See or Broadened Observation.* To **see** *opportunities* beyond the obvious—see those that others don't in everything, and *anticipate the unexpected* to avoid being blindsided
- *Sow or Extensive Innovation.* To **sow** those opportunities by *unleashing your passionate pursuits,* by taking action and being courageous and sowing the right way, which leads to growing and sharing
- *Grow or Strategic Focus.* To **grow** those opportunities with *an entrepreneurial spirit* and build momentum by remaining strong but adaptable
- *Share or Generous Purpose.* To **share** those opportunities with *a generous purpose* (being able to trust yourself enough to share the momentum you are building with others) and embrace your cultural promise to *leave a legacy* to multiply success and be more significant

The results of the Serendipity Quiz and the Workplace Culture Assessment (you can take the latest version here: http://glennllopisgroup.com/assessment/workplace-culture-assessment.php)—in which an 80 percent score in any of the four skills is proficient and 100 percent is mastery—show the same thing I wrote about in *Earning Serendipity*:

People are most proficient at execution of the work they are assigned to complete but unable to see beyond the obvious opportunities (see Figure 1.1). They lack the required strategic focus and entrepreneurial mindset to multiply the opportunities (grow) for the initial task they are asked to complete (sow). In other words, the workplace has trained and conditioned employees to be doers (sowers) as opposed to thinkers (growers). An execution-minded workplace makes it difficult to see, sow, grow, and share opportunities. It is all about sowing. People think that sowing means you are in survival mode. But survival mode forces you to see, sow, grow, and share. (Immigrants are always in survival mode.) The conclusion: Employers are not training their employees to be better growers to harvest the full potential of opportunities from what they sow, and they are creating execution-minded organizations and leaders as opposed to market-driven organizations and leaders. This explains why organizations forgot to evolve.

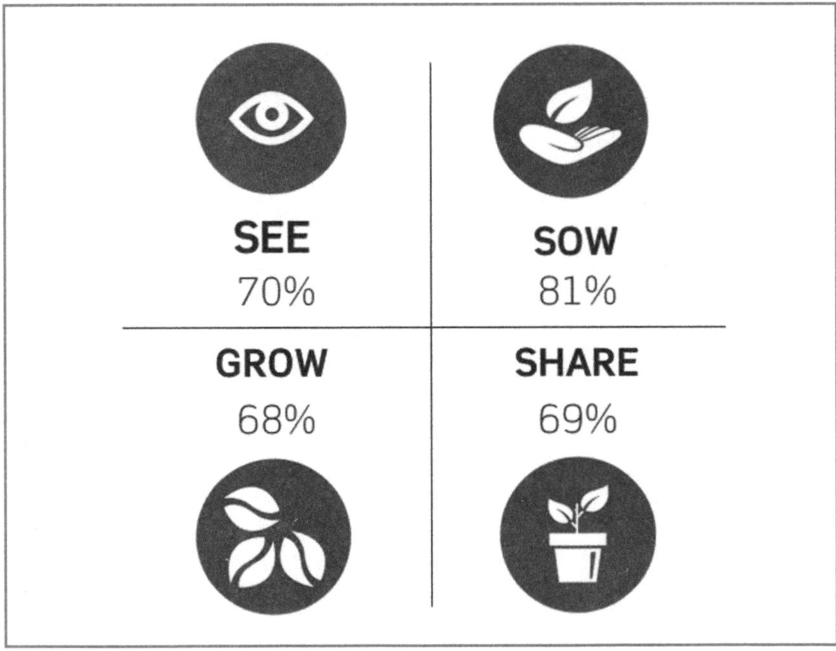

Figure 1.1—The Business Is Owning Us! We Sow, but We Don't See, Grow, or Share

It doesn't matter what industry you are in. These numbers correspond within a few percentage points of the scores generated by the teams at companies as diverse as a multinational food and beverage company (see, 73 percent; sow, 81 percent; grow, 68 percent; share, 70 percent), a global professional services firm (75, 86, 71, 63, respectively), and a national big box retailer (77, 82, 67, 64). None of that surprises me. When clients tell me they are bringing in the best of the best of their client relationship teams to my leadership programs, I always ask, "What does that mean?" They'll tell me how they are bringing in people who have done really well—their personality and attitudes have translated to results, but they don't think they have or know how to reach their full potential. One client even said to me, "We don't even know if they know how they got to that performance level." *What?* That client just told me they are incentivizing people for being the best of the best, but at the same time has no idea why they are the best? That's a fundamental and revealing flaw that is in no way limited to that company. Incentivizing people for being successful but not knowing why they are successful? We do this all the time. In life, we do it in youth sports where everyone gets a trophy for participating. In business, we create incentive programs like that only to incentivize people to *show up and do*—in other words, sow—which is why sowing is the only thing we are moderately good at overall according to those assessments. Diversity be damned if it doesn't help us sell more. If we need to sell to diverse populations, we can hire Hispanics to show up and sell to other Hispanics without understanding or allowing them to connect in ways their market understands. That's inauthentic sowing!

We don't think diversely. We think about diversity, which leads to silos and buckets and not seeing the people we are solving for—including ourselves.

Sowing must be the linchpin between seeing opportunities and then growing and sharing them—and then resowing them.

As disheartening as all this sounds, it also strangely gives me hope, because if people like doing what they are told, let's tell them to do something different like the way Xavier did. Let's get away from the compliance and complacency that compromise our competitive advantage and break free using the six characteristics of the innovation mentality.

The Six Characteristics of the Innovation Mentality

The six characteristics of the innovation mentality (Figure 1.2) help leaders help themselves and the people they manage understand why they are successful, why they don't know what they don't know, and what they need to do to make sure they can self-evaluate that success in the future.

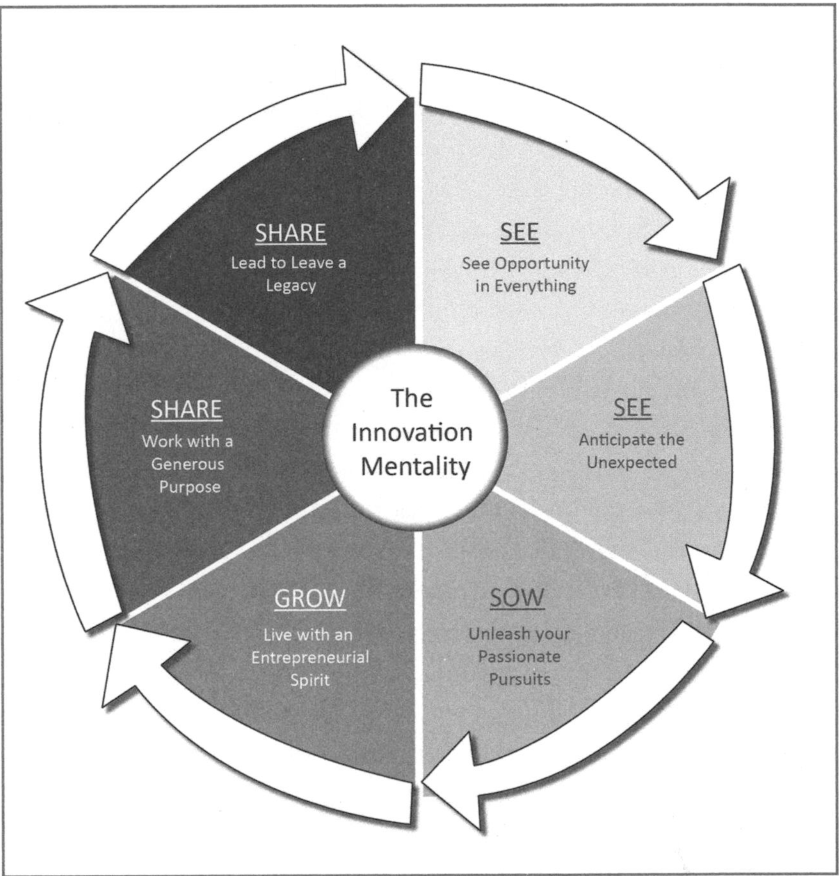

Figure 1.2—The Innovation Mentality Framework

Self-awareness is key. They need to not only see the value in taking calculated risks but also *take them*. They need to trust themselves and focus on opportunities, not just objectives that lead to more sowing without seeing, growing, and sharing.

Here's the simple truth about business today: The old templates for doing things have created gaps in the workplace and marketplace that breed stagnation rather than new roads to opportunities for growth. We need to innovate—to shift our mindsets, reinvent leadership, and sustain growth by unlocking business opportunity in the next decade and beyond. Based on my organization's proven methodology for strengthening corporate cultures, values, and leadership, the best way to do this and stay focused on innovation and remain competitive is to adopt the six characteristics of the innovation mentality.

These characteristics may have grown out of what I call the immigrant perspective—and I may use the word "immigrant" in describing them—but we need to have the wisdom and courage to get beyond words. The innovation mentality is about diversity of thought, not labels or demographics—and its characteristics are how you get there. You also need to see the six characteristics as interconnected. Their impact becomes greater as they build on one another and become a natural part of your leadership and company identity. That said, no situation requires you to use all six skills at once. The idea is to have balanced proficiency in all six to be able to use them appropriately when the situation arises. In Part II, we'll put that into practice. For now, let's do a deeper dive into understanding them.

Characteristic One: See Opportunity in Everything

Leaders need to see that opportunities are everywhere, every day, and that they need to make the most of those that cross their paths. They need to think like immigrants who come to a new country with nothing but faith, hope, and love. There can be no myopia where opportunities are concerned. Opportunities are everywhere, and the immigrant's gaze sees those that others miss. When you are in survival mode—not based on fear but on having to find a way—you have to be inventive. You know there has to be a better way, a different way to grow beyond just throwing money at the problem.

This is what my Dad did when he built his darkroom in his dorm at Massanutten Military Academy. This is what Andrew James Viterbi, an Italian immigrant, did in 1967 when he invented the Viterbi algorithm, an error-correcting code, which has been used widely in cellular phones. He went on to co-found Qualcomm Technologies, Inc. And it's exactly what Pierre Omidyar, an immigrant from France, did when he revolutionized the selling and purchasing of goods by founding eBay, and what propelled the immigrant founders of 44 of the 87 startup companies valued at more than $1 billion in the U.S. These are just a few of the many examples of immigrants who have seized opportunities big and small to create a market *previously unseen.*

But it is not like large established companies cannot seize opportunities to create markets. CVS Health is a 50-plus-year-old Fortune 10 company that has seen opportunity to evolve from retail pharmacy to healthcare provider with clinical services such as those at its MinuteClinics. To get there, CVS Health bucked trends and took a huge loss to invest in its future and reposition itself. "I tell people that CVS Health is one of the oldest startups in America," says Lisa Bisaccia, chief human resources officer for CVS Health. "We have worked diligently to reinvent ourselves to remain relevant in the today's market. This mindset led us to be the first retail pharmacy to remove tobacco from our stores, which accounted for two billion in revenue for the company." Adds David Casey, chief diversity officer for CVS Health, "That decision was crucial to a more expansive future. Tobacco sales are clearly incompatible with being a health-focused company. But it exemplifies how we must not simply react to current consumer demands and what's in our current line of sight, but to think about what an increasingly diverse market will want and need from us before our customers even realize what they want and need from us. Seeing that opportunity requires diverse perspectives around the table who are encouraged and empowered to see the art of the possibility."

Consider what Odilon Almeida, president of the Americas and European Union at the Western Union Corporation, told me: "I hail from São Paulo, Brazil, and live in the U.S. For some, my home country may be considered a remote part of the globe. Immaterial of where you are from, immersing in diverse cultural and personal norms may make it feel that accomplishing a task may sometimes be impossible. However, in my view, impossible is not an absolute, and situations often require more time and a lot of resilience. I have seen people struggle with reality and spend much time and effort to deny it. Denying reality is a loss of time and energy. From my life experience to date—in several countries with distinct and unique cultures—I have found that once you can develop a shared sense of the reality you are approaching, bringing people together to share a journey and a vision can lead to infinite possibilities."

Almeida's words support diversity of thought as a foundation for seeing opportunity and then moving through the remaining five characteristics. You don't need to *be* an immigrant to remember what it is like to have this perspective. In the end, it's not experience but diverse thinking that is the true mother of success. We all come from somewhere, and that is what makes us who we are. Diversity of thought simply allows leaders to be their authentic selves, bringing those unique identities to the forefront to drive that same diversity of thought for their companies to propel initiative and innovation. *That is the kind of diversity that unites rather than divides and promotes evolution over substitution.*

Associated Behaviors and Workplace Characteristics: Seeing Opportunity in Everything

- Visionary/forward-thinking
- Seeing the glass as half full
- Seeing things others don't
- Introducing new ways of doing things
- Hopeful, positive attitude

What Opportunity Gaps Does "See Opportunity in Everything" Solve For?

- Recognizing and closing gaps
- Guiding principles
- Nothing left off or on the table
- Ambiguity

- Broadened perspectives
- Close mindedness

Leaders who are proficient in this characteristic work in a company that provides its people with a high-performance environment to challenge one another to seize opportunities previously unseen. It doesn't restrict new ways of doing things and encourages an optimistic, glass-half-full environment where employees are free to share their ideas and ideals. Leaders in this organization are forward thinking and see with broadened observation to ensure the company maintains a market leadership position. They know how to define high-performance standards and can identify talent that is capable of delivering to those standards. In those workplaces, people have the opportunity to advance in their careers, as the corporate values do not place limitations and restrictions on innovation and initiative.

Ask Yourself

- Does your authentic self and your heritage (who you are and where you come from) influence your business perspective? Are self and business aligned?
- Write down one value that comes from your heritage. Does that value match with who you are and what you do in business? Why or why not?

Ask Your Company

- Do our people believe that work is a place where everyone is given the resources and tools to thrive?
- Are our people challenged to try new ways of doing things in their jobs to improve outcomes?
- Are our clients empowered enough to contribute and be heard? Do our external partners understand our business well enough to help us see previously unseen opportunities?

Characteristic Two: Anticipate the Unexpected

During times of *adversity*, how often does your gut tell you to be courageous and act, and you don't? During times of *prosperity*, how often does your gut tell you to be courageous and act, and you don't? Good times, bad times, it doesn't matter. You wait until those around you begin to take the actions that you were hesitant to take. All leaders need to develop an ability to take calculated risks by seeing around the corners up ahead. Don't wait for permission—seize the opportunity now!

Estée Lauder didn't wait. The child of Hungarian immigrants, she created a family dynasty by proactively managing change in the cosmetics industry. In the post–World War II consumer boom, women began to request samples of Lauder's cosmetic products before buying them. Lauder noticed and responded by taking a risk and giving away some to get more, pioneering two marketing techniques that are commonly used today: the free gift and the gift-with-purchase.

Mike Fernandez, chairman of MBF Healthcare Partners, told me he looks for the same risk-taking in his talent: "The type of individuals who lead are natural risk takers and we encourage them to make mistakes. There is no penalty for making mistakes when you take a calculated risk. There are actually rewards. I remember years ago walking down the hall at one of our companies. I passed an office with the door open. Someone in the desk chair with his back to the door is talking on the phone, and it sounded like *me*. I mean actually like my voice, and he was telling the person on the other end of the line, 'I need the report by Monday, and I don't care what you have to do to get it to me, but I need it by then." He then hangs up and swings around in the chair, sees me, and jumps back. I came to find out he was 19 with a GED, which did not afford him the best opportunities in life, but he had learned to mimic my voice and saw opportunity in that. He would call our data center and pretend he was me to get what we needed from the people there and break the bureaucracy. That man still works for me today. He recently walked away with tens of millions from the sale of one of my companies. So, yes, we encourage mistakes and risk. You can't become risk averse. Risks are necessary companions to opportunity."

Many immigrant families know risk and opportunity go hand in hand through the crisis and change they experienced in their mother countries. As a result, they became proficient at anticipating unexpected outcomes, false promises, and crises. Like my father, they learned to manage change before circumstances forced their hands. I call this "circular vision." Filtering leadership advancement and business opportunities through this lens allows you to put your options into proper perspective with much greater clarity. This circular vision also provides you with a healthy skepticism and prevents you from getting too comfortable, even in times of great success, because someone else is always looking to get the advantage over you. This is not being negative; it is a way of being cautious and strategic and to avoid being blindsided.

Consider what Lou Mercado, the former vice president of inventory management at CVS Health, told me. His role impacted retail, which translated into making decisions for the largest pharmacy chain in the U.S., comprising nearly 8,000 stores and 18 distribution centers, a responsibility in the tens of billions of dollars. What foundation did Mercado draw on for handling these decisions? The immigrant neighborhoods he grew up in: "If you look back at where I came from, growing up in Harlem and Washington Heights, New York, I learned early on that change is inevitable. So it's important to prepare yourself for change, to always be ready for it, and to be extremely flexible when it comes. The needs of customers are always changing and evolving, sometimes on a grand scale. If you don't understand these changes and aren't nimble enough to change with them, you're not going to be successful in the long run." What leaders like Mercado also understand is the need to be nimble in the workplace is a corporate competitive advantage: Encourage not only the people who work for you but people across departments to embrace and value this line of thinking and lead by example.

Associated Behaviors and Workplace Characteristics: Anticipate the Unexpected

- Strategic focus
- Change agent
- Crisis management is second nature
- Adaptable/flexible/instinctive
- Works well under pressure

What Opportunity Gaps Does "Anticipate the Unexpected" Solve For?

- Risk mitigation
- Security shield
- Situational awareness
- Linear thinking
- Minimizing disruption
- Preparedness/readiness

Leaders who are proficient in this characteristic promote strong change-management disciplines in the ways people think, act, and innovate, and support people who are strategic and embrace change, encourage innovation and initiative, and anticipate the unexpected for the betterment of the entire organization. They work in high-performance environments in which people work well together under pressure and can readily adapt to a constant wave of change to stay ahead of the market and the competition. Leaders in these companies embrace risk as the new normal. As a result, those companies can course-correct or reinvent themselves to adapt to the changing needs of its people and clients/customers. In search of the best marketplace talent to support this culture and stay ahead, these companies believe in continuous growth and development.

Ask Yourself

- How often do you practice circular vision, take risks, and think about the unexpected?
- What is one competitive threat that could come from a company that is not currently in your marketplace? (Remember, Kodak was riding high with film and never invested in digital until it was too late, even though one of its own engineers invented the digital camera in 1975.)

Ask Your Company

- Are our people challenged to constantly scan the news and community happenings to find opportunities for themselves and the company to recruit new talent?

- Do the people in our workplace and marketplace believe that our company actively gives back to the communities it embraces?

Characteristic Three: Unleash Your Passionate Pursuits

How many times have you been in a meeting when someone says, "That's a great idea, you should do something with that"? Then what happens? Nothing. Sure, we all recognize that we should act and create strategies for change. Most people just don't trust themselves enough to take the first steps and define their strategies, since this is the basis for accountability. They would rather be held accountable to others' expectations than their own. Simply put, those people lack passion, and passion defines your strategy and propels action.

History has shown many immigrants to be potent pioneers, blazing paths few others would go down, and seeing them through to the end. Immigrants are natural explorers, looking for where they fit and people to understand them. They have a lot of value to bring, but they also look and sound different, so they also strive to blend in without dimming their passionate sense of purpose. As long as that remains consistent and authentic, it will open new doors. Having passionate purpose also allows you to be more open to the passion of others. As one senior executive said to me during one of my executive forums, "I get it, and I won't forget it: This isn't about multicultural populations. It's about all people feeling they do not have a voice." When I hear words like that I am heartened but sad to think about just how much passion has been undermined or driven out of us by the way we work and act. This is why my father would always ask me after speaking with him every day after work, "Did you see possibilities that you didn't even know existed? If not, keep going, son! Keep going!" At first, I didn't understand what he meant, but he kept asking me every day—*every day*. And then I realized it: His goal was to make sure I always took *ownership* of everything I did. He wanted me to own what I did and maximize my influence through those passionate pursuits; he wanted me to be a "natural explorer" for the betterment of a healthier whole.

What did my father mean by this? I found his words echoed in a 2013 study by the Deloitte's Center for the Edge called "Unlocking the Passion of the Explorer." In that study, Deloitte identified three "explorer" attributes: commitment, quest for improvement, and new challenges that push us to new levels of performance and connecting. To do all this, the study said, "Worker passion is essential. Organizations have an opportunity to redesign their work environments to ignite, amplify, and draw out worker passion within all of their workers—from management to the front line. [But many] companies today are structured such that they actively discourage passion. In 20th-century corporations built for scalable efficiency, jobs were well defined and organized to support processes designed to meet plans and forecasts. Workers were trained to protect company information, and any collaboration with those outside the organization was highly monitored or even discouraged. Most innovation was driven from within the company's four walls, often without feedback or customer interaction. In these environments, the Explorer's attributes are threatening."

This is just one of the reasons "passionate pursuits" is the most threatening of the six characteristics to the status quo in business and leadership. Its absence is conspicuous only when people have it, and it threatens their way of doing business. This explains why in the early stages of my career I was made to feel that being a natural explorer wasn't in the organization's best interest. When you don't unleash your passionate pursuits, you stay restricted and confined to the environment you are associated with, which is how you allow the environment (i.e., the business) to control you. Individuality be damned, just do what you are told.

What's wrong with doing what you're told? Nothing at first. "Passionate pursuits" is about sowing, and if you're sowing because someone else told you to do something, then you are striving for excellence in support of your team and the organization; you want to do what you are told, and do it extremely well.

But if you keep sowing without seeing, growing, and sharing, then you operate with linear vision and miss opportunities. You are merely being proficient in what you sow. That's when complacency sets in. Complacency widens opportunity gaps, because your thinking is not evolving enough to begin closing those gaps. How do you shake yourself (and your people) out of complacency? Unleash your and their passionate pursuits and get everyone in exploration mode. When you are in exploration mode, you never stand still or go backwards. You may be moving forward or side to side, but you are sowing in a way that leads to growing and opportunities that drive growth. Sowing is most effective when it enables you to see, grow, and share better, and identify those people around you who can as well. If you're sowing while seeing (using the first two characteristics), you see the wisdom in growing and sharing with those people, and then resowing together as you work with a generous purpose and lead to leave a legacy (the last two characteristics). When you are courageous about sowing this way, activating your own beliefs, pioneering, and ultimately exploring endless possibilities, that exploration moves you from linear to circular vision and living with an entrepreneurial spirit (the next characteristic). That's the key to mastering the right ways to sow: Mastery means you are activating the entire innovation mentality mindset—all six characteristics—with focus and purpose to achieve excellence and influence evolution.

To do this, you have to explore your environment and learn to lead *through* it, then get other leaders to engage so you can ultimately lead through it together. That doesn't just mean the people on your team but anything or anyone your leadership touches. To own this, you have to think and be mindful of others. You also need wisdom—and courage—just like the explorers who first set off around the globe.

As senior partner at Deloitte Tax, Jorge Caballero takes responsibility and has unleashed his passionate pursuits to developing a more inclusive workforce and advancing more diverse leaders into senior leadership roles where they can have more of an impact and greater influence. As the needs of the marketplace rapidly evolve, he has long recognized that diversity of thought is crucial for business growth and evolution, and he works to cultivate authentic relationships built on collaboration and trust. Where many organizations remain fixated on playing a numbers game, Caballero is focused on finding the right talent and maximizing their full potential as the means to grow and compete and remain relevant: "When I was starting out in the 1980s, there was very little value placed on my uniqueness. The conventional wisdom was that you needed to assimilate. You needed to be like everyone else (i.e., the majority). Fast-forward to today, and from the top of the organization on down, there is real recognition of the value in being authentic, in leveraging what makes us unique, not only as it relates to the work of our client service teams but in terms of actually interacting with our clients—and, ultimately, to the continued growth and success of our business."

So, are you taking ownership? Allow your ability to be a "natural explorer" to unleash your passionate pursuit for excellence and impact. Think about what excites you most.

Are you living this every day in your work? Think about those you associate yourself with. Are they supporting and fueling your passionate pursuits? Do you fuel theirs? Are you vulnerable enough to care and open your heart to take action and make a difference for those around you? Is it a one-sided relationship? This is why most people feel stuck in the workplace. We give so much of ourselves to those who don't reciprocate. If your passion doesn't impact others, your influence will be short-lived, and your passionate pursuit will lose its momentum.

Associated Behaviors and Workplace Characteristics: Unleash Your Passionate Pursuits

- Belief
- Courageousness
- Pioneering/trailblazer
- Striving for excellence
- Explorer of endless possibilities

What Opportunity Gaps Does "Passionate Pursuits" Solve For?

- Complacency
- Exploration (adding value)
- Overcoming fear of failure
- Persistence
- Resiliency
- Taking ownership

Leaders who are proficient in this characteristic strive for excellence by believing in individuality. They support what their employees stand for to propel the exploration of endless possibilities. They leverage individual strengths and empower people to be their most authentic selves to ensure that opportunities are seized and then seen through to the end. These leaders are trailblazers, pioneers in search of the next big thing or idea. They are courageous enough to unleash their passionate pursuits to ensure the marketplace doesn't pass them by. They trust themselves enough to be vulnerable, knowing they don't have all the answers and might fail at times. They are wise enough to learn from experience and from others, and encourage their people to do the same so everyone in the company can become potent, passionate pioneers while still supporting the company's mission. In other words, they encourage people to think and explore new frontiers to strengthen their relevancy and importance to others at the company, its leaders, the clients it serves, and its overall core beliefs and values.

Ask Yourself

- What gets me going in the business? What brings me to work every day?
- There are four types of people in business and in life: Leaders, Lifters, Loafers, and Leeches. How do my friends and associates fall into each category? How do I put those people in proper perspective? How do they fuel my passion?

Ask Your Company

- Do we embrace diversity of thought, and are we extremely mindful of leveraging individual strengths?
- Are our employees empowered to bring their whole selves to work every day—their cultures, personal perspectives, and passions? Do they own what they do and strive to explore endless possibilities?

Characteristic Four: Live with an Entrepreneurial Spirit

My father always told me that money divides people, but the wealth created through authentic relationships advances commerce, stimulates society, and benefits all. Your return on investment will thus be measured in the outcomes of those relationships and how they helped you achieve your goals while benefiting those around you. Seizing these opportunities to build relationships that advance commerce and improve humanity is a survival mechanism for many immigrants. This is the logic of chain migration and the glue of new immigrant communities. Leadership development and advancement must be approached with this same hunger for entrepreneurial relationships, because today, entrepreneurship is no longer just a business term; it's a way of life.

You don't need to be an entrepreneur to be entrepreneurial. You just need to cultivate the entrepreneurial mindset: You must continuously invest in yourself to sustain your relevancy. This investment will not be driven by money alone. In fact, it will require you to find the right people who can further guide you and teach you how to invest in yourself. Once again, the immigrant perspective provides guidance. In America, you have a choice to be an entrepreneur. In developing countries, you must be one to survive. Innovation thus becomes second nature. Volatile markets, hyperinflation, constantly changing economic plans, political instability and corruption . . . all many immigrants have had is their core beliefs and the willingness to keep investing in themselves through all the chaos.

I shared this perspective with the President of Colombia, Juan Manuel Santos, and he replied, "I couldn't agree with you more. I call the people of Colombia informal entrepreneurs, and we work to transition them from being informal to formal entrepreneurs so they can become more self-aware of how they can reach their full potential and develop as people. And how collectively as a country we can prosper more rapidly—organically from within—to reinvigorate our economy." And don't think this goes unnoticed even if Colombians are struggling to accept peace: For his efforts to end 50-plus years of civil conflict in Colombia, Santos was awarded the 2016 Nobel Peace Prize.

Sound familiar to what is happening in the U.S. today? We are experiencing the reinvention of our economy—or at least agree it must be reinvented so we can grow and prosper from a greater awareness and strategic use of our own resources? We are coming to the inevitable conclusion that we must all transition from being informal to formal entrepreneurs so we can grow and prosper from a greater awareness and strategic use of our own resources, including one another. Robert C. Wolcott, cofounder and executive director of the Kellogg Innovation

Network (KIN) and a clinical professor of entrepreneurship and innovation at the Kellogg School of Management, Northwestern University, calls this the foundation of "corporate entrepreneurship," which he and Michael J. Lippitz literally wrote the book on (*Grow from Within: Mastering Corporate Entrepreneurship and Innovation*). What does corporate entrepreneurship mean? According to Wolcott, "We define the term as the process by which teams within an established company conceive, foster, launch, and manage a new business that is distinct from the parent company but leverages the parent's assets, market position, capabilities, or other resources. Corporate entrepreneurship is more than just new product development, and it can include innovations in services, channels, brands, and so on. Traditionally, companies have added value through innovations that fit existing business functions and activities. After all, why would they develop opportunities that can't easily be brought to market? Unfortunately, this approach also limits what a company is willing or even able to bring to market. Indeed, the failure to recognize that new products and services can require significantly different business models is often what leads to missed opportunities. Corporate entrepreneurship initiatives seek to overcome such constraints."

Associated Behaviors and Workplace Characteristics: Live with an Entrepreneurial Spirit

- Connecting the dots with focus and purpose
- Effectively using resources
- Valuing relationships/investment in people
- Focus on building momentum
- Always looking to make things better

What Opportunity Gaps Does "Entrepreneurial Spirit" Solve For?

- Aligning expertise
- Breaking down silos
- Eliminating mediocrity
- Growing with people
- Operationalizing change
- Figuring out ways to evolve

Leaders who are proficient in this characteristic embrace an entrepreneurial mindset that reverberates throughout the organization. Sharing of ideas and ideals is encouraged. Innovation and creativity play important roles. People are incentivized to connect the dots in an environment that encourages outside-the-box thinking. Embracing a workplace culture that demands strategic focus encourages employees to unleash their full potential. And it is what allows the organization to grow opportunities that have the greatest potential and helps ensure that marketplace opportunities never pass it by. By valuing relationships, maximizing the utilization of resources, investing in its people, and always looking for ways to improve strategic resource sharing, the business sustains momentum. This defines the essential foundation of having an entrepreneurial mindset.

Ask Yourself

- How can I nurture and develop a relationship that invests in mutual success for the future rather than what I need now?
- What is an entrepreneurial opportunity that is sitting right there in front of me in my area, department, business, organization, and marketplace?

Ask Your Company

- Do we encourage our employees to actively share their ideas and ideals?
- Does our workplace culture value employee relationships and encourage entrepreneurial mindset in their work?
- Do we allow our external partners to play an influential role within our ecosystem?

Characteristic Five: Work with a Generous Purpose

An entrepreneurial spirit does not mean looking out only for yourself. In business, you should trust yourself enough to share your intellectual capital as a strategy for growth through relationships. Seizing opportunities to build relationships, advance commerce, and improve humanity is an inborn survival mechanism for immigrants. But these relationships take time to cultivate and require a commitment to collaboration and giving. It is also in the immigrant's nature to give. In the immigrant populations that my organization researches, children are often raised to consider others' needs as much as their own. This begins with giving inside our family when we are young and then, when we are older, as part of a larger community or "family" around us. Our propensity to give to others from our harvest ensures us a perpetual harvest.

"My joy in helping others comes from my parents," says Mike Fernandez, chairman of MBF Healthcare Partners. "It's another one of the cultural values they instilled in me. We didn't have much growing up, but they were always giving to others, even if it was just their time. No one succeeds on their own. I know what I can do, but I also know my limitations. I know what was driven by the people around me. Gratitude is a great gift, and when you're grateful for what you have and what you've been able to accomplish, you want to give back to those who helped get you there." (Which is why Fernandez not only gives back to his people in the workplace, but he listens to recordings of customer service calls every week.)

People don't share and give back to society in more meaningful and purposeful ways, because they don't trust themselves enough to stand for something that they can share with others unconditionally.

That level of sharing Fernandez talks about in business begins with trust, and trusting yourself to do this first is one of the most critical success factors in your work and career. In *Earning Serendipity*, I wrote, "The wise man forfeits his fortune when he does not trust himself."

Today's brave new workplace must be centered on sharing, standing for something, and making those around you better. It's not just about one's country of origin or identity but knowing how to understand and leverage the distinction of your origin and identity that allow us to solve things better together in a global market environment. It's about collaborating—uniting, empowering, and inspiring those around you to support a societal cause your business can influence. Most organizations refer to this as corporate social responsibility (CSR). Immigrants defined CSR before it was a term. It's about giving and sharing and making those around you better.

I agree that today's leaders must begin to understand that they have an important role to play in CSR and must activate those around them to do the same. But I believe the sharing that comes from working with a generous purpose connects to all individuals in a company as a strategy for business growth and innovation. These are the leaders who intimately know the mechanics involved with each line of business, trends, recent challenges, competitive pressures, and where the growth opportunities exist. They are not afraid to change the conversation as corporate entrepreneurs and constructive disruptors that seek to change paradigms, challenge the status quo, and enhance existing business models and client relationships.

Associated Behaviors and Workplace Characteristics: Work with a Generous Purpose

- Promoting honest and direct feedback
- Trust and transparency
- Promoting the spirit of giving and sharing
- Advancing themselves by serving others
- Having each other's backs

What Opportunity Gaps Does "Generous Purpose" Solve For?

- Cohesion/unity
- Shared beliefs
- Development of people
- Mentorship/sponsorship
- Selfishness
- Leading by example

Leaders who are proficient in this characteristic know the wisdom behind having each other's backs and work in a place where everyone's best interests are taken to heart, regardless of hierarchy or rank. Corporate culture values transparency and promotes honest and direct feedback, and thus empowers people to break down silos and build bridges to strengthen communication, clarity, and understanding. In other words, it promotes the importance of working with a generous purpose where the sharing of knowledge and know-how is encouraged to create competitive advantage by maximizing and leveraging the intellectual capital that lies within the organization, its employees, clients, and external partnerships. Leaders embrace this mindset fully and advance themselves by serving the needs of their people. They are genuine about making their employees feel valued and their clients appreciated, because they see it as not only the right thing to do but also a competitive advantage. In today's world of work, everyone's perspectives should be valued, especially when you consider the complexities of the workplace and marketplace. Be grateful, respect others' unique points of views, and allow them to see opportunities previously unseen. By being mindful of the needs of those they serve and associate with, the entire company brings people closer together and builds an ecosystem of continuous prosperity.

Ask Yourself

- What do I stand for? How many of my friends, colleagues, co-workers, customers, and clients know what I stand for? Can they articulate it in three words? Can *I*?
- How do I give back? How could I share my expertise beyond my everyday work?

Ask Your Company

- Do our people, customers/clients, and external partners believe that our company promotes sharing among and giving back to our people—and the communities and causes they and the company embrace?
- Are our employees and leaders encouraged to work as volunteers in the community in addition to their paid work?

Characteristic Six: Lead to Leave a Legacy

According to a Harvard Business School study, family firms are often able to take longer-term, more strategic approaches and keep stronger relationships with their customers. In fact, family-controlled firms outperformed their public peers by 6 percent on company market value, and one-third of all companies in the S&P 500 index are run by families. You don't need a family business, however, to succeed on this level. You just need to treat people like they are family. Some of the strongest bonds in business, across the entire value chain, occur when employees, partners, and clients alike are treated like family. If legacy is the establishment of traditions that can be passed on to future generations, the family business is a good model. They have an intimate approach to their business, and they have taken time to understand it.

Sadly, too many leaders have forgotten what this means. Our cultural promise is driven by our ability to have a generous purpose and defines our "significance factor." Wisdom teaches us not to seek recognition alone but to primarily seek respect, which is more lasting than recognition. This goes back to a theme I discussed in *Earning Serendipity:* Leaders who do not desire to be significant are solely in search of recognition; leaders who desire to be significant are in search of respect. *Recognition* explodes and subsides. *Respect* reverberates and multiplies. There's nothing wrong with recognition, but too many people have become recognition addicts. The recognized person appeals to the head where things are easily forgotten. The respected person appeals to the heart—and the heart doesn't forget. We must value respect before recognition. Leaders cultivate wisdom in others when they genuinely respect differences and those who disrupt the status quo for the betterment of a healthier whole.

The innovation mentality must be focused on respect to lead to leave a legacy. Again, I can't think of a better story from a person to explain what this means than Mike Fernandez. Fernandez was a penniless immigrant who became a business mogul in health care as well as a philanthropist, who is well connected in his industry, leadership circles, and politics. He commands an audience. But he doesn't hesitate to remind other leaders, especially nondiverse ones, the perils and pitfalls of lacking respect for those people and communities who don't look or think like you. Fernandez says, "I told a bunch of attorneys general, mostly Republican, who were sitting with me in my home: 'Think of people who picked cotton, picked tomatoes, packed fruits, cleaned hotel rooms, cleaned animal cages. I know a person who cleaned animal cages all through high school. I know that person went through a very difficult time and got a job making $500 a month when he got out of the Army. That person? You happen to be sitting in his home today.' Don't assume that as we are picking tomatoes that this is where we are going to stay. If you don't change your mindset and the way you treat the rest of us, your days are numbered."

Remember, Sam Walton not only wanted to shake the janitor's hands at every store he visited, but the janitor wanted to shake *his*. Or consider another great American brand: Hershey's. Milton Hershey lived the six characteristics and broke all the molds of the American food industry to leave a lasting legacy that the company is now working to resow as it tries to become a global player in the business, not just a North American player. Change for them begins with simply heeding their founder's number-one lesson: "One is only happy in proportion as he makes others feel happy. And only useful as he contributes his influences for the finer callings in life." Hershey was famous for authentically caring about everyone his company touched, including his community. That community may have been a company town, but he felt morally, not just economically, attached to it. So he made the company feel like the moral pillar of the day: home.

When you take the trolley ride at Hershey's Chocolate World and learn about the history of the man behind the company and the chocolate, this story comes through in every image from his work with disadvantaged children in creating the Milton S. Hershey School to the creation of the Milton S. Hershey Medical Center at Pennsylvania State University. In short, he saw no difference between good business sense and genuine care for employees, customers, and the community. That was his legacy. You still feel that legacy today in the wonderful people I met as they wrestled with the questions I asked that connect directly to that legacy: What does Hershey solve for? What do people and American enterprise expect from Hershey's? The answer goes way beyond the quality and service behind its products. That answer is not strong enough, because that's what people have been expecting from Hershey for years. I suggested they take the tour, because Hershey solves for exactly what their founder left: helping leaders live and understand what "lead to leave a legacy" means. It is an embedded part of what Hershey's represents.

Hershey, like Sam Walton at Walmart and the founders of many successful companies that survive in America, used the innovation mentality. They saw the wisdom in magnifying the harvest of the seeds they had sown and used it to guide their thinking, mindset, and overall attitude. In other words, they understood the power of resowing success to create significance—a core component of leading to leave a legacy. The most prominent example of that today is Apple, which went from iMac to iPod to iTunes to iPhone to iPad and beyond, resowing its successes into more significance—and growth. Every new product strengthened the foundation of what got them there and integrated the power of the individual—from its leader right down to the customers—to fuel their innovation mentality. Is some of that resowing based on simply repurposing or reimagining a product they had done successfully? Yes, but Apple did so while seeing opportunities to build on those successes. Each introduction and launch was about seeing things better, anticipating the future, and identifying opportunities with the greatest potential, as well as continually exploring, sharing, and resowing them to build not just success but significance by sustaining and growing the power of the brand *and increased intimacy with the individual.* Companies and people who resow this way evolve their legacies. Those who remain stuck in substitution mode? They also stay in sow mode. That's what happened to Kodak with film or Blackberry. They get stuck in substitution and lose control of their legacies.

> *Leaders and companies who get stuck in substitution mode lose control of their legacies.*

In a time of tremendous change in America it is of utmost importance that all companies begin to reacquaint themselves with their own individual legacies. Turns out, this is what Hershey's was already talking about: How do we communicate internally and externally about how we should be doing things differently as a global player and better leverage the assets of the organization? That's a great start for a company that feels challenged as it spreads its partnerships outside of Hershey, Pennsylvania, and feels they are losing touch with the legacy of their founder.

But legacies are not defined by locations. Leaders define legacies. Allow your leaders to lead and be held accountable not to a job description but for the expertise they bring to the table and the legacy they will renew, reinvent, and refresh as it relates to the current culture under which everyone is operating. Let them ask, "What is my purpose? What am I here for?" and then create that within the constituency they are engaging. Leaders have a responsibility to uphold the heritage and traditions of those that came before them. But equally they must hold themselves accountable to build on those traditions to further strengthen the culture, human capital, and brands of the organizations they serve. You have to build on the strong traditions and not get stuck in the past without evolving. Ensuring the long-term sustainability of a company involves embracing change and evolution but not just any change. It has to be authentic and personal.

That's how leaders and businesses will ultimately make the decision to deliver on their cultural promise to support workplace cultures and the marketplace—their entire ecosystem—in everything they do and how they act. Think about this carefully. Your promise to your people, customers, clients, and external partners should be centered on being a community-minded leader that is not only accountable for the advancement of yourself but also for the well-being and advancement of those around you.

Consider what Hamdi Ulukaya, the CEO of Chobani, did for 2,000 of his employees that could make them millionaires. According to *USA Today*, "Ulukaya told the company's 2,000 full-time employees at its upstate New York plant [that] they'll receive shares worth up to 10 percent of the company's value when it goes public or is sold. 'This isn't a gift,' Ulukaya said in a letter to employees. 'It's a mutual promise to work together with a shared purpose and responsibility. To continue to create something special and of lasting value.'" And who is Ulukaya? A Kurdish Muslim and immigrant from Turkey who has courageously urged businesses to hire more foreign refugees and welcomed those the federal government has sent to his plant in Twin Falls, Idaho (the world's largest yogurt factory), in spite of the political climate and local protests.

Ulukaya knows what we all should: Wholeness in work and life is what leading to leave a legacy stands for—the cultural promise that continuously propels a sustainable workplace and encourages innovation for the advancement of a healthier whole. This should be your legacy.

Associated Behaviors and Workplace Characteristics: Lead to Leave a Legacy

- Significance over success
- Treating others like family/cultural promise
- Sustainability/resowing
- Respect before recognition/reciprocity
- Protecting what others stand for

What Opportunity Gaps Does "Leave a Legacy" Solve For?

- Fragmentation
- Great teams
- Sustainable growth
- Building a great culture
- Culture inefficiency
- Embracing one's ideals

Leaders who are proficient in this characteristic are wise about the future, and their companies' core values are rooted in the belief that success comes to those who are surrounded by people who want their success to continue. Thus, the workplace promotes a team-first mentality and treats its employees, clients, and partners like family. It is an environment where people are treated with respect, integrity, and dignity, because the entire business is mindful of protecting everyone *and* everything: people, products, services, and brands. In other words, leaders are focused on the sustainability of the organization's success. They have a deep desire to protect and strengthen the legacy of the brand and its promises and are intentional about investing in helping their employees reach levels of performance and significance through their contributions in the workplace and the industry they serve.

Ask Yourself

- What is your cultural promise? Have you created a culture that people thrive in?
- What is the legacy that your promise has created for those around you?

Ask Your Company

- Do our employees feel that the workplace is an environment where everyone treats one another like family? Do our customers, clients, and partners feel that we treat each other this way? Do they treat each other this way?
- Do our employees believe that their jobs are not just jobs—they are opportunities to shape their legacies? Do our customers, clients, and partners know that we believe this? Do they have the same belief?

Remember, legacy is not about what you can achieve in the present and immediate future but how much are we willing to do some real sharing. We may not see the results of our efforts while we are still living, let alone leading. But we must start and be motivated to do so. Because in the end, successful leaders love being leaders not for the sake of power but for the meaningful and purposeful impact they can create. When you have reached a senior level of leadership, this impact is about your ability to serve others and can't be accomplished unless you genuinely enjoy what you do. The six characteristics play to both sides of this equation: your enjoyment and success and the enjoyment and success of others.

If you are thinking all this is obvious, well, it is.

Common Sense Is Not Easy

The six characteristics of the innovation mentality are like many great ideas: deceptively simple. That's the point: They awaken you to new opportunities and possibilities through the simplest language that can be applied to all aspects of leadership. For example, the most popular article I ever wrote for Forbes.com was on the 15 things leaders must do automatically, every day, to be successful in the workplace. These 15 things ultimately allow leaders to increase the value of their organization's brand, while at the same time minimize the operating risk profile. They serve as the enablers of talent, culture, and results:

1. Make others feel safe to speak up.
2. Make decisions.
3. Communicate expectations.
4. Challenge people to think.

5. Be accountable to others.
6. Lead by example.
7. Measure and reward performance.
8. Provide continuous feedback.
9. Properly allocate and deploy talent
10. Ask questions and seek counsel.
11. Problem solve and avoid procrastination.
12. Have positive energy and attitude.
13. Be a great teacher.
14. Invest in relationships.
15. Genuinely enjoy responsibilities.

Millions of people read, responded, and shared this post. Why? Certainly not because the list is so groundbreaking. Do these 15 things sound new, counterintuitive, or complex? Of course not. Like the six characteristics, they are simple to say and clear in their direction for how we connect with, market, impact, and influence all people. We can't do these things most effectively and consistently unless we can maximize the potential of everything our leadership touches/influences. In an execution-oriented environment, how is this possible? I'll let you in on a little secret that might help: Every one of these 15 things is drawn from and connected to the six characteristics, like the following, for example:

- Measure and reward performance: See opportunity in everything.
- Ask questions and seek counsel: Anticipate the unexpected.
- Properly allocate and deploy talent: Unleash your passionate pursuits.
- Invest in relationships: Live with an entrepreneurial spirit.
- Provide continuous feedback: Work with a generous purpose.
- Lead by example: Lead to leave a legacy.

Can you figure out the rest? While you think about it, realize this connection to the six characteristics extends to the work most companies aspire to every day, such as serving customers (anticipate the unexpected and work with a generous purpose) or striving for excellence (live with an entrepreneurial spirit). That's the common sense behind the six characteristics; they apply and are adaptable to all aspects of business and leadership, as well as being simple to grasp and eminently memorizeable.

So, now that you have done a deeper dive into each characteristic, go back through them again and ask yourself:

- How do you live each characteristic in your work?
- How can each characteristic propel innovation and initiative in your department?
- How can each characteristic contribute to the success and betterment of others?
- How do others experience each characteristic in your leadership in the workplace?

For example, consider six brand strategies (below) that most chief marketing officers (CMOs) fail to execute to heed the rapidly evolving ground rules for branding that are challenging brands to think differently.

1. *See consumer engagement that others don't.* Stop doing what everyone else is doing, and be creative about how your brand engages with consumers.
2. *Establish an identity that is easily relatable.* Consumers want brands to be deliberate with their identity—straightforward while at the same time forward thinking.
3. *Have a lifestyle platform that inspires people and communicates hope.* A holistic approach to branding that gives people hope will accelerate your ability to earn consumer trust and loyalty.
4. *Show continuous innovation with flawless timing and execution.* Consumers want to know that you are ready when they are; that means your timing must be in perfect sync with their demands.
5. *Promote the genuine spirit of giving.* The spirit of giving must be a central part of every brand's DNA. Make it a point to show your gratitude to the people and communities your brand is serving.
6. *Serve others to leave a legacy.* What is the experience and/or product association you are attempting to leave behind for your brand, and what will your audience remember most about how it impacted their business or lifestyle?

Sound like the six characteristics? They are! As I have developed this work over the past 25 years, I've realized that I can apply the six characteristics to how we connect and do the right things to any workplace or marketplace opportunity. In this case, CMOs learn the six characteristics through these brand strategies; each is equally important and builds on the other to create and sustain the ultimate customer experience. They force CMOs to be accountable to their needs and take responsibility to keep the momentum of the relationships moving forward. That's how you build a power brand for the 21st-century consumer.

But if these six characteristics are simple to say and grasp for any leader in any department and industry, they are certainly not so simple to embrace, let alone operationalize. That requires creating new systems and approaches. Which pretty much sums up the feedback I got from CMOs and marketers to that list: CMOs are "naive to other avenues of marketing" for ROI; "most brands are not structured to handle these!"; or "CMOs are only familiar with strategies they have used in the past."

Responses like those are why I anchor change of this scale to something simple: the six characteristics. And remember, I am not saying everyone lacks all these characteristics, nor do they need them all every day; like the four skills of opportunity management, they simply lack mindful and balanced proficiency in all of them. Only that balance will allow them to deploy the appropriate ones when needed. Think of the characteristics as a progressive but interactive ecosystem, like essential ingredients in your kitchen pantry for the recipes you know by heart. Not every recipe requires every ingredient, so you don't use each ingredient every day, but in the course of a week, month, or year, you need them all to create the best dishes for your family. These skills are ingredients for your workplace and marketplace families. One characteristic can be used to solve a given problem, but, as we will discuss in detail in Part II, deploying a second characteristic to support the solution elevates and propels it to a whole other level. Not all the characteristics need to be applied at any given time, but knowing they are at our disposal, we understand how much strength there is in that knowledge—and as we achieve mastery of the characteristics, our knowledge is converted to wisdom. *It then becomes our wisdom that guides our thinking, mindset, and overall attitude.*

For example, look again at that list of 15 things leaders must do automatically, every day, to be successful in the workplace. Number five is "be accountable to others," which has a strong dependency on passionate pursuits (characteristic three: believe not only in yourself but in those you are accountable to), but to make the accountability even stronger, requires generous purpose (characteristic five: caring and having the backs of others).

Again, in Part II, we'll learn how to master the characteristics by applying them to solve certain scenarios. The important point to retain right now is leaders and businesses must understand the need for balanced proficiency. Over time, leaders must master the fundamentals of the four skills of opportunity management and the six characteristics so that they can understand, propel, and implement the innovation mentality throughout their companies and the people who work there—to instinctively apply them, moving in and out of each characteristic to achieve mastery of them. It doesn't do any good if you have a leadership team of, say, seven people in the c-suite, but only one is thinking with the innovation mentality, and the rest have mastered only some of the skills and characteristics. That c-suite must think together like any other operating division or department should. This is why the leadership identity crises we will discuss in Chapter 2 exist and lead to a "sowing" default at most of the companies I have worked with. Team members must complement one another to celebrate individuality, freedom of expression, and collaboration. The leaders who do have balance must take responsibility to drive others in their organizations toward change to evolve. Sustainability of the six characteristics is a product of shared beliefs and values and a culture the impact and influence of which grows stronger over time. In fact, these six characteristics give leaders the foundation for success and significance.

> *Does your organization support a mentality to connect and empower its employees enough to affect evolutionary and transformational change?*

Are You Vulnerable Enough to Listen?

Most companies don't have these leaders. I have done assessment surveys and consulted dozens of companies on their workplace cultures. Their impact and influence grows stronger as they build on one another. All these companies and leaders believed in the four skills of opportunity management and the six characteristics of the innovation mentality. But our assessments and findings confirmed that what they said is not translating to actual change. None of these companies, from the Fortune 10 on up and down, were fully and consistently stimulating and incentivizing diversity of thought, even those companies that had statements like "respect individuals," "our people are our point of difference," or "value our and all people" as part of their mission statements.

Think you are? Diversity of Thought is the lifeblood of the six characteristics of the innovation mentality, so I invite you to take my "Diversity of Thought Assessment" at www.glennllopisgroup.com/diversity-of-thought-assessment.php and find out. (You can see and answer the questions in Figure 1.3, but I urge you to answer them online to get your results before continuing.) The assessment measures your ability to be open-minded enough to think differently in your quest to achieve workplace and career goals through different pathways and approaches. If you do not have access to the internet, I have listed the questions below. Make sure you answer them before you continue.

Diversity of Thought Assessment

1. Are you mindful of your employees' and/or colleagues' unique differences? ❑ Always ❑ Sometimes ❑ Rarely ❑ Never
2. Do you embrace diversity of thought and use their individual strengths? ❑ Always ❑ Sometimes ❑ Rarely ❑ Never
3. Do you encourage your employees and/or colleagues to share their ideas and ideals? ❑ Always ❑ Sometimes ❑ Rarely ❑ Never
4. Do you create a family environment in your department? ❑ Always ❑ Sometimes ❑ Rarely ❑ Never

Figure 1.3—Diversity of Thought Assessment

Diversity of Thought Assessment

5. Select the word in the pairing below that is most important to you as a leader in order to effectively serve your employees and/or colleagues:
   - ❑ Connection or alignment
   - ❑ Influence or control
   - ❑ Professional development or maximizing each person's potential
   - ❑ Success or significance
6. What do you believe is more important for your employees and/or colleagues to advance in their career?
   - ❑ Self-promotion by employee
   - ❑ An environment for your employees and/or colleagues to seize opportunities
7. Are you vulnerable with your employees and/or colleagues?
   ❑ Always ❑ Sometimes ❑ Rarely ❑ Never
8. Rank the following in order of what you believe encourages your employees and/or colleagues to be their most authentic selves:
   - __ Trust and transparency from their supervisor
   - __ Feeling valued and respected
   - __ Permission to take action (responsibly)
   - __ A safe environment where no is judged
9. Do you encourage your employees and/or colleagues to live the organization's core values? ❑ Always ❑ Sometimes ❑ Rarely ❑ Never
10. Do your employees and/or colleagues share the unique ways their cultural values influence how they think?
    ❑ Always ❑ Sometimes ❑ Rarely ❑ Never
11. How often do your employees and/or colleagues influence your decisions at work? ❑ Always ❑ Sometimes ❑ Rarely ❑ Never
12. Do you empower your employees and/or colleagues to challenge your opinions and perspectives? ❑ Always ❑ Sometimes ❑ Rarely ❑ Never

Figure 1.3—Diversity of Thought Assessment, continued

More than 10,000 senior executives at 65 Fortune 500 companies, many of who lead diverse employees, have taken this survey, and their answers were shockingly similar and extremely complimentary. I won't cover all of them in this chapter, but looking at the answers to these questions that directly relate to what I have discussed so far, you would think I was preaching to the proverbial choir:

- *Question 1.* Are you mindful of unique differences? Always: 70 percent; Sometimes: 30 percent; Rarely: 0 percent; Never: 0 percent
- *Question 2.* Do you embrace diversity of thought? Always: 77 percent; Sometimes: 23 percent; Rarely: 0 percent; Never: 0 percent
- *Question 3.* Do you encourage sharing of ideas and ideals? Always: 83 percent; Sometimes: 13 percent; Rarely: 4 percent; Never: 0 percent
- *Question 7.* Are you vulnerable? Always: 14 percent; Sometimes: 73 percent; Rarely: 11 percent; Never: 2 percent
- *Question 10.* Do your employees/colleagues share how their cultural values influence how they think? Always: 20 percent; Sometimes: 70 percent; Rarely: 3 percent; Never: 7 percent
- *Question 12.* Do you empower your employees to challenge your opinions and perspectives? Always: 71 percent; Sometimes: 24 percent; Rarely: 4 percent; Never: 1 percent

How do these answers compare to yours? Chances are, pretty close—not because I think you are dishonest but because most leaders answer all the questions the way they *should* be answered or think they are actually leading. They will not be vulnerable enough to admit that they don't know how to embrace diversity of thought, even though 87 percent of them say they are always or sometimes vulnerable with their employees and colleagues. But when I show the answers to those employees and colleagues, the problem is immediately clear: Their evaluations of their leaders are the mirror opposite with every "always" becoming a "never" and every "sometimes" a "rarely." That said, those same employees, especially the diverse ones, wouldn't react that way if there were nondiverse supervisors in the room. Why? Because they don't feel safe to do so. Which is the right answer to Question 8: What do you believe encourages your employees and/or colleagues to be their most authentic selves? The answers from those who took the assessment in order of what they ranked first:

1. Feeling valued and respected (48 percent)
2. Trust and transparency from their supervisor (37 percent)
3. A safe environment where no one is judged (12 percent)
4. Permission to (responsibly) take action (3 percent)

The answers from their diverse employees and colleagues:

1. A safe environment where no one is judged
2. Feeling valued and respected
3. Trust and transparency from their supervisor
4. Permission to (responsibly) take action

Why do so many leaders not get that their employees just want a safe environment where no one is judged? Because they aren't listening to the people. *They don't understand that recognition is more important than respect.*

That needs to change. Our leaders must adopt a new mindset that embraces the six characteristics of the innovation mentality, breaks free of the templates of the past, and evolves past substitutional thinking to challenge the status quo. They must understand the requirements for business agility and leadership acumen in the 21st century; the wisdom our employees, partners, customers, and clients need; and how our leadership can create and sustain a competitive advantage for our future, the future our businesses, and the people we impact and influence every day.

Leaders must guide the right conversations, set the right tone, and maximize the potential of others. But that requires listening, and listening requires intimacy and leaders who trust themselves to share their authentic leadership identity with a generous purpose to strengthen our well-being and overall satisfaction at work. Unfortunately, many leaders have no idea what their leadership identity is and thus perpetuate an identity crisis in the workplace. Being intimate with the business elevates our self-awareness and broadens our observations to see opportunity in everything and opportunities previously unseen. That self-awareness requires leaders to have an authentic awareness and understanding of what their leadership solves for—to be truly accountable to and take ownership of their leadership identity. You can't acquire wisdom unless you are being your most authentic self. Instead you get trapped in what others want you to be. You can't acquire wisdom without consistently living your ideals and ideas that can then be influenced by and influence others. You can't create your own wisdom unless you are being your most authentic self and sharing it. But as we will see next, even the best nondiverse and diverse leaders lack the ability to do much or all of this through their leadership identity, because they are trapped in a leadership identity crisis.

Take the Assessment!

In addition to the "Diversity of Thought Assessment" (www.glennllopisgroup.com/diversity-of-thought-assessment.php), the Glenn Llopis Group website features the other two baseline assessments cited in this chapter: "The Workplace Serendipity Quiz," which measures your opportunity mastery skills (www.glennllopisgroup.com/workplace-serendipity-assessment.php), and "The Workplace Culture Assessment" (http://glennllopisgroup.com/assessment/workplace-culture-assessment.php), which determines if your corporate culture adheres to the six characteristics of 21st-century leadership that influence your proficiency in opportunity management. Each one has been taken by thousands of leaders and is free.

CHAPTER 2

USE THE INNOVATION MENTALITY TO STRENGTHEN YOUR LEADERSHIP IDENTITY

At 26, I became the youngest senior executive at Sunkist in the company's history. It was also my first corporate executive position. Thankfully, I had several mentors to guide me through it all, and I have never forgotten the first piece of advice one of them gave me: Leaders must touch the business as much as they lead; whatever you do, don't ever forget that the minute you stop touching the business is the minute you stop understanding the business. He explained that while the company had been growing rapidly, it was also losing touch as it grew. The company's leaders were focused on growing rather than understanding. Most times they had no idea what was going on beneath the numbers or how to anticipate any problems, because they did not touch the people in the field or know how consumers were experiencing our juice products. They didn't talk to the people in distribution and delivery, connect directly to what was happening in the stores, or see the looks on customers' faces. And it had cost the company time and time again.

This is how I learned the power of vulnerability. I can't say I completely understood all this at the time, but my mentor's words stuck with me. Today, I understand them completely and know the problem was hardly unique to Sunkist or any industry. It was and is a problem with leadership and executives at those companies who become self-satisfied and complacent in times of rapid growth and change, and thus followed outdated business templates, and sowed and sowed and sowed without seeing, growing, or sharing. As a result, those leaders have lost touch with the very thing that drives our businesses and indeed our lives: people.

It is people who define whether any organization is successful or not, which is why business and leadership today must become a more personal experience. We need this intimacy to identify and understand how to convert unique differences into seeing opportunities previously unseen—the first characteristic of the innovation mentality. The more we personally touch our businesses, the more we can appreciate the value in those differences and support the people we serve and give them a safe environment to speak up without judgment. Leaders must be proactive in providing this genuine recognition to discover the full potential in others by appreciating their unique needs, which in turn helps them understand the unique needs of the entire business as well as its external partners, clients, and customers. That's how authenticity thrives in the workplace and extends to the marketplace to engage with the unique identities of the consumers and clients we serve on a more genuine level—it moves from the inside out.

To do this, we must allow diverse thinking to flourish in our leadership and become the new normal. Which is exactly what most leaders don't do. They don't engage diversity of thought enough to understand what it really means and how it connects to their leadership: that diversity of thought fuels the innovation mentality, which, in turn, fuels their leadership identities and makes leadership a personal experience. That's exactly how people get caught up focusing on what they are being asked to do rather than taking responsibility to do much more. The status quo performance metrics don't measure intelligence; they measure an employee's ability to be what the company wants them to be rather than encouraging them to be who they really are and help the company evolve. That's how people get stuck working on the things that are right in front of them and why they only do what their job descriptions say and nothing more. That's how they develop skills to execute only the tasks assigned to them but not any other leadership skill. Sowing becomes their proverbial carrot for the horse.

Simply put, people fall back into sowing because they can't lead authentically. Sowing is the battle line between assimilation and authenticity in leadership and business. When they are authentic, the paradigm shifts from business to individual, and evolved solutions come from the individual, not the business. That's how all people will feel they are making contributions and align their goals, ideals, and ideas with their leaders' and their companies' goals—authentically as individuals who create shared cultures that drive change and foster growth. To do this, we must accept what this paradigm shift means for leadership and business today:

IT'S BECOMING LESS ABOUT THE BUSINESS
DEFINING THE INDIVIDUAL

AND MORE ABOUT
THE INDIVIDUAL
DEFINING THE BUSINESS

Leaders must be accountable to this—they need to have the wisdom, courage, and vulnerability to turn the spotlight of accountability on themselves first! Most leaders have no idea how to do this—or care to. Instead, they continue to take the road most traveled and manage by the templates of old. They cannot evolve to be the leaders America needs, because those templates stripped them of their identities and left them insecure about who they are and how to face change.

Diversity of thought and the innovation mentality belongs to those who are fearless about this change, renewing and reinventing themselves to propel initiative and innovation—whether or not they are winning. Only then will our untapped potential strengthen everyone's standing in the country we call home. America and the rest of the world has yet to experience and benefit from true collective wisdom. That's how we make the path easier for the future of our children—by applying our collective values and strengths to help cultivate economic prosperity and the sustainable well-being of America. That's how we renew and reinvent ourselves as a country, as a world, as businesses, and as leaders—we get back to what we once knew. This is why understanding and strengthening your leadership identity is the first real step in embracing the six characteristics of the innovation mentality. And that starts with the question every leader must ask and keep asking before diving deeper into the six characteristics of the innovation mentality: What is my leadership identity?

This may seem like an easy question to answer, but most leaders I have met have trouble with it, because they have very little experience answering it. You may understand that your leadership identity defines who you influence and how you influence business evolution, but what defines your leadership identity? The answer: your personal brand and its value proposition (what your personal brand solves for). The evolution of your personal brand (knowing who you are) is the foundation for defining and shaping what your personal brand solves for, which ultimately defines your leadership identity. Your leadership identity then evolves to drive change through the business and lead through rapid changes in the workplace and marketplace as they extend beyond the speed of business, globalization, and connectivity to include the demographics, gender, race, ethnicity, culture, and personal brands served by you and your company (see Figure 2.1 on page 49).

Defining your leadership identity starts by defining the personal brand of the individual you have the most control over: you. You can't turn around a division, a department, or a company until you turn around yourself. Understanding who you are and what you solve for is how your leadership will define the evolution of the business in the new normal.

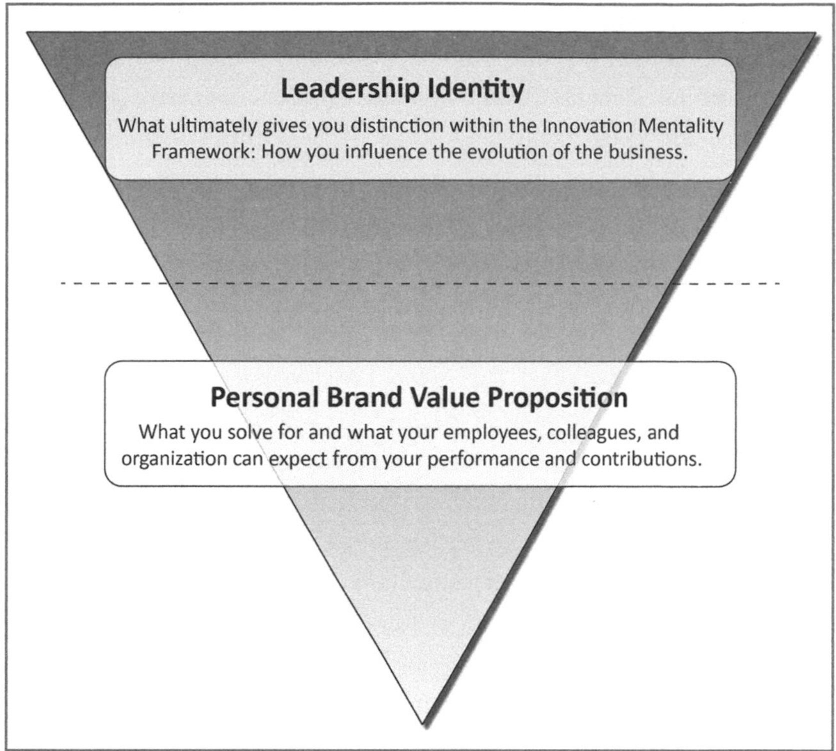

Leadership Identity
What ultimately gives you distinction within the Innovation Mentality Framework: How you influence the evolution of the business.
Personal Brand Value Proposition
What you solve for and what your employees, colleagues, and organization can expect from your performance and contributions.

Figure 2.1—What Defines Your Leadership Identity?

Your Authentic Identity

We each have a unique identity and points of difference. Mine happen to extend to my name: I am the only Glenn Llopis in the world, which is great for Google relevancy but lousy when it comes to pronunciation. To help people get past this, I met with a linguist at Merriam Webster's to get the phonetic pronunciation of my last name as it would appear in its dictionary: ʽyō-pēs. For those who can't read that, it sounds like something a hippie might say to a soldier in the 1960s: "Yo, peace!"

The story of my name is part of every introductory presentation I make, because long ago, I promised my parents to trust the authentic identity that I was born with and make it represent what my name stood for—a perfect expression of how my Cuban and American sides combine to create something unique: Glenn (for legendary American big band musician Glenn Miller) and Llopis (to reflect my parents' Cuban heritage). I use that uniqueness to introduce people to and celebrate my family, our stories, and my Cuban/Hispanic heritage, and how they have shaped and influenced my values. Why I do this goes beyond me as the messenger of my story. It is about the message: It is an educational moment for my audience on diverse thinking and the profound nature of how our personal brands shape our leadership identities.

Not everyone has a unique and difficult-to-pronounce name like mine, but our core identities are still profound, extremely relevant, and lie within and all around all us. This is why I wish remarks like those made by venture capitalist John Doerr at the 2015 TechCrunch Disrupt conference were atypical. Doerr, an investor in Google and Facebook among other tech companies, was at the conference to discuss diversity in Silicon Valley. According to Anna Holmes in her *New York Times* article "Has 'Diversity' Lost Its Meaning?" Doerr explained that his firm, following a sexual discrimination suit, had "begun putting its employees through training in unconscious bias. The 64-year-old Harvard Business School graduate professed [that he was] 'deeply committed to diversity,' adding: 'We have two new partners who are so diverse, I have a challenge pronouncing their names.'"

Doerr later apologized for his "unfortunate joke," but Holmes called him out as an example of how diversity has become "a convenient shorthand that gestures at inclusivity and representation without actually taking them seriously." She was beyond right. This is the difference between people who take things for granted and those who make the extra effort toward and are unafraid of intimacy and being vulnerable. How can you expect people whose names are mispronounced all the time to believe that the person who is mispronouncing those names and dismissing them with jokes is making a genuine investment in wanting to know more about who they are as individuals? How do you expect those people to be willing to invest in you and your differences if you are not willing to invest in theirs? That's why I invest so much in helping the leaders I work with be more comfortable about my last name. If leaders can't invest enough to know who people are at this most basic level, then why would the people who have these unfamiliar (if not complex) last names make an investment in their companies and their brands? According to my survey of thousands of leaders, less than 20 percent of them ask their employees the following question: Who are you, and what do you believe gives you distinction? Given that, why would people feel those leaders and their companies are authentically considering their individual needs? That's what those partners were thinking when Doerr said what he said.

Too many leaders are creating tension—often unknowingly—through their words and actions.

That's also how I felt the day I read the *New York Times* story. I was on a short business trip, and six different people at the airline pronounced my name incorrectly. Even after I corrected them, they said it wrong again . . . and again. Can you imagine how long it truly takes for leaders to embrace our larger unique differences and change the culture of their businesses if they struggle so profoundly with our names? In fact, on that same trip to consult for a multinational food company, I heard one of the company's executives use the same expression Doerr did in his speech: "unconscious bias." He proudly told me that as part of his company's work on diversity "they recently had a discussion around unconscious biases." Just like I thought about Doerr, I wondered what that meant to this executive and the company. Unconscious biases may go beyond diversity, but they exist only where we lack diversity of thought, and diverse thinking can exist only when people allow themselves to listen and recognize the value that people bring when they embrace unique differences. None of the executives I spoke to even considered that in their discussion.

Can that executive, Doerr, the people at the airline, and anyone who faces this "problem" firsthand accept this and truly change? Not from anything I experienced that day or at most companies, because businesses have not traditionally bought into or valued diversity and inclusion, let alone diversity of thought. So, how do you get them to change? What do you say, and how do you say it and show them that it not only matters but also is a necessity? How do you take the workplace culture and change it to embrace diversity of thought and the six characteristics of the innovation

Individuals defining the business must be the new normal.

mentality that remains dormant? You have the wisdom, courage, and vulnerability to call those people out and tell them that individuals defining the business must be the new normal.

This is why I explain to audiences up front that my name is not "Lop-iss" or "Lopez" and tell them to think of it as "Yo, peace!" When I say it that way, everyone gets it almost immediately and never forgets. When I deliver this message about my name the right way, they never forget and have opened up to hear more. I showed them something tangible that subtly made them understand why we need to embrace diversity of thought and the innovation mentality. This is why Caroline Wanga (pronounced wan-*ja*, not wan-*ga*), vice president of corporate social responsibility at Target Corp., told me she also makes sure people honor her request to pronounce her last name correctly: "There's sometimes courage in helping people help you feel bold, and one of the ways I do that is helping people pronounce my name. For me, it is such an important part of my identity. I'm Kenyan. There's pride in saying Wanga. Whenever I hear my name mispronounced, I feel you are taking a little bit of me away from me."

Let's stop taking that away from anyone. Wanga's actions, like mine, are just a couple of small steps toward changing the template and replacing dismissive jokes and unconscious bias with intimacy and diverse thinking—and valuing it authentically. Until then, the lack of intimacy and genuine caring for people will continue to create unnecessary tension that ignorance cannot excuse. People want to feel valued for who they are and are tired and frustrated with being misrepresented and battling the gulf between assimilation and authenticity.

Aren't *you*?

Most leaders privately say they are, yet they still devalue authenticity in the workplace and marketplace. It's time to transform that thinking and connect on the most intimate level, which is absolutely crucial in a 21st-century workplace that is more mobile, transient, flexible, diverse, and personally branded than ever before. We must become leaders who use diverse thinking to be completely authentic in who we are. That's your authentic personal brand.

Go Beyond Personal Branding

The concept of personal branding—the idea that success comes from how you authentically present and market yourself and your career as an individual—may date back to 1997, but the workplace has not encouraged us to develop our personal brands, let alone live them and use them. Thus, a lot of leaders talk about personal branding, but few connect it to leadership in this way and thus hold themselves accountable to it to evolve. According to my organization's research, fewer than 15 percent of leaders have defined their personal brand, and only 5 percent are living it every day. But why would they and how can they if deep down most of them feel that brand is inauthentic?

Think about this yourself as it relates to your leadership identity: Are your differences clearly understood? Do you provide clarity, or are you unknowingly creating tension? Are you unknowingly creating conflict because you haven't transitioned your knowledge into wisdom? As I explained in the introduction, leadership is transitioning from knowledge-based to wisdom-based and is becoming less about what you know and more about what you do with what you know. In this new economy, the importance of a personal connection to leadership—of touching the business every day as I learned from my mentor at Sunkist—cannot be understated, as it defines your leadership identity and your ability to value differences and enable the full potential of others: your team, your clients, and *yourself.* This book is not about doing what I tell you, but being wise enough to listen to and learn from what I tell you so you can listen to and learn from others.

> *You must know yourself to be mindful of and value other people's brands.*

To educate and define who we are as people and how we want to contribute to the success of the company, we need leaders to have the courage to listen to us—all of us, not just those of diverse backgrounds—as they simultaneously deconstruct and reconstruct themselves to embrace the innovation mentality fueled by diversity of thought. Your people want to know where they fit and where they can best contribute to their organization and the reinvention process. They want to be part of a workplace that allows them to be their natural, authentic selves. Only then will they become custodians of the workplace culture and become more accountable to it, driving that authenticity into being more intimate with your clients and customers and seizing new marketplace opportunities. To do this, people need leaders with strong identities that provide clarity and understanding for what their leadership solves for—leaders who have a strong identity that supports their personal reinvention efforts to be more purposeful, responsible, and accountable in how they lead and influence others. The moment you walk into the workplace you have to be more accountable to reach greater levels of influence by working with a generous purpose and leading to leave a legacy—the fifth and sixth characteristics of the innovation mentality.

This is one reason I believe that many leaders today shouldn't be leaders in the future. Leadership is about the desire to be significant, not just successful, which is what the innovation mentality stands for. You just need to be *courageous* and vulnerable enough to take action and be your most authentic self in everything you do to understand people and what their brands represent and solves. Do that and your leadership identity will have incredible influence for driving change through your people. Often, leaders think they have to be the one to drive things, but you are really leading when you are maximizing the potential of others. It is not just about what we are solving; it's about "who" you are solving for—the people in the room. If we don't know them, we tend to retreat, grow complacent, and perpetuate the silos, instead of leading new conversations much like we do in serving the unique needs of everyone—the foundation for the survival, renewal, and reinvention America and indeed the world needs.

Have you ever asked your employees or clients what they expect from your leadership? Do you know the added value they want you to deliver every day as a leader?

We must allow all people to contribute in ways that help leaders better understand what they should be solving for to ensure the business evolves. You have to know what you're solving for to see, sow, grow, and share together with balanced proficiency. Because in the end, leaders must be accountable to solve for both the organization and people they serve. When you don't know who (or what) you are solving for, you are just answering questions. Much like when you're stuck in sowing, all you're doing is sowing. You are not solving for anything evolutionary when you are just sowing; you are just substituting the templates of old—creating slow progress—which makes it difficult for you to evolve as a leader and your company to evolve at all. For years, businesses and their leaders and managers didn't value all people. Now they can't prevent them from having an identity and sharing their unique perspectives, nor would they want them to if the strategy is to evolve the business. When we all know how to live our personal brands and leadership identities, and allow them to cross-pollinate across the company and beyond, that is when the company truly begins to act like a powerful and focused innovation lab that can consistently identify and close opportunity gaps and capitalize on those gaps to avoid getting stuck in sowing.

So, what have you done to enable the full potential of "yourself"? To cultivate new possibilities previously unseen through the six characteristics, you must break free from the outdated workplace template that devalues individuality and clearly define your personal brand. But even then, *knowing* your personal brand does not go far enough, which is why personal branding has become less useful as a concept disconnected from leadership identity. You can't just define your personal brand and connect it to your leadership identity; you have to know what its value proposition is—what it is and what you solve for. As you live your personal brand and it continues to evolve, you gain experience to manage opportunities properly. You establish your personal brand's value proposition as it relates to those opportunities. You must then use that value proposition to forge a leadership identity that is a catalyst for *evolution.*

What Does Your Personal Brand Solve For?

Problem is, since most leaders and their personal brands are disconnected, they don't know what they are solving for. They may *think* they know. They can even sound smart when they say it, like the analyst I met who claimed to be "an expert in solutions with SAS software." You don't have to know anything about technology to understand that an analyst's "expertise" has little connection to her personal brand or its value proposition. Software ability is a *skill*, and specific skills do not solve for anything general enough that can cast a wider influence on the business—they are just about what you *do*. In other words, *sowing*, which is how that analyst will get trapped in a sowing mentality.

Here are some other answers I got from people at companies across various departments in retail, insurance, health care, financial services, and beyond when I asked them what they solve at the *start* of our work together:

- Inventory replenishment
- Sales
- Doing my job
- Being an expert

None of these things are about what these people influence. They are based, like that analyst, on what they sow. That's what happens when we associate our brand's value proposition with the wrong things. We never truly know what we are accountable to solve for, and thus we can't identify how we can fit in and best contribute to the organization. When you understand that, your wisdom shapes your thinking. You become the go-to knowledge resource, guide growth strategies, and provide the best recommendations for implementation. You touch the business every day and take personal stock in being more accountable for its evolution. You become opportunity experts in your domain.

Your Personal Brand Value Proposition

What opportunity gaps does your brand solve for? As you may have guessed, this question is not as easy to answer as it sounds. I asked a senior executive at a Fortune 500 company this question, and he said, "Talent." I told him it was more than that. He just looked at me, so I asked him, "Can you define your personal brand proposition?" I listened as he talked for two minutes, never quite finding the right words. And he was one of the smartest executives I have met. When he stopped talking, I said, "So, you solve for *potential*. Not just the potential in people or the potential of the best practices that will carry through to the business but something bigger than that: Your role is to solve for the potential of the business through the individuality of the people. That's what will then drive the growth and evolution of your organization." That executive could do that by creating metrics that make the human resource department a profit center, not a cost center. How does he do that? By valuing it, using his ability to embrace and enable diversity of thought in others. This is how the individual will define the business rather than the business defining the individual—by valuing everyone's brand value proposition, starting with your own.

In no way do I think this leader was unusual in his inability to articulate or see this. Over the course of four months in 2015, I interviewed three dozen senior executives, and not one could clearly or succinctly answer what opportunity gaps their personal brand solves for, and only 25 percent of these executives provided answers that were close to being strong responses. For example, one marketing executive told me he "identified competitive threats." That's good. But what he really solved for was "lack of innovation." The difference between his answer versus my suggested response is they lead to different outcomes. His response leans toward a leadership approach where substitution and evolution are inconsistently applied, whereas my suggestions require a leadership approach that supports constant evolution with a strong endgame in mind—where "the solve" is always clear. When leaders lack this clarity and understanding of what the answer is, they are unable to effectively strengthen their own personal brands, let alone the personal brands of those they serve. More important, when you can't respond to these questions with 100 percent belief and clarity, it's impossible to consistently lead with an approach that fosters evolution over substitution.

What Outcomes Do You Enjoy Solving for the Most?

This lack of clarity and belief is how leaders end up solving for the wrong things more often than you might think. This is why my workshops, summits, roundtables, and keynotes combine understanding of the innovation mentality with real-world workplace scenarios to test and improve the participants' ability to be their most authentic selves as leaders. By being their authentic selves, they can influence the effectiveness of their

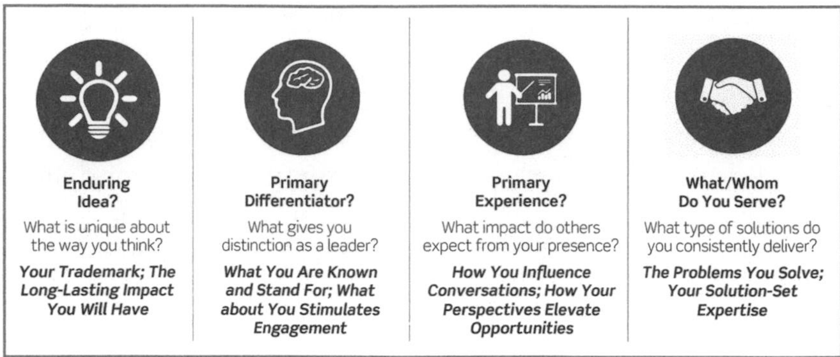

Enduring
Idea?
What is unique about
the way you think?
Your Trademark; The
Long-Lasting Impact
You Will Have
Primary
Differentiator?
What gives you
distinction as a leader?
What You Are Known
and Stand For; What
about You Stimulates
Engagement
Primary
Experience?
What impact do others
expect from your presence?
How You Influence
Conversations; How Your
Perspectives Elevate
Opportunities
What/Whom
Do You Serve?
What type of solutions do
you consistently deliver?
The Problems You Solve;
Your Solution-Set
Expertise

Figure 2.2—Define Your Personal Brand Value Proposition

decision making; seize new marketplace opportunities; enable their full potential and that of others; and solve for the most promising opportunity gaps. All this must be viewed through the lens of their personal brand value proposition as it relates to your leadership identity, which is why I make each participant answer four "Personal Brand Value Proposition" questions that fall into four categories (see Figure 2.2).

Now, it's your turn: Answer those four questions. Keep your answers to four words or fewer if possible, and remember there are no wrong answers. Write them down. As you do, keep in mind that the categories and questions are sequential, and, like the six characteristics, each of them build on one another. They tell the story of your personal brand value proposition. This sequence and story is essential to understanding who and what you serve, what others can expect from your leadership, what your personal brand value proposition is and solves for, and how your leadership identity influences the business. Don't just say these words; realize this power.

If you're struggling to come up with your answers, you're not alone. Some of the smartest leaders I have worked with struggle, too. It's hard to find words to describe what we solve for when we have not been taught to understand and/or have not been held accountable to know what we solve for. We have been conditioned for the business to define that for us.

To help you overcome this obstacle, I'll take the same approach those leaders really respond to in our workshops. First, Figure 2.3 on page 59

Name	Enduring Idea	Primary Differentiator	Primary Experience	Who/What Served
Edgar	fresh perspectives	desire to excel	exceeding expectations	those who demand long-lasting impact
Dana	connecting the dots	methodical	high speed, high quality	continuous improvement
Rick	catalyst	always a way	optimism	potential
Sandy	fierce simplicity	crave common sense	gets to the point	clarity
Angela	preparedness	seek to understand	momentum	advancement
Robert	changing the game	path less taken	think outside the box	trailblazers

Figure 2.3—Examples of Defining Your Personal Brand Value Proposition, Part 1

provides six examples that are based on the work I have done with hundreds of companies across a variety of departments. The names are completely made up.

Once you process those answers, try this "speed-branding" exercise. You can do it alone, but it is much more effective in groups of four or five.

1. Draw a chart like the one in Figure 2.4 on page 61 with the names of the people in your group.
2. For each person, go around the room and ask everyone—excluding the person being discussed—to say out loud what they think that person's enduring idea, primary differentiator, primary experience, and who or what they serve are. Try and keep the answers to four words or fewer.
3. Write them down as they are called out.

4. Switch the note taker and complete steps one through four until each person is done and everyone has taken notes.
5. As a group, go deeper. Think again about each person and ask, "What is unique about the way they think or act?" Refine your answers.
6. Consider the words for each person: Are the words right, or did you just say them? Is the sequence right?
7. Do an elimination process: Take out the words and answers that are repetitive and not strong enough—make sure each answer is now four words or fewer.
8. Refine, again. Go back to the examples I provided. Do they have a logical sequence and build on the one before? Can they tell the story of that person's brand value proposition? This time, narrow the number of words for each category to no more than three words if possible.

Once the answer to that last question is "Yes!" you are ready to tell that story and say what your brand value proposition is, and even give it a tagline. Here's how that works. Consider Sandy. Her sequence is as follows:

1. *Enduring Idea:* Fierce simplicity
2. *Primary Differentiator:* Craves common sense
3. *Primary Experience:* Gets to the point
4. *Serve/Solves for:* Clarity

Sandy and her group looked at these words the same way a business looks at its brand: They took the words and looked for a brand value proposition that was a title for the story those words told. They took Sandy's words and defined her brand as "Focused Igniter." Her tagline was, "Accelerating strategic focus to reach the endgame." Figure 2.4 on page 61 lists the other answers for each person.

If you're still struggling, don't worry. These answers are powerful, but they are often unfamiliar, despite their deeply personal nature, because the business has defined you as an individual. And a business like that can provide no guidance. The answers can't be found in job descriptions. In fact, job descriptions are part of the problem. Job titles are creating more

Name	Brand/Tagline	Tagline
Edgar	Beyond Borders	No wall too tall to climb
Dana	Task Master	Getting it done right, one task at a time
Amy	Optimistic Explorer	Unleashing the full potential in others
Sandy	Focus Igniter	Accelerating the endgame
Angela	Endless Possibilities	Making progress happen
Robert	Changing Lanes	Blazing new paths for growth

Figure 2.4—Examples of Defining Your Personal Brand Value Proposition, Part 2

silos and fueling hierarchical, bureaucratic infrastructures. Employees get buried under and blinded by those titles and accompanying job descriptions. Labeling their role and listing their responsibilities can make them feel trapped and boxed in by a limited set of expectations, uncertain how to unleash their full potential and that of others.

Political bureaucracies define the traditional workplace, where silos slow down productivity, as opposed to the new workplace that is fueled by innovation and initiative. Employees are eager to be more creative and express their opinions. When they let their job titles limit their ability to stretch themselves, it makes it more difficult for their talent to get discovered, and thus their distinction remains unnoticed. As a result, employees are finding it more difficult to navigate the requirements for success in the workplace; the many layers of management bureaucracy make it challenging to be proactive, and even leaders have difficulty making decisions.

Zappos CEO Tony Hsieh certainly understands the barriers to advancement that job titles create, which is why he eliminated them in a program called Holacracy. He said that for the majority of companies, "There's the org chart on paper, and then the one that is exactly how the company operates for real, and then there's the org chart that it would like to have to operate more efficiently. With Holacracy, the idea is to process tensions so that the three org charts are pretty close together." A wholesale Holacracy program may not be for every company, but small substitutional course corrections to what has been done in the past won't lead to evolution either.

I recently met with a Fortune 50 executive who shared with me that his company is experiencing an "organizational engagement crisis": Beyond employees feeling stuck behind their job titles and descriptions, the high prevalence of change management that the organization is experiencing is making it difficult for not only employees but whole departments and their leaders to engage cross-functionally. As this executive described it, "People are afraid to make decisions and are hypersensitive to ensure that every title is represented in the room in order to reach consensus. People are not willing to be courageous because they don't want to be held accountable for the outcome. The lack of organizational engagement has made our company more reactive and is putting our market leadership at risk."

Do You Work in an Environment that Works to Get By?

What that Fortune 50 executive asked me is why I believe job descriptions will be dinosaurs in the future. Individuals will define their job descriptions in the future as statements of accountability for specific job functions. The description will be one paragraph of what that individual's core responsibilities are and what he or she solves for; the rest will cover how that individual will solve for those responsibilities based on their personal brand value proposition. That brand value proposition will define how the job function is performed and will also influence KPIs, or key performance indicators, that directly align with the organization's mission, vision, core beliefs, and values. Individuals thus influence the evolution and identity of the organization's culture and brand value proposition and create a powerful, airtight ecosystem among leadership and beyond through which they can drive the innovation mentality. They are part of integrated employee and employee-branded communities and the center

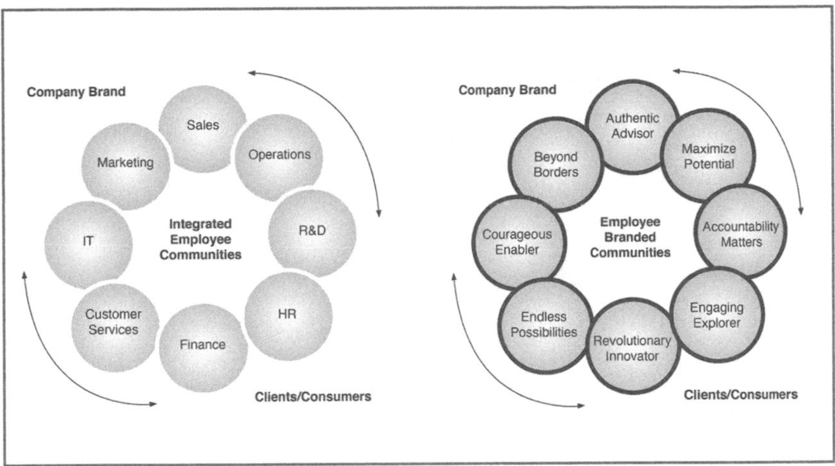

Figure 2.5—The New Workplace: Integrated and Employee-Branded Communities

of the workplace that influences the business and guides how they and the organization operate (see Figure 2.5).

This is why those individual brand value propositions are so important: They are at the center of this new workplace. Look at Figure 2.6 on page 64, which illustrates what would happen if the six personal brand value propositions described before cross-pollinated in a department or business to create a community that solves for the business's problems and opportunities collectively.

Can you honestly deny the power in this? Together this group can solve for so many things: adversity, project management, change management, a turnaround operation, mergers and acquisitions, business development, and beyond. Think about your own workplace and consider the following ways that your and other job titles and descriptions might be disrupting productivity and innovation and disconnecting you from your personal brand and its value proposition. We do not even know how to break free from the templates because we are so sucked into them. The problem is individuals don't believe they have influence. Although the business is saying or showing them through models that it wants them to have more influence, it is not letting go enough. As a result, despite

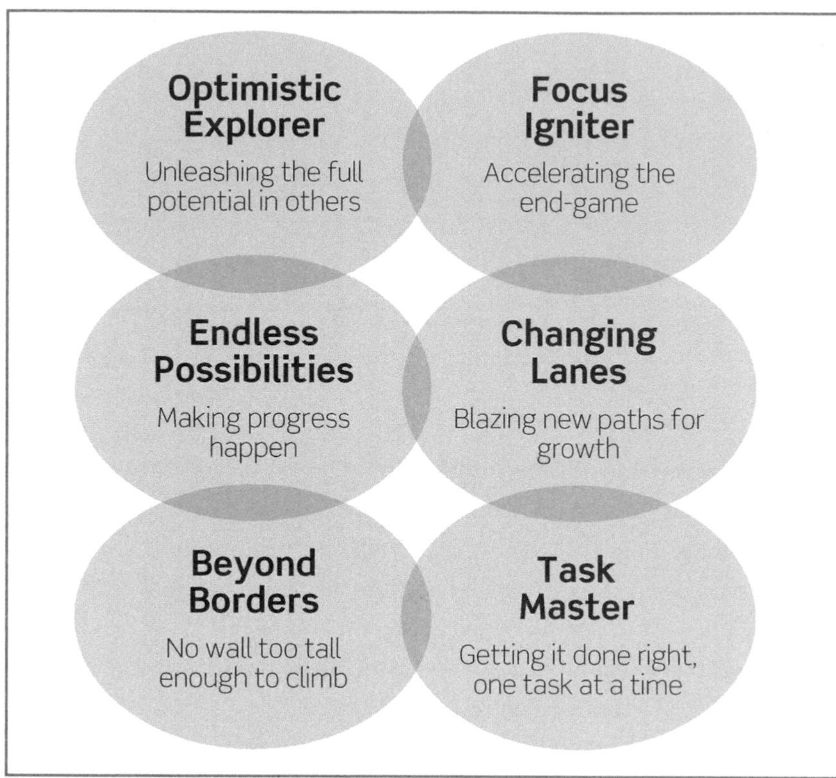

Figure 2.6—The Cross-Pollination of Leadership Identities to Strengthen Teams and What They're Solving For

or perhaps in spite of their best intentions to foster a culture of diverse thinkers, companies more often than not seek to control the performance of their employees based on outdated ways of thinking. They played it safe, conforming to existing workplace engagement practices and fostering that "I just do what I am told" approach. Most companies are fine with this or don't know any better. After all, this approach has been "fine" for a long time, which is why many leaders have become followers and masters at sowing and nothing else. If no one sees or goes after more than the obvious opportunities, and those are moving the bottom line, then who needs to see beyond the obvious? Who needs to use "circular vision" to anticipate the unexpected or to appreciate or pay attention to their people and their individual efforts? Everyone just keeps doing what they are told.

But you have to wonder if everything can truly be fine when employees feel unappreciated and the workplace isn't innovative enough to value the individuality and their personal brands. You have to wonder how long an if-it-isn't-broken-don't-fix-it attitude will hide the deeper problems. How long can "fine" last? The results of my corporate assessments back this assertion, but more likely than not you don't need an assessment to understand that on some basic level. It's what you have experienced or are experiencing now.

Resistance to Individuality Makes Evolution Difficult if Not Impossible

I remember my first job at a large wine and spirits company. It had a top-down, best practice, zero-defect, career-path, fear-based culture. Everyone was accountable to someone or to some set of policies and procedures. I was taught the ten steps to managing my sales. I was told I had to perform, or I would be out in 30 days. I was not encouraged to freely express my individuality. The only thing that mattered was the transaction. It was a "what have you done for me lately" environment. It wasn't about me or anyone else at the company. *It was about control.*

In the classic way of bureaucracies, this approach created big problems in this company's leadership. The best salespeople had been promoted into management where they were floundering, because they needed different types of skills to succeed. A great salesperson is not necessarily a great manager, but this company didn't see that or care about the consequences that created. This was a linear-thinking, cookie-cutter, no-individuals-for-hire-here culture. And I did well enough in it at first. In fact, I won several sales contests and awards. But soon I began to realize I was working in a culture that didn't value diversity in its people or client relationships. I may have learned valuable lessons about the importance of discipline, structure, and protocol, but without any personal growth and development of my potential that would help me find success and eventual significance, the financial incentives were not enough to make me perform better or commit for the long term. It wasn't long before I realized this culture simply didn't allow me to perform and contribute at the highest level. I knew I was not evolving. I didn't believe that I had been given permission to go above and beyond what I had to do for them and invest back in the company. I started doing only what the company wanted me to do, and like many others before and after me, I soon left—and it was not because I thought I was special or deserved special treatment.

Like so many employees today—from the top to the bottom at countless companies across every industry—I just got tired of fighting for other people's agendas and wanted to find things that mattered to me, gave me purpose, or made me feel like I was contributing in meaningful ways. That's what happens to people when they do not reinvent themselves. They focus too much on what others want them to be rather than what they seek to be themselves. They don't have *courage* to be who they authentically are, so they don't even know how to get started reinventing themselves. Eventually, they get tired of fighting and default to the dead-inside response, "I just do what I am told." Or as a woman in the audience at one of my keynotes said to me, "Glenn, I am a really aspirational person, but I stopped believing that my differences are valued, so I am no longer as aspirational as I once was. What's the point? They're not going to get it anyway. So I stopped fighting the fight."

My message to this woman was: "You are fighting the wrong fight. That's why you are tired." That was how I felt and why I turned to my dad for help in reinventing myself as I struggled—the very moment that led me down the path to understanding the innovation mentality. This is why my personal motto is, "I will never advise others about something I have never experienced or done myself." If I was going to evolve and was willing to fight, then I was going to put that energy into reinventing myself and help companies and leaders do the same for themselves and their employees.

Maybe generations before my time approaches like I experienced worked at that wine and spirits company but not when I got there and surely not today. The rate of change has been exponential, even if our businesses have not kept pace. Companies like these may look great from the outside, but greatness is built on the backs of their employees. And in today's marketplace, employees have changed and demand more. They want to feel like they're having an impact, like they're making a difference. Too often, they can't see what they are doing matters, let alone applies beyond that company. These traditional workplace environments are so internally focused, they don't prepare employees to move around or up. They wire workers to be successful for the task at hand at that company—and only for that company. Employees can be fooled by this. Often, executives or leaders want people to be fooled in this way, because whose agendas are they trying to drive forward? Is it the executive's decisions? The individual's? In the end, many people spend their time sowing because their bosses are not solving for the right things. As a result, they waste a lot of time not evolving because management keeps substituting through sowing, rather than maximizing the potential of the right things (growing).

Stop focusing on what others want you to be, rather than what you seek to be yourself.

This is when leaders in the workplace lack the strategic focus to define their personal brand value propositions and identify the opportunities of greatest potential (growing). Job titles, job descriptions, and departmental silos only cloud that focus further. As a result, most leaders don't know what they solve for in the business and, like that Fortune 500 leader, just keep sowing what they think their expertise is (e.g., talent), never evolving to see, grow, or share what it really is (potential). Leaders must be accountable to what they solve for. But to do that, they must also overcome a catch-22: They must fully develop their brand value proposition for their employers to discover, but in our post-recession, resource-constrained corporate landscapes, many businesses no longer support employees with an array of resources and professional development to help. They expect a person to get by with less, which means leaders must be more resourceful in ways they never have to before. As a result, we must live with an entrepreneurial spirit and break free from the templates and excuses that restrict us, enable new resources, invest in people the right way to create new opportunities for the betterment of a healthier whole, and be willing to turn everything we know upside down and be beginners again.

That's what I described in the introduction when I realized I needed to get beyond diversity in my thinking. I did it again when I realized my business was delivering the wrong message about Hispanic populations. My message had been: "Hispanics are the future of America, because they bring the thinking we need to lead us out of the demographic changes affecting this country." I said this because Hispanics (like blacks, Asian/Pacific Islanders, Arab Americans, and other recent "minority" populations in the U.S.) had been forced to embrace and live what I then defined as "the immigrant perspective on leadership and workplace innovation" and has now shifted to "the innovation mentality." As such, they understand survival, renewal, and reinvention. That is true, but few businesses understood that message, valued it, and knew how to apply it on a deeper and broader enterprise-wide level when I said it that way.

I was continually met with blank stares when I tried explaining to companies how an individual's cultural heritage provides the organization with some distinction that creates competitive advantage. But when I identified the things that diverse populations can and have done that have broad effects and real value that can be measured and translated to the bottom line, *that* they listened to.

Because I was willing to evolve my thinking on what I solved for and identify what worked and what was limiting about its message, I did not fall into the same trap I was trying to get leaders and companies out of. On the surface, this may sound like simple exercise in semantics, but the reality is this process is extremely complex. It requires not only a deep understanding of the behavioral changes and/or perspectives that you are attempting to deliver but also being in tune with the message and content that your audience is thirsty for. This is why my content—my blogs and articles, keynotes, roundtables, summits, conferences, social and traditional media, books, and whitepapers—are focused on the innovation mentality and what it solves for: *leadership*. I want leaders to engage and share my experience and thinking with their teams as steps for translating that thinking into something transformational for themselves and their companies.

So, when was last time you shared your story and what your brand stands for and solves? The best content-marketing strategies drive consumer engagement by solving growing tension points and/or narrowing demand gaps in the workplace and marketplace. When engagement is converted into sustainable revenue, you know that your content strategy is on the mark. Leaders can do this on an individual level, which is why I encourage those who already embrace diversity of thought and respect the power of the individual to help others be their most authentic selves by sharing it with the company.

- Can you identify the ten best practices you have created because you understand and value diversity of thought?
- Can you share new operating procedures that you defined?
- Can you talk about how you conduct meetings differently simply by getting everyone involved in the conversation and valuing and respecting everybody's point of view?

Find your personal brand value proposition and a way to share it—give it life to propel engagement with your workplace, external partners, and marketplace. It could be as simple as what this Fortune 10 senior executive told me: "I put my personal brand value proposition and what it solves for on my office door. My team asks me about it, and it helps them understand who I am and what they can expect from my leadership, and then helps them share who they are the second they walk through the door."

That's the power your personal brand value proposition has to define your leadership identity—who you influence and how you influence business evolution.

People in today's workplaces and marketplaces are speaking louder than ever: We *all* want our unique needs and contributions to be discovered—to feel we are valued by our leaders, companies, and the products and services they sell. We must have the wisdom diverse thinking gives us to listen to this and understand what it means—to connect and do the right things by our employees and, in turn, design the best strategies for customers and clients. That's because in the 21st century, talent and market development are connected like two sides of a coin: You may see only one side at a time, but they must coexist, unavoidably connected. The side your leadership identity must connect to first, however, is the talent in the workplace.

Your Leadership Identity—and Identity Crisis

At a pitch to the leaders of the merchandising department at a Fortune 500 company, I closed my presentation by asking the leader of the team,

"What are you trying to solve for?" She didn't know how to answer it. Neither did the other leaders on her team, because only those who have lived their personal brands openly and genuinely and understand their value propositions have taken the steps to break free from their *leadership identity crises.*

These leadership identity crises are real, severe, and have created dysfunction both within the teams those leaders lead and how consumers are identifying with the company and/or its brands and services. They have not only minimized trust but also diminished companies' performance and influence, reduced productivity, and set people back in their careers. These people lost their distinction and their sense of self in the process of having the business define them as individuals. As a result, too many leaders have been acting inauthentically, managing by the templates of old, and cannot evolve to be the leaders their company needs, because those templates stripped them of their identities and left them uncertain about who they are and how to face change. They've lost their leadership identity to the corporation through assimilation and how it wants them to be defined, suppressing or checking their personal brand value propositions at the proverbial door. Perhaps they are assimilating to a mandate or just a philosophy that is undefined—both of which over time make individuals lose their leadership identities in the process if they don't feel aligned to it. This becomes even more apparent when companies refresh their value propositions only when the people at the top are replaced or shareholders and boards demand it and force that change on the rest of the employees. That's the business defining the individual.

Shouldn't we be doing the reverse or at least the same when high turnover reaches critical mass in the middle or in the roles where people touch the business every day to ensure alignment between their goals and the company's?

Simply put, corporations are smothering people and not letting them be who they are. The bigger issue, though, is so many companies don't even see the bigger picture: that what they are doing is perpetuating the problems they are trying to solve. I spoke to leaders from an organization that later told me, "Glenn, we can't support your leadership program as it doesn't support our current leadership development curriculum."

I accept that. But when I asked about the curriculum, the executive in charge laid out a program that was familiar to me from hundreds of companies: an amalgam of the same leadership materials I had seen for decades—a mismatched mix of perfectly good but very different content thrown together that didn't align with what the company solved for and the type of leaders it wanted to create. In fact, this executive, while he clearly articulated the curriculum, couldn't even tell me why he and others had to go through the program. He was unclear of what the training solved, even if he was clear that it offered credible content and material.

This is how leadership identity crises are born.

American Leadership Is Suffering from a Leadership Identity Crisis

Here's how a senior executive from a Fortune 50 company explained this workplace frustration and his identity crisis: "My company brand defines me. My job title is my credential. My quarterly evaluation binds me. I am told that I am next to being promoted, only to find my boss is leaving the organization. My boss controls my future. I am forced to start over by proving that I am still worthy of the 'next in line status.'"

I am sure this executive's words sound familiar to many of you. It's what most people sound like when their identities have become marginalized and their employers define them as a headcount liability rather than valuable assets. It's what people resigned to this fate sound like when they've become dependent on others rather than *themselves* for their self-worth and would rather value more what others think or believe.

When companies don't value individuals like this executive and simply train them on what they want their leaders to be, it is easy for those leaders to forget why they are in business. As illustrated in Figure 2.7 on page 72, you can easily see why personal brands and value propositions are losing their meanings and a leadership identity crisis results; what value does anything personal have?

When the people at the top have these leadership identity crises, those in the middle of the organization on down find it difficult to begin their

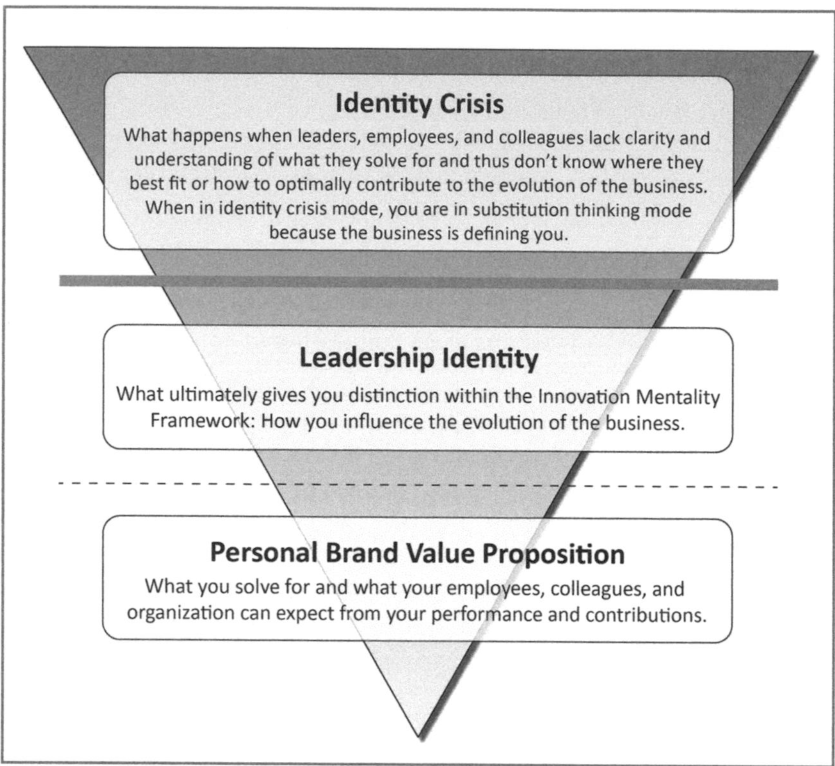
Identity Crisis
What happens when leaders, employees, and colleagues lack clarity and understanding of what they solve for and thus don't know where they best fit or how to optimally contribute to the evolution of the business. When in identity crisis mode, you are in substitution thinking mode because the business is defining you.
Leadership Identity
What ultimately gives you distinction within the Innovation Mentality Framework: How you influence the evolution of the business.
Personal Brand Value Proposition
What you solve for and what your employees, colleagues, and organization can expect from your performance and contributions.

Figure 2.7—How Your Identity Crisis Affects Your Leadership Identity and Personal Brand Value Proposition

journey to develop their personal brands and value propositions. This is especially dangerous, because the people who are driving the evolutionary thinking are the ones in the middle of the organization—who also tend to be the most diverse—while the ones stuck in the substitutionary thinking are at the top of the organization. Thus, the middle faces a choice: Act authentically and establish their own leadership identities and be marginalized, or assimilate to what the company expects. Is it any wonder those people are confused, stuck, and anxious to be recognized during a time when most are doing more for less? They don't know how to fit in a workplace that is fueled with false promises and unexpected outcomes without preparation. Because if they don't know themselves, how can they know anybody else and truly invest in them as individuals? How can those

Are You Dictating Your Path?

Meet "Christine," a client of ours who gave us permission to use her story but not her name. As you read, think of how you can relate to this situation and the way she course-corrected.

Christine's colleagues and peers were not taking her seriously as a leader. She had a reputation of not being assertive enough in meetings, too soft-spoken with senior leadership, and not being sufficiently active in company functions and industry networking. Though she was well liked and a strong performer, she played it safe rather than finding ways to leverage her likeability—whether to enable positive outcomes, be more politically savvy, or open new doors of opportunity for herself, her direct reports, and the teams that she led.

Simply put, Christine had allowed the workplace environment to define her personal brand value proposition and leadership identity because she focused too much on being well liked and fell into the trap of complacency. As a result, she became focused on driving results—sowing, sowing, sowing—and lost sight of her other responsibilities as a leader, which was to be a great decision-maker; to be strategic, visionary, collaborative, and entrepreneurial; and to employ greater focus on making those around her better. After three years on the job, she wasn't leading; she was managing. She felt stuck, unable, and unsure how to navigate her career into a more elevated leadership role within the organization to have more impact and influence.

Christine was an extremely qualified and experienced leader, but she had never defined her personal brand value proposition well enough to manage her reputation and establish her leadership identity. Thus, like so many leaders, she was unknowingly being irresponsible to the organization and the people she served. As she battled the gulf between assimilation and authenticity, her employees looked for consistency in her approach, more authoritative presence in her style, and heightened performance standards

Are You Dictating Your Path?, continued

for her teams. They wanted a leader who was confident in whom she was and deliberate in leveraging her strengths. Christine needed to dive into her full potential as a leader to help others grow and prosper in their roles. Until she did, her employees would feel she was putting their careers and their own reputations at risk.

When Christine realized this in our workshop (using the same exercises I just covered), it was a wake-up call to break free from her leadership identity crisis. She stepped back and re-evaluated her leadership skills and those characteristics that came most naturally to her. She became determined to live her most authentic self. She identified her strengths, asked her colleagues to provide transparent feedback, and started to align herself with the right people and organizational resources to elevate her leadership presence. She stopped micromanaging people and started to define roadmaps for their success. She ultimately took control of her reputation by viewing herself as the enabler of her full potential rather than depending on the organization. She trusted herself enough to actively put her ideas and ideals to the test and soon began to find her leadership rhythm.

leaders understand what others solve for and help others guide and define that for themselves?

In today's new normal, people want to be part of a workplace culture that allows them to be their natural, authentic selves—one that supports their efforts to be more purposeful, responsible, and accountable. Everyone (from the front desk and mailroom on up) wants a role to play. Instead, they are losing their identity and their skill sets are becoming outdated while their employers try to figure out their future. This is also what makes consumers less trusting, because they don't believe a brand's intention is authentic. That's why consumers are asking, "If you are trying to market to me, do you have more of me in leadership? Do you support me through more than just corporate social responsibility?" If companies continue to hold their employees hostage to the problem, workplace performance will be strained and dissatisfaction will continue to rise with no real solutions in sight.

This is how companies can write beautiful presentations about new brand strategies or diversity and inclusion plans but not be able to answer the question regarding what these strategies or plans actually solve for. They say all the right things in their PowerPoint presentations, like "we want a more personal engagement for our brand with consumers" or "we want to create competitive advantage through diversity and inclusion" or "we will develop a diverse employee and leadership pipeline" without understanding what those words *mean*. Without that meaning and thus a clear sense of what they are doing—let alone *why*—those companies are going to lose the competitive advantage they thought they would claim, not to mention current and future employees and customers.

That's why everyone would benefit if leaders broke free from these identity crises. To do this, you need to see with wide-angle, circular vision to manage your leadership identity with proper focus. Yes, these days our visions are clouded with distractions, data overload, and the uncertainty of the global economy. But you must stop getting trapped in all the noise and focus on adopting a new mindset. You have to shift your thinking from the organization as provider to the organization as enabler. In a more profound sense, you need to start thinking of yourself as a participant in a larger whole rather than merely a worker at a particular company. You're part of a greater community, one defined by those areas of expertise and interest that you share with people well beyond the limits of the organization itself. So while your position may feel riskier in some senses, in other ways you will begin to feel greater security as you explore, develop, and inhabit that community. You can regain a perspective and authenticity that makes you capable of surviving and indeed thriving as a leader who transforms the workplace culture through your people, who strengthens your business's brand and impact in the marketplace.

You have to walk away from only sowing and start growing. Sowing alone fuels complacency and your identity crisis.

Embrace Constructive Disruption

There are many reasons this transformation hasn't happened already in business and leadership: fear, entitlement, uncertainty, disconnection, and greed, but the biggest reason is that transformation is hard. We don't like to change. It disrupts what is comfortable and familiar. Forget about embracing transformative leadership that creates constructive disruption of business as usual to drive new ways to enable growth. That's the key word here—*growth*—personally and to our companies' bottom lines. True innovation must create something sustainable with enough impact and influence that it continues to resow its own seeds in the future. But that kind of sustainable growth does not happen by being comfortable and playing it safe. To stop playing it safe, leaders must stop clinging to the hidden agendas and political maneuvering that causes their employees and customers to distrust their intentions. Without that trust, you can't do any of the work ahead. How can you expect people to trust you if they don't know who you are? Thus, the first step in establishing or re-establishing this trust is to get out of this identity crisis management mode.

- **STOP** saying, "What about me?"
- **START** being other-directed and seeing yourself *and* others as personal brands that have different perspectives and want to grow and compete together.

And that means *all people.* I used to think the leaders most affected by these identity crises came from nondiverse backgrounds—those who have led by existing templates and default to inauthentic corporate definitions of who they must be and who they serve are. Today, I understand leaders from diverse backgrounds can have the *greatest* identity crises, because the leaders they learned from have lived with their crises even longer. Those leaders never become intimate enough to understand their diverse leaders, even if they wanted to, and thus enabled those diverse leaders' own identity crises. Is it any wonder then that leaders fail to see value or understand members of their increasingly diverse workplace and marketplace, even if they are part of those diverse populations? If you don't know what gives you distinction, how can you be distinctive or help others find distinction?

Is it any wonder that we are living in an age of identity crises? They don't even understand themselves!

For years, we've allowed people who don't even know their own identities to help shape the identities of others! All because no one embraces diverse thinking and sees the value in being other-directed. Instead of connecting the dots with focus and purpose, we stay silent, lacking the self-trust to lead with distinction and our leadership identities and what they solve for.

What you solve for equals recognition. Leadership identity equals responsibility.

So, how do we truly break free from these identity crises, re-establish our leadership identities, and redefine our corporate cultures for the future? We use the six characteristics of the innovation mentality. Embracing these characteristics gives us permission to own this diverse thinking. They enable the new ideas and ideals that leaders and businesses have not been courageous and vulnerable enough to own. That's how we will see the bigger opportunities, reawaken our entrepreneurial spirits and passionate pursuits, and build strong ecosystems where collaboration and diversity of thought are embraced as opportunities to build a strong legacy.

The workplace and marketplace demand leaders who are connected with individuality and value diverse thinking, who understand that people domestically and globally think differently and want to be accepted and respected for who they are. It wants diverse thinkers who are courageous enough to invest in closing the growing business opportunity gaps between themselves and the company and people who don't look, sound, act, or live like them, or lead in support of a healthier, collective whole.

Simply put, we as leaders must turn the spotlight of accountability on ourselves to strive for excellence—to help guide the evolution of our organizations' futures and that of our clients and customers. We must be passionate in our pursuits to explore endless possibilities, anticipate the unexpected so change is welcomed, embrace an entrepreneurial spirit to make things better, create stronger alignment, and build momentum. What we need is a new mindset, one that takes us from melting pot to mosaic, substitutional to evolutionary thinking, knowledge to wisdom, business to individual, and survival to reinvention. Your ability to see, sow, grow, and share as a leader using the innovation mentality creates an environment that allows others to see, sow, grow, and share, and develop their personal brands and their own leadership identities.

This is not the leadership we learn how to do in school or by imitating other companies. Again, consider Tony Hsieh. His leadership brilliantly defines his company's marketing and publicity plan. He pays employees to leave, lives in a trailer, and got rid of corporate hierarchy and moved to a system of self-management. Agree or disagree, that's diverse thinking. Notice I called Hsieh a diverse thinker, not just diverse (though he is a first-generation American-born child of Taiwanese immigrants). That's because *diversity of thought* rather than of demographics defines his and other leaders' innovation mentalities. When uncertainty is the new normal and growing tensions between leaders and their employees are creating productivity challenges, Hsieh and diverse thinkers like him trust in who they are. They act and face change fearlessly and authentically.

Remember, at its core, the innovation mentality is all about leaders who are genuine, fearless about starting over, and changing their mindset from one based on resistance to one based on continuous survival, renewal, and reinvention.

Leaders suffering from their identity crises have been disconnected from this innovation mentality in corporate America. Does that mean the innovation mentality will eventually put nondiverse leaders out of a job once the nondiverse leaders connect to the diverse thinking they have lived but been forced to repress? No. You don't need to be Hispanic, black, a woman, a Millennial, or any other group who has been struggling with their identities both in and outside of the workplace to be a diverse thinker and embrace the innovation mentality. Just like belonging to any or all of what we call "minority" groups in the workplace and marketplace doesn't guarantee you know your leadership identity and embrace the innovation mentality. Those leaders can't see diverse thinking as a threat to their position within the status quo. This is not baseball in the Jackie Robinson era. This is business in the *Modern Family* era. No one has a target on their back. *All* leaders—regardless of race, ethnicity, sex, sexuality, age, or religion—can and must leverage what they have to advance and include everyone to grow. They must provide enough clarity and understanding to others, or they, like John Doerr at the 2015 TechCrunch Disrupt conference and other nondiverse leaders, will unknowingly create tension and conflict. They must have the wisdom and courage to step back, be a little vulnerable, and get in tune with what and who their leadership identity contributes and influences.

Actually *Modern Family*, the smash ABC sitcom, provides a quick and enjoyable primer on what I mean by the importance of personal brands as they relate to the innovation mentality. Look beyond the comic entanglements and fights that make the show so funny and consider how every character on the show lives their personal brand consistently. And while the result is comic chaos, in time, they learn to value each other's unique differences and solve for their problems. In doing this, though, none of the characters ever diverts from who they are, what they represent, and their authentic selves. Of course, they grow and evolve, but they stay true to their brands, even as they learn and live who they are in every episode. As we watch, they and we discover depth in those brands beyond the words used to describe them (i.e., "the ditzy daughter," "the hot tempered Colombian bombshell," "the high-strung gay couple").

Imagine if you did that with and through your leadership identity—if you used diverse thinking to appreciate the value in their unique differences. Would you create distinction? Yes. Would you know where you fit? Yes. Would you have the experience of authentic relationships with who you are and what you represent as an individual? Yes. Would you be able to influence innovation and initiative because other people would know what to expect from you since you have established your leadership identity? Yes.

Then why don't you?

This is where the six characteristics come in. They enable you to do this as you reinvent or course-correct for any situation you encounter in 21st-century workplaces and marketplaces. As a result, great leaders get the most out of every situation they are faced with by seeing the opportunities they present. They anticipate the unexpected by managing crisis and change before circumstances force their hand. Their passionate pursuits of excellence open new doors of endless possibilities that they aim

Remember, great leaders never take their success for granted. They aim to be significant by finding new ways to elevate the expectations others have of them.

to share with others. And those are just the first three characteristics.

As my mentor at Sunkist told me—and I have lived every day since then—the minute you stop touching the business is the minute you stop understanding the business. That's also the moment leaders stop adding value and their effectiveness begins to wane along with their reputations. The six characteristics of the innovation mentality tests your ability to authentically lead *and* own your leadership identity and the deep responsibility associated with it. Because that's what the six characteristics of the innovation mentality solve for: leadership that continuously and consistently touches the people it serves in the workplace and marketplace and builds trust, and relationships that add value to all our careers, experiences, and lives it influences.

And this is exactly what you'll need to get through the next step. The time has come to take these characteristics, the innovation mentality, and our rediscovered leadership identities and convert this country's melting pot of differences into a mosaic that fuels strategies for growth, innovation, and opportunity to maximize the full potential of people, brands, and businesses. What I call the Cultural Demographic Shift™ (CDS) is upon us, and what it is telling us is this: The days of taking one-size-fits-all approaches are over. We need to capitalize on the opportunities diverse communities present. They are redefining business models that will bring people with many differences together, united under the same corporate values and missions.

It is from the CDS that we truly begin to understand that it has become less about the business defining the individual and much more about the individual defining the business.

CHAPTER 3

CONNECT THE INNOVATION MENTALITY TO THE CULTURAL DEMOGRAPHIC SHIFT™

In 2015, I hosted an executive business summit for senior leaders representing more than 20 Fortune 500 companies. The number of conferences these leaders had previously attended surely numbered in the thousands. I guessed from their reactions that few if any of those conferences included attendees arriving to find drums at their seats . . . 7 A.M.

I watched as the executives examined their drums. Some placed them between their legs as they sat down; others placed them to the side of their chairs. A few refused to decide what to do and instead went to get one more cup of coffee, waiting until compelled to come inside. That moment came as the drumming group I hired took the stage. Their beats filled the ballroom, jolts strong enough to negate jet lag and wake anyone who had not finished their first cup of coffee. As sound and rhythm filled the air, those with the drums between their legs started to play along. Most of the others picked their drums up and joined in too. A small number resisted but not for long. The drum leader soon had everyone following her lead and playing with a passion that had this child of a former Cuban musical star beaming.

The drumming that day spread over the room like a wave at a sporting event, contagious and undeniable. As it moves from the intrepid true believers who start it to the fans in the next sections who take up their call to those across the stadium, a wave becomes undeniable in its movement. When it really rolls, you feel its energy as it approaches; it absorbs differences, unites a sea of individuals, forces even the most resistant minds and bodies into action and their faces into smiles. A wave compels us to see things differently. It changes our focus from the field to the stands, and those who refuse to participate are metaphorically drowned as it passes them. But soon the wave slows and stops, its momentum gone, its transformative power spent. People sit and focus returns to the game at hand.

That could have been the case at the summit that morning as the drumming stopped. The summit, however, was not a game. Instead, the leaders had taken up the call to join a wave that is critical to the future of American businesses and our global competitiveness. They have already become change agents for their companies and the industries they serve. Specifically, those leaders were at the summit to hear and share ideas about embracing and operationalizing the innovation mentality by uniting with a wave that I call The Cultural Demographic Shift™. Those leaders at my summit see the CDS as I do: a game changer for American business and leadership in embracing diversity of thought, engaging developing markets domestically and globally, and retaining and developing the leaders and talent of the future. The "drumbeat" of its approach is one no leader or business can afford to ignore.

Understanding why that is, what it means, and how it connects to all of our futures is our next step in embracing the innovation mentality.

What Is the Cultural Demographic Shift?

First, let's define what we mean by Cultural Demographic Shift (see Figure 3.1 on page 83). The Cultural Demographic Shift, or CDS, is my organization's term for what happens when large cultural segments of the

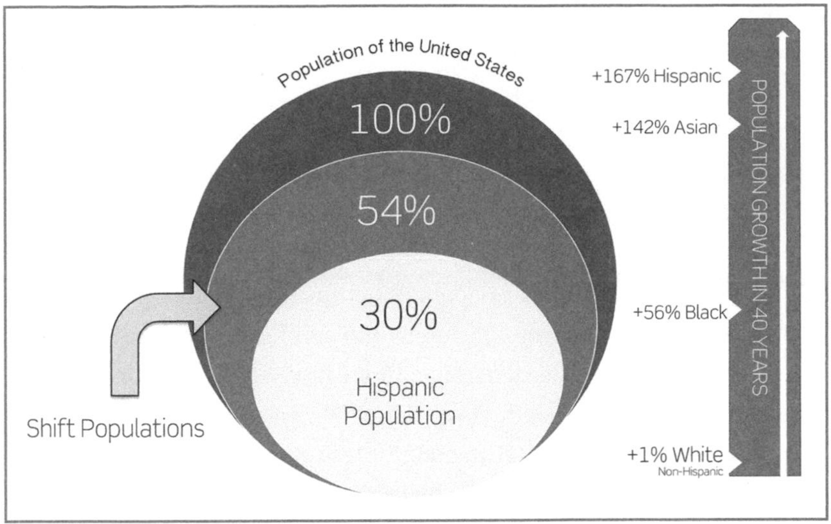

Figure 3.1—The Cultural Demographic Shift

population reach critical mass or numbers sufficient to have a significant effect on what we do and how we act.

According to Nielsen, diverse, or "shift populations," are projected to represent 54 percent of the U.S. population by 2050. But we are already at critical mass with those populations—what we traditionally call "minorities" or "multicultural populations" in the U.S. (i.e., nonwhites such as Hispanics, Asian/Pacific Islanders, and black Americans). Hispanics alone will account for 30 percent of the U.S. population by 2050, a projected increase of 167 percent from 2014. The Asian-American population is expected to grow 142 percent during that same time, blacks 56 percent, and whites (non-Hispanic) only 1 percent. According to PBS *NewsHour*, just four states were majority-minority in 2014 (places where shift populations are a greater percentage than whites). By 2060, there will be 22 states.

Are you and your business prepared for the power of the CDS? Shift populations not only represent the shift in cultural demographics in the U.S., but they are introducing "paradigm shifts" that are influencing reinvention and innovation (new ways of doing things) across all industries, products, and services. The influence of shift populations are compelling all industries to serve the needs of larger, broader populations of employees in the workplace and customers (or patients) in the marketplace and also impact how external partnerships are defined and formed. They are forcing organizations to engage more authentically, embrace diversity of thought, and consider strategies that break free from existing templates to evolve in new ways to create distinction and enable sustainable growth.

If 2050 or 2060 sounds like a long time from now to worry about all this, then consider right now population growth in shift populations is driving major shifts among consumers and employees who are influencing the changing marketplace. Hispanics alone have accounted for nearly half the U.S. population growth since the 2010 census. According to CNN, every 30 seconds two non-Hispanics hit retirement age and one Hispanic turns 18 years old. According to the Selig Center for Economic Growth at the Terry College of Business at the University of Georgia, Hispanics alone will generate 74 percent of our labor force growth by 2020. By 2019, Hispanic buying power is expected to total $1.7 trillion with all other diverse groups totaling $2.5 trillion for a total of $4.2 trillion, or 26.7 percent of the U.S. total of $15.7 trillion. (In 2014, the combined buying power of blacks, Asians, and Native Americans was $2 trillion—117 percent higher than its 2000 level of $916 billion—which amounts to a gain of $1.1 trillion.) That buying power is represented at all income levels. For example, there are more than 15 million upscale Hispanics in the U.S., and 24 percent of Hispanic U.S. households earn more than $75,000, up from 14 percent in 2000. Most of these households are looking to invest, send children to school, buy products, cars, homes, insurance, etc.

But beneath all these numbers there's a problem that should concern anyone. On the face of it, the buying power numbers for Hispanics and other shift populations may look strong and growing. Yet they are low compared to the overall population, especially when you consider market and workplace representation as compared to the overall population growth. Latest estimates from the U.S. Census Bureau show that the non-Hispanic, white population continues to decline, approaching 60 percent overall, but carries outsized weight in buying power. Why? One reason is unemployment. Overall "white" unemployment numbers are about 30 percent less than Hispanic unemployment and 50 percent less than blacks.

Another reason is the age of the populations. According to a special report on America's Hispanics by *The Economist*, nonwhite populations are "making America much younger. The median age of whites is 42; blacks, 32; and Hispanics, 28. Among American-born Hispanics, the median age is a stunning 18." But here's another reason: underemployment in higher-paying positions. The same study by the Selig Center showed that 96 percent of Hispanic professionals are in the earlier stages of their careers or stuck in lower-paying positions. That's a big reason Hispanics are performing at only 40 percent of their full potential. Imagine what would happen to their employment numbers and buying power if this number increased not just for Hispanics but all shift populations? Imagine what it would mean for the American economy.

Why hasn't this happened? Because Hispanics, just like all shift populations, have different values, needs, and beliefs as consumers and employees, and they feel disconnected and devalued, unproductive and disengaged. As David Rennie, Washington Bureau Chief for *The Economist,* wrote in his survey for the magazine, "Some conservatives would retort that most Hispanics are white. They argue that the creation by federal bureaucrats in the 1970s of a new box on forms turned hard-working migrants into an artificial new race, trapping them in a ghetto of grievance politics and government welfare. But that is too glib. For generations Hispanic-Americans were whites on paper only, denied equal access to everything from schools to restaurants or town cemeteries."

This is a major reason why, according to a study by my organization, 81 percent of Hispanics believe their unique perspectives are not valued enough. In other words, they don't feel listened to and recognized by leadership. Our study also revealed an overall lack of cultural intelligence at companies that is perpetuating workplace engagement tension, employee misrepresentations, and stereotypes, which results in lower workplace productivity and engagement among Hispanic employees. Yet companies still try to force Hispanics and other shift populations to assimilate to the status quo instead of joining the wave of the CDS that engulfs *all* populations (diverse and nondiverse). Instead of seeing everyone as uniquely different segments, they force shift populations to battle the gulf between assimilation and authenticity at work. My conclusion is that these factors significantly contribute to the low number of Hispanics and diverse employees represented in senior executive roles as well as the revenue opportunity gap of more than $10 billion across the top three market leaders in all major U.S. industries, whose businesses depend on these consumers for future growth and to remain competitive. A $10 *billion* opportunity gap.

> *Think about the unique differences in people and the factors that influence how people think, act, perform, and are motivated to buy. Collective differences make us stronger and lead to growth.*

Simply put, the CDS requires diversity of thought—new approaches for businesses and their leadership than in the past when the critical mass was mostly white and largely undifferentiated. These shift populations should be changing the ways companies think, act, communicate, perform, and buy—and, in turn, strengthen the overall U.S. economy. Yet too many companies still have their proverbial hands in their laps, watching the wave of the shift pass them by. In these companies, diverse workers and consumers feel the most ignored, insulted, undervalued, misrepresented, misunderstood, and undefined. Sure, these companies and their leaders will tell you that they historically have tried to target Hispanics and other shift populations, and it hasn't been successful because it is very difficult to measure sustainable return on investment (ROI). I understand that, because that was my mentality, too. But it is a different time now. It is not about history or guessing but establishing a competitive advantage by allowing cultural intelligence to be a strategy for growth.

According to my organization's study, while 89 percent of Hispanics perform best in a culture where they feel valued, not judged, and can work with an entrepreneurial spirit and sense of purpose that strengthens overall contributions, only 20 percent of the workplace and corporate values that matter most to Hispanics are represented, authentically applied, and lived in Fortune 500 companies. But then again, whose are—whether they are Hispanic or not? This goes back to what we discussed in Chapter 2: Leaders don't trust themselves enough to live these values and hold each other accountable to do the same. Instead, they hold themselves accountable to what the company wants.

That's how they ended up in an identity crisis. No wonder 92 percent of Hispanics do not gravitate toward their non-Hispanic supervisors because they find them self-absorbed, judgmental, and disrespectful of diverse employees. These types of managers tend to lack the cultural fluency that can increase workplace engagement with their Hispanic and multi-ethnic employees, which helps explain why only 30 percent of Hispanic professionals are actively engaged at work and only 75 percent of Hispanic professionals believe they lack the networking, connections, and relationships to advance.

Although these statistics pertain to Hispanics, similar numbers can be applied to all populations in the CDS. (The Hispanic population represents the largest segment of the shift and serves as a model, a guide for best practices to serve other shift populations.) As David Rennie of *The Economist* told me, "Hispanic populations will soon become an important part of American enterprise and the anchor that will fuel new marketplace investments both from the inside-out and the outside-in. That diversity in leadership will reinvent industries, drive innovation, and change how brands engage with culture and the potential associated with them. America's growing melting pot will soon become a mosaic that will be much younger—and more entrepreneurial—in its pursuit of both success and significance. We just need to realize its full potential."

Listening to and recognizing people is an act of courage, vulnerability, and wisdom in leadership.

Exactly! In fact, as my discussion with Rennie concluded, these diverse audiences will no longer assimilate to white Anglo-Saxon Protestant values the way other immigrant groups have in the past. Instead everyone must use the six characteristics of the innovation mentality to embrace the CDS. These diverse groups will change elections, businesses, and the mindset of America by defining success and significance on their own terms. Isn't that at least part of what this country was founded on? This gets back to what I wrote about in the introduction: We need the courage and wisdom to see this and *listen* to all people and the message of the CDS (see Figure 3.2 on page 88).

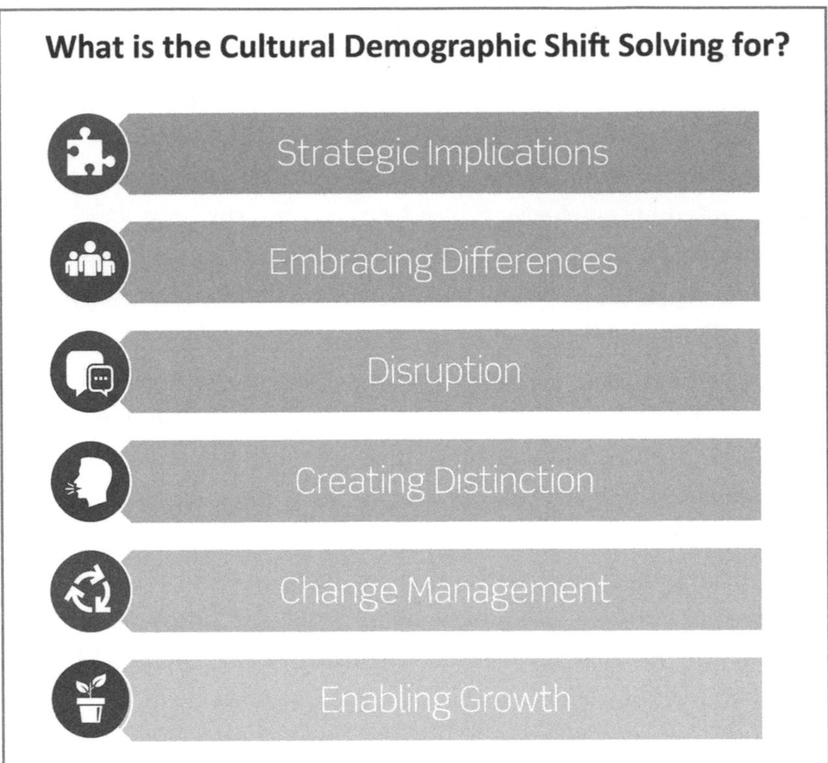

Figure 3.2—What the Cultural Demographic Shift Solves For

Businesses need to be educated on what this means and what makes each group unique, then over-deliver on it, instead of making excuses about how hard it is to measure ROI. Of course, when the one delivering that message is Earvin "Magic" Johnson people tend to listen faster.

Magic Johnson, the Innovation Mentality, and the Cultural Demographic Shift

As chairman and CEO of Magic Johnson Enterprises, Magic Johnson has proved to Sony, Starbucks, and many other brands that urban neighborhoods are not an investment wasteland. How would they know that the demand for products and services doesn't already exist in these neighborhoods? None of the c-suite executives at Sony grew up in or go to the urban neighborhoods that Magic is connected to. He saw how people there had to drive more than an hour outside those neighborhoods to get quality services and goods. Using the first characteristic of the innovation mentality (see opportunities in everything), Magic saw a way to bring Fortune 500 companies looking for growth to drive ROI in urban America—as long as they were willing to adjust how they came in to those urban neighborhoods.

As Magic told leaders from Fortune 500 companies across the U.S. at my summit, "Preparing U.S. Leadership for the Seismic Cultural Demographic Shift," "Urban America is different. You have to tailor to fit in. I know the urban consumer. But before you go in, you have to talk to the people. Explain why it is important to them. You have to educate them why the brand is important. Why your brand is going to make their lives better. I didn't try and create demand. Demand was already there. I understood what the people wanted and then over-delivered on it. Do that and they will become loyal customers and make you money."

Consider Sony, Magic's first target. He knew minorities were the number-one group of people going to the movies, but there were no theaters in the black neighborhoods of Los Angeles just a few miles from Hollywood. So, Magic approached Peter Guber, then chairman of Sony Pictures and offered a partnership: If Sony would deliver the theaters, Magic would deliver the customers. The naysayers said it was not going to work, but Magic practiced what he preached: He went in before the theater opened. He spoke at churches, neighborhood councils, and community groups. He explained why Sony was coming, why he was involved, and how they were going to provide services tailored for urban consumers and jobs for the neighborhood.

Not that Sony listened to everything Magic said—at first. When the food service providers refused to listen to him and gave his theater the same amount of hot dogs they gave suburban theaters, they sold out in a weekend what it took to sell out in a month in suburbia. Magic knew what Sony did not: Minorities don't go to dinner and a movie like suburban customers—they eat *at* the movies. More hot dogs soon arrived to be washed down by grape, orange, and other flavored soda that Magic knew urban customer preferred. The result? "My per caps were so high, we had the highest food sales in the industry," Magic said. "We became a top-ten national theater for the Sony chain in the first year. All because I understood that if you understand the people and you deliver what they want, then you are going to be successful. You can't do urban America from the corner office 3,000 feet in the sky."

Of course, Magic Johnson is a celebrity, as well as a beloved and exceptional basketball player and human being. But his use of diversity of thought to leverage his personal brand and develop a platform for change makes him much more than your typical celebrity sports spokesperson: His work goes beyond the wonderful but limited effort of many athlete's charitable foundations. That's because Magic was a partner in those businesses. That stake made his work was far from charity. It was about providing jobs and services for the communities he cares deeply about.

Because Magic listened, he knew that the people his business employed and served were not loyal to a brand because it was chic or it elevated them; they wanted societal advancement and a connection to the brand's story. In the same way consumers want to know the story behind the products they are buying, shift populations don't want to be sold, they want to be educated. They want to feel that they can advance. If they are not advancing, they can't continue to grow.

It's the concept of resowing to leave a legacy, which is what Magic has left with his partnerships. But that was just his final step. His conversion of a demand in the CDS to sales comes down to one thing any leader and business can do: He embraced six characteristics of the innovation mentality. He saw an opportunity for growth, anticipated the unexpected by talking to the community, pursued his passion for people from the neighborhood, showed his entrepreneurial spirit right down to the food being served, worked with a generous purpose for both the community and his business partners, and left an undisputed legacy that brought business to urban neighborhoods nationwide.

> *Leaders are more like-minded than they think. Just because you are on different paths, doesn't mean you are thinking differently.*

Most leaders and businesses don't hear their own "magic" and are "siloing" demand that already exists, thus missing significant investment and growth opportunities. They are listening to the same things over and over, so they fail to see the unique differences and uncover the business's full potential.

Listening to the Cultural Demographic Shift

Consider my experience in the financial services industry. This industry knows there is an immediate growth opportunity to tap diverse markets, which historically do not keep their money in banks. According to the most recent numbers from the Federal Deposit Insurance Corporation (FDIC), Hispanic households alone represent $53 billion in unbanked wealth—more than double the U.S. rate. In addition, only 33 percent of high-net-worth Hispanic individuals have retirement plans. Knowing this, a major financial services company invited me to present at one of its large annual meetings. After my presentation, I met a Colombian couple who worked as representatives at the company and was succeeding in attracting Hispanic households. As I listened to their amazing story, I realized I should train all my leaders to understand their mindset, because Hispanics are going to fuel my immediate growth needs and represent the future of my clientele. *Every* leader could learn how best to serve this underserved community by recognizing what's important to them. But that requires *courageous listening*, which means you must be vulnerable to the people who are most critical to you.

Yet nobody at this company was doing that. This is not unusual in financial services firms, even when they create diversity and inclusion plans to ostensibly support shift populations once they are hired. How are you going to retain them and make them feel valued and comfortable and like they fit in? You will need to reinvent your leadership team. You could recruit people and inspire them with a "dog and pony show." But what are the validators you will provide? What will get them to make the commitment? I get the government is all over certain sectors like finance to make this commitment, but I'm convinced these businesses only have strategies to get them in the door. Why would they stay?

Later that evening, when I ran into one of the company's executives, I told him, "I want to introduce you to two of your representatives, but if I do, there are some ground rules: First, I just want you to listen. Thank them for being part of the organization, and ask them, 'What can I do to help?' Second, I want you to stay for at least 15 minutes and *really* pay attention to do that. And third, tomorrow you have to send them an email and tell them you appreciate the time that you spent with them."

Those are the first steps to celebrating differences within your organization and embracing the wave of the CDS. It sounds so simple. Then *why* wasn't this company doing it? After all, they were wise enough to *hire* this couple. Why did they lack the wisdom to embrace what they had to offer? That's basic first characteristic understanding: See opportunity in everything and everyone.

And quite frankly that opportunity for growth isn't hard to see. According to an analysis of EthniFacts and the CDS conducted by Nik Modi of RBC Capital Markets, Equity Research, August 22, 2014, marked the exact day that the U.S. officially became a "Majority Interethnic Society." As Modi says, "While Non-Hispanic white Americans compose most of the U.S. population, [they] are often married to, living with, or nearby people of a different ethnicity, leading them to make multicultural consumption decisions."

As Modi further explained to me, "Consumer companies that have been around for a long time may have a rich history, but it's not necessarily one that is multicultural. What they find is that they have such an ingrained way of doing business that the pace of change around the Cultural Demographic Shift is moving way too fast for them. They're used to very low levels of volatility in how things operate, and consumer preferences shift. That's why authenticity is so important. Every company talks about it, but not many understand why it matters so much—or how powerful it can be when you get it right. Every aspect of a company—how they manage business, create strategies, promote from within, market to consumers, etc.—must revolve around authenticity. But you can't create authenticity with a distribution-led model. It has to grow organically over time to be authentic. A good example is Corona beer. It took time to go mainstream, but once it did, it became a multicultural brand that was authentic to everyone, whether you were a first-generation Hispanic living in downtown L.A. or a young professional working on Wall Street."

Investing in the cultural intelligence and know-how to correctly approach Hispanics—the largest and fastest-growing segment of the

CDS—will give organizations a fresh template they can use for all other cultural demographic employee and consumer segments. And as you prepare your organization's leadership for the CDS, you will be creating the ideal ecosystem to ignite sustainable growth for your business.

Unfortunately, that is not happening quickly enough in authentic ways. My experience at this financial services company was not unusual. Too many nondiverse leaders and thinkers don't see potential like this. That is why many leaders at my CDS summit have been working hard to get their own companies to embrace the shift, working hard to push it beyond its confinement to corporate diversity programs. And those are people from companies that ostensibly *want* to change. This shift remains largely a topic for closed-door discussions among executives who feel uncomfortable discussing it because they are being challenged in their abilities to personally connect and relate to it.

This is what happens when too few diverse thinkers populate c-suites and boardrooms. According to a June 2013 survey by executive search consultants Russell Reynolds Associates, a significant share of Fortune 250 boards lack representation from specific diversity groups while 17 percent are composed exclusively of white directors. And according to the "Board Monitor" report from executive search firm Heidrick & Struggles, of the 399 new directors selected for top company boards last year, Hispanics claimed only six seats.

When I asked the COO at Aramark, Victor Crawford, why we can't move faster to embrace the CDS, he told me, "You would think that there is not just a business sense to do so but a moral sense to advance this topic a lot faster than we do. But you have to carry a torch for all these folks who are in leadership today. I think those folks are afraid. The current leaders are intimidated that they will no longer be needed if they embrace this change. So they dismiss it, even if they buy into it—or worse: They buy into the ideas but believe it does not apply to them. It's not me; it is someone else. It is like the movie *Groundhog Day*, but not quite, because every time this movie starts over another company is gone."

For those of you who haven't seen the movie Crawford's analogy is perfect. *Groundhog Day* stars Bill Murray as an arrogant TV weatherman from the big city who finds himself forced to relive the same day in a small town covering the annual emergence of the groundhog from its hole. How did the main character in that movie break the vicious circle of living the same day over and over again? He finally owned his leadership identity. He showed he had the wisdom, vulnerability, and courage to confront the failures of his past attitudes, actions, and desires, and create a future that authentically celebrates and serves others despite how uncomfortable it initially feels. In many ways, he embraces the six characteristics of the innovation mentality in one ever-repeating day to effect real change in himself and others, which is why the movie is used as a reference in many self-improvement books and speeches.

The Cultural Demographic Shift compels leaders to embrace the innovation mentality.

But this isn't a movie. To own what we need to do in the face of this CDS, leaders must take responsibility for rethinking entire business models. The CDS compels leaders to embrace the innovation mentality. We must be fearless about starting over and shift our mindsets from ones based on resistance to ones based on continuous survival, renewal, and reinvention. To do this, we must see the CDS as a profit center (investment) linked to individuals defining the business, not a cost center (expense) linked to the business defining the individual (see Figure 3.3 on page 95).

The impact of the CDS is a big enough "burning platform"—a natural and evolutionary "crisis" that forces change—to merit full attention. After all, the changes it brings will affect nearly everything about how a company:

- Plans for future growth
- Allocates capital management resources
- Creates new brands, products, and service opportunities
- Defines the most effective workgroups and organizational teams
- Strengthens external partnerships and strategic alliances in search of the right intellectual capital
- Authentically engages its clients and customers in support of its own business model

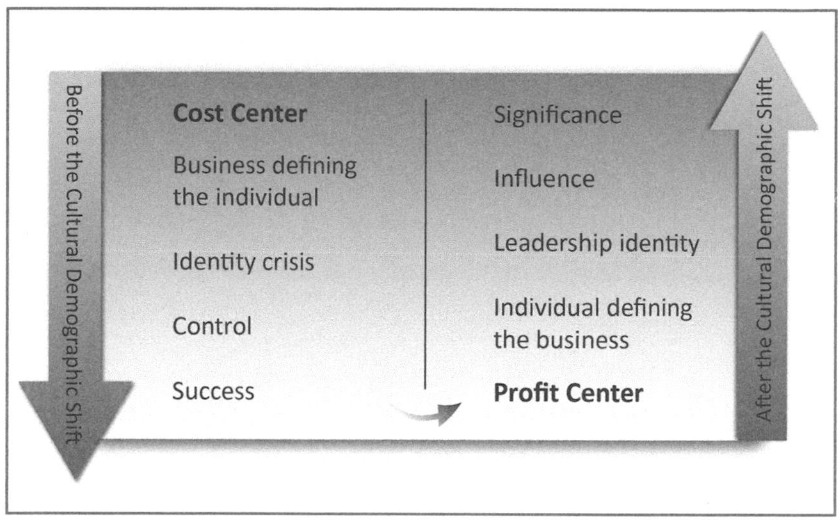

Figure 3.3—See the Shift as a Profit Center, Not a Cost Center

The CDS is more than the new "diversity flavor of the month." It's a seismic *business* adjustment that is revising the standards and best practices by which our businesses lead, recruit, and retain top talent, as well as innovate, market, and sell to the new American consumers overall (not just diverse populations). The CDS and the global market represent the new normal—the core elements that must be embraced for leaders and their organizations to welcome change in order to evolve. Seeing and participating in the CDS becomes a competitive advantage for *any* company that stands up and learns to ride this wave. Think of the CDS as the enabler to make your overall business smarter, more sustainable, and wiser. The six characteristics are the strategies to break through old templates that blind us to this and rediscover our leadership identities to guide the new ways to work and lead. Now it is time to use the characteristics to see and feel the CDS coming, anticipate the bumps, and capitalize on hundreds of billions of dollars in opportunity gaps. If that's not enough to get you serious about this, the odds are very much in favor that someone else who sees the CDS as a growth strategy will.

CHAPTER 4

SEE OPPORTUNITY GAPS THROUGH THE INNOVATION MENTALITY

As Magic Johnson showed in Chapter 3, those who are slow to make decisions, fail to take action, or take things for granted as the wave of the Cultural Demographic Shift gains strength will be washed away, replaced by those who act to own the market. Mike Fernandez, chairman of MBF Healthcare Partners, made the bulk of his fortune doing exactly that. Fernandez gained his competitive advantage by using the innovation mentality to pioneer in health care, an industry that had underserved shift populations. To understand how, we must learn why the industry has struggled to evolve.

An Opportunity Gap Case Study: Health Care and the Cultural Demographic Shift

The health-care industry did not ride the wave of the CDS from the beginning and has found itself in a hole with shift populations as it moves from a cottage industry to big business. According to Top

Issues Confronting Hospitals 2015, a report by the American College of Healthcare Executives (ACHE), issues like "patient satisfaction" and "personnel shortages" are on the rise, especially among shift patient populations. That's because shift populations do not always feel welcomed by the health-care industry. They tend to associate doctors with hospitals and hospitals with a place to die, not get better. This is why many first-generation Hispanics would rather have a major surgical procedure performed in their mother countries than in the U.S. This is a bigger issue when you consider businesses across all industries are realizing wellness among employees and customers is essential to sustained success in business, especially customer engagement and career advancement.

Let's consider the Hispanic population more specifically. This population represents the largest shift population segment of the health-care market and can serve as a model to guide businesses on how to serve other groups represented by the shift. Historically, Hispanics have not managed their health well. They are often not proactive with their preventive care and thus disproportionately experience major health problems later in their lives. For example, according to the American Diabetes Association, compared to non-Hispanic whites, Hispanics have a 66 percent higher risk of being diagnosed with diabetes and 43 percent more are obese. (For blacks, the percentages are even higher—77 percent and 48 percent, respectively—though blacks represent a smaller percentage of the population.)

Addressing health disparities and inequities in the Hispanic community is becoming more urgent as the nation's demographics shift. Without a course correction, the threat to the U.S. economy and impact on global competitiveness will be catastrophic. This community needs doctors and nurses who can speak Spanish and understand cultural nuances to educate Hispanics about health and more. Yet according to a 2015 study by UCLA, in 1980, there were 135 Hispanic physicians for every 100,000 Hispanics. By 2010, that number was 105 for every 100,000, a 22 percent decline. In California alone, Hispanics surpassed whites as the largest racial/ethnic group with 39 percent of the state's population, yet in 2014 only 4.8 percent of the state's physicians and 8 percent of registered nurses were Hispanic. This mirrors what is happening nationally: The national percentage of doctors who are Hispanic is at 5 percent and declining, and for nurses it is 7.5 percent and only slightly growing. Exact national figures for Hispanic patients are not available, but you don't need to be a statistician to realize that if the Hispanic population increased by 243 percent between the 1980 and 2010 censuses, the number of Hispanic patients nationwide has only grown. According to the U.S. Department of Health and Human Services, the uninsured rate among Hispanics dropped by more than 25 percent since 2010. Yet at the same time, the number of physicians and nurses has declined, leaving a huge cultural deficit between workplace and marketplace. The result is Hispanics are insured but are still terrified to go to a doctor. Like many shift populations, when Hispanics come in, they want to talk as well as get the health care they need. This is why the National Institutes of Health "recognizes a unique and compelling need to promote diversity in the biomedical, behavioral, clinical, and social sciences research workforce."

What are health-care businesses doing about this?

I visited a major southern university hospital—one of the best in the country—and asked them what their strategy for Hispanic engagement was. Their answer (and this is not a joke): "Oh, we just hired a translator."

What? That's not evolution—that's putting the tiniest bandage possible on a serious wound. Unfortunately, that answer is pretty typical and applies to shift populations as customers and clients in almost every industry.

With health care evolving to a patient-centered model, health-care providers must change their businesses to a relationship-based model in which they grow together with their patients and customers from birth to end of life. Patients want to see people who look like them and understand their unique needs that are influenced by their cultural heritage. They want people who know and respect their culture and their values and do so in a legitimate and authentic way. But this is at odds with health care getting progressively consolidated, regulated, and systematized in the age of the Affordable Care Act (ACA), which fuels tension instead of trust, as organizations continue to unknowingly perpetuate an identity crisis among shift populations. Too many of these organizations don't know how to authentically serve shift populations. They don't understand their culture or how they think, and as a result, fail to allow these populations to take ownership for their own health let alone pursue health-care careers.

This is why the CDS is driving a revolution in healthcare businesses in the U.S. As the percentage of individuals from fast-growing shift populations become insured and gain access to health care through the ACA, the ratio of those who are culturally fluent enough to serve them is on the rapid decline. And it is not just doctors and nurses who lack this fluency. Insurance companies (payers) and providers have reached out to my organization for what they often call "cultural fluency training," because they don't have employees on their teams to sell health plans to organizations that serve shift populations. Health care is stuck in the silo mentality in which people, groups, and departments lack the intellectual capital and know-how, which makes the industry inefficient and ineffective when it comes to the CDS. They hear terms such as "diversity and inclusion" and default into compliance mode, rather than seeing the broader growth opportunity to evolve with their shift patient populations. Whether they are providers or payers or anywhere on the health-care spectrum, companies that have the right intellectual capital and best practices to lead through the CDS shift will win the war for diverse talent. They will also help strengthen health-care delivery and overall decision making to best serve shift populations and create new private/public partnerships and revenue streams in the process.

Preparing U.S. health-care executives for the CDS is a logical and essential evolution from the recent health-care delivery discussions around value over volume. The idea is that to improve health outcomes, providers and payers need to move away from rewards for volume-driven care and shift to value-driven care, which rewards providers for keeping people healthy and reducing costs. But without approaching the CDS as a strategy for growth, it becomes more difficult to deliver real, sustainable value to shift patient populations that are trying to trust in and engage with the health-care system.

All this makes health care a perfect example of failing to heed what I talked about in Chapter 2: Talent and market development must represent two sides of the same coin. The unique health-care needs and lifestyle perspectives of shift populations and consumers have rarely been understood or valued enough, or they would be reflected in organizational missions, business models, and brand value propositions. As a result, the gap is widening not only between those who are gaining health insurance and access to health care but also between those people and the physicians, nurses, and staff that are reflective of them and/or culturally equipped to serve them. You can't put together strategies for attracting customers without effectively recruiting and employing the people who connect to those customers and can lead and manage through the CDS. You can't just pay people and expect them to do it for you either. You need to have people intelligence. And you can't have that unless a business and its leaders see it as a true opportunity gap.

Mike Fernandez saw this lack of people intelligence and saw opportunity (the first characteristic of the innovation mentality) long before anyone else—and it netted him billions of dollars. According to Fernandez, his success did not start with him spending millions to make millions. It began with him using his entrepreneurial spirit (the fourth characteristic) and having the wisdom to spend the time, energy, and thought on strategies that would evolve his businesses. That and realizing it was OK to do well and do good and help the community he is a part of (the fifth characteristic: generous purpose).

When Fernandez started his company, most health-care businesses focused on the majority of the population. They assumed (and still do) that the minority would adjust to what the majority buys. "The non-Anglo-Saxon population is tens of millions of people," said Fernandez, "You expect them to adjust? As an economy, the Hispanic population alone would be the seventh largest in the world, and their purchasing power would be the sixteenth largest. What would you pay to start a company to capture a market of this size? You have a market bigger than Brazil in your backyard with a growing purchasing power, and you can spend a fraction of what it would take to get that market in Brazil and get to know it. That's what I did. I built it for this population, and then someone buys it. Today, I've been involved in 28 companies. Of them, two have failed and the rest were acquired because they were great companies." As Fernandez said to me, "Ownership is the difference between wanting to be relevant and someone who just allows life to pass them by."

Don't let life pass you by. Do what everyone who has ridden the subway in London or elsewhere is told lest they fall into the space between the train doors and the station platform: "Mind the gaps."

That's what Paul Heredia, chief human resources officer at Citrus Valley Health Partners in Covina, California, did to lead change management efforts, starting with a mindset shift among physician leaders used to thinking that the doctor-patient relationship is all about them. After all, even if we had dozens more Xavier Universities, it is not like new doctors who reflect the diversity of the patients can be minted quickly, so diversity of thought needs to be driven through the existing leadership while more diverse doctors are trained. As Heredia explained, "Today, connecting with the patient means a complete transformation, starting with the realization that it's no longer about you, the doctor. It's about understanding the patient communities you serve and the demographics they represent. It's about a clear focus on patients and patient care that's specific to those communities. Without that alignment in mindset, a 'me mentality' will be perpetuated instead of the learning that needs to take place about the populations and the people that we serve."

His advice for a company struggling with this old school "me" mentality with their customers? "You can't just tell people they've got to change. You've got to educate leaders by showing them something compelling: the data," says Heredia. "For example, we know that patients want three basic things from their doctor: heal me, don't hurt me, and be nice to me. You may think you're a good doctor, but with regard to these basics, what are your patients saying about you? Are you courteous and respectful, do you listen to them and make them feel like you are taking good care of them? Changing the mindset starts with this level of education around the data and the voice of the patient. Besides the patient, you've got to look at things from the point of view of the next generation. The up and coming talent is realizing that 'what got us here is not going to get us there.' For example, why are diabetic rates in our service area—which is predominantly Hispanic—three times that of the national rate? When you see differences like this, you have to ask how you can better serve Hispanic patients. How can you help them improve their health and well-being, which affects every facet of their lives, including the next generation modeling their behavior? If you can help the

Hispanic community grow and prosper, then you're making a real impact not only with their health but their financial well-being, their educational and social status, and even their spiritual well-being. If you're not doing this, you're not going to survive because your patients will be lined up outside the doors of the doctors who are."

Angela Patterson, vice president at CVS Health, and chief nurse practitioner officer of CVS MinuteClinic, would agree and added this point about the health-care industry mirroring the communities it serves, so it can engage those communities. She says the industry has to realize that "health is something that for the most part happens outside of health-care facilities, and where it really takes root is within the families and communities we serve. You also have to think of health in more than just physical terms. There are social determinants that come into play where health is concerned, be it culture, the economy, the school system, even the system of sanitation in your neighborhood. These all can have a powerful impact on the health and well-being of the community, so in addition to reflecting the patient population, we have to create systems that are representative of community needs."

This is affects us all, not simply Hispanics. It is shocking to most medical institution executives I've talked with that this amount of intellectual capital already exists but not when you consider that historically there has not been clarity around the importance and benefits of serving Hispanic patients. As such, there has not been any alignment among leaders within each major functional/departmental area. This is why the health-care industry is not in a position to lead change management efforts to best serve the CDS during a time when the demand for it is at an all-time high.

This goes way beyond health care, however. It explains why so many organizations have difficulty aligning their internal brand (the perceived workplace environment) with their external brand (what customers expect from their products and/or services). When the realities of both are not in alignment, it makes it difficult to sustain any real momentum and a positive reputation that matters to employees and clients. This is why leaders must have clarity in purpose and focus and an alignment of strategic philosophy and resolution goals for their change management objectives. There must be a common language that guides execution, monitors progress, and allows for course correction along the way. There must be a culture where leaders are willing to share all their intellectual capital, and everyone throughout the organization values teamwork and the urgency of breaking down silos. Above all, there must be a well-thought-out, clearly defined, and communicated strategy behind any change management effort—that's where you can begin to show real leadership clarity and alignment.

To prepare for and own the changes wrought by the CDS, you must do what Hernandez and Heredia did: Use the innovation mentality to recognize opportunity gaps, identify why they exist, see their potential, and solve for them using the six characteristics. That's the path to growth. That's also how Magic Johnson won over Sony: He brought diversity of thought to the entire business strategy, model, and approach so he could capitalize on a huge growth opportunity in urban America. He broke through the barriers in which people, groups, and departments refuse to share with others, which not only makes those businesses inefficient but also contaminates the culture, especially when it comes to the CDS.

Seize the Cultural Demographic Shift Opportunity

When you have your own silo, and other leaders and groups are stuck in theirs, this shift doesn't mean anything. You can understand it and use what you learn to solve problems that we are all dealing with so that you and your business learn to value the potential in our differences. That's how you wind up with strategies that are about substitution (doing what you've always done) not evolution (doing what needs to be done to change). That's how you end up treating the CDS as a cost center (an expense in substitution) rather than a profit center (an investment in evolution) and telling everyone they are unique and different but never talking about, let alone recognizing, how it contributes to the bottom line. To do this and seize business opportunities and ROI in any population represented in the shift the way Magic did, you can't just sell to people. You need follow these four steps:

1. *Educate leadership* (define and commit to what you are solving for; be committed; build a strong foundation to educate others).

2. *Over-deliver value* (don't sell; selling without understanding unknowingly creates tension; serve the unique needs of your workplace and marketplace).
3. *Embrace mutuality* (convert diversity of thought into opportunities previously unseen to benefit everyone).
4. *Define your platform* (evolve and multiply what you are solving for).

The best way to appreciate these steps is see them as part of the scale in Figure 4.1, "Seize the Cultural Demographic Shift Opportunity."

"Educate Leadership" is about committing to evolve and changing the template—re-educating ourselves and helping to define what we are solving for. The reason corporate templates don't work is that people don't understand what they mean. They don't know how to translate them into tangible desired outcomes and how their own leadership identity can best support them. Corporate frameworks become words that unknowingly create tension.

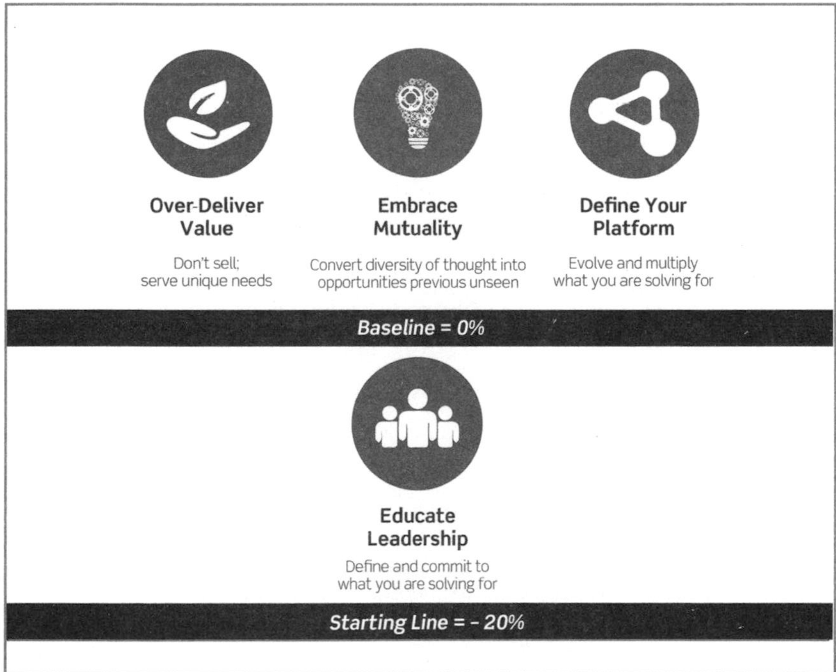

Figure 4.1—Seize the Cultural Demographic Shift Opportunity

Note how the "Educate Leadership" step gets you only to the baseline in the scale. Given our inability to embrace the CDS populations, your starting line is actually –20 percent. For some companies, it can start or drop even lower if people believe you are focused on initiatives that never develop any meaning or sustainable actions. Remember, that offends any target audience and creates unnecessary tension because it looks like you are throwing a bone to people, rather than presenting an evolved strategy that represents commitment. You will only get to zero percent when you engage with your employees, customers, and external partners and define and commit to what you are solving for. And every time you don't fully commit or take ownership and live the characteristics, you fall backward into the negative and must recommit yourself to get back to the baseline.

Not only do you fall backward, but you get into situations like the city of Los Angeles found itself in. In 2013, the populations of the CDS had already become the majority, with the nonwhite Hispanic population alone surpassing whites as the city's largest demographic group. Moreover, the number of Los Angeles residents born outside the U.S. was approaching 40 percent. Yet fewer than 1 percent of the city's elected officials represented first-generation ethnic populations. As a result, those leaders struggled to authentically connect with those populations. They didn't know how, because they followed the old template—right down to the voting. Los Angeles County may be home to the largest voting jurisdiction in the U.S., but voter turnout is at record lows, and whites are over-represented at the polls while shift populations are underrepresented.

As a result, city leaders kept falling backward from the baseline and starting over at –20 because they couldn't engage with their local community from a leadership standpoint. This lack of education and connection affected the Los Angeles economy on a *global* scale by severely hindering the city's ability to authentically reach out and enhance foreign trade across Latin America, Mexico, Asia, and India—populations that are clearly represented in Los Angeles.

Since 2013, Los Angeles has taken several steps to stay above the baseline, including more than $10 million in statewide spending to boost voter turnout and the creation of the Los Angeles Area Chamber of Commerce's New American Leaders Program, which was designed to find leaders who represented the city's overall demographics and seize the broader opportunities. But even if these and other programs succeed, the city would still find itself only at the baseline. Only when the education is complete do you have the opportunity to grow past zero and face the choice to lead people or sell to them. When you lead them, you are advancing yourself by serving others (i.e., innovation mentality characteristic five: working with a generous purpose). You aren't selling to people when you understand and serve them. That's how you "over-deliver value"—by serving others and embracing their unique needs. Selling without that level of understanding unknowingly creates tension. Over-delivering value eliminates the tension leaders too often unknowingly create (by feeling a sense of entitlement to force those who already do not feel they are understood or are valued to adapt to the majority, which is exactly what Mike Fernandez saw happening in health-care delivery).

When you are selling to people without being aware of their unique needs, that sale comes across as if you are taking advantage of them rather than educating a community that demands reciprocal relationships. When you do that, you are embracing mutuality, creating opportunity with and for these shift populations, and giving them influence in the process. Listen and observe what they do and why, and how they do it to understand their value of, approach to, and style in the things that matter to them. Consider Magic Johnson, who over-delivers value in every partnership and reimagines the templates of leaders and their companies who believe there is only one way to conduct business. You should never do something one way until you have reached the finish line by embracing mutuality and creating authentic relationships that define your platform. At that point, the one way should be about mutual discovery so everyone feels they are growing and defining your platform becomes about staying committed.

Too often, leaders and companies think they have reached the finish line after their initial successes. No! They are still at the midway point at best and still must evolve and multiply. We must be courageous and vulnerable enough to take ownership and reinvent the approach constantly to avoid slipping back into substitution after making so much evolutionary progress.

In some ways, this is just common sense. As Caroline Wanga, vice president corporate social responsibility at Target Corp., said at my Cultural Demographic Shift summit, "Nobody questions you when you give extra attention to a product that is underperforming. You have to identify what to do about it before returning it to your total portfolio because your goal is for all your products to perform on par with what they were expected to do. So when we talk about diversity, it's really an effort to get to parity, not to give competitive advantage to anyone. We have to dismantle that myth, because what it's really about is giving everybody the same experience of opportunity. It's about equality and equity. I like to say that my job is not to give everybody a shoe; it's to give everybody a job that fits."

What Wanga notes is not a Target problem; it is a global problem. And it requires much more than businesses simply cutting a check for diversity training or sponsorships and paying lip service to the idea of an ideal. We have plenty of loud calls for change and diversity, but there is no substance behind them. We've gotten very good at pointing out the problem, but we continue to substitute the failed solutions with more failed solutions instead of evolving to truly confront and solve the problem. That's what puts us at –20 for the starting line in Figure 4.1.

I get that we are all trying to be inclusive, and I don't think our efforts are malicious. But while I understand the intentions are good, the outcomes are not always. They are well meaning, but most of the time they lack the wisdom of courageous thinking and are lazy when it comes to engagement, leaving everyone tired of the same uninspiring conversations.

Will that wisdom and courage eliminate the mistakes and missteps of the past? Of course not. Fernandez admits he has made mistakes. For example, he failed to anticipate the unexpected and see the nuances in the Hispanic market. Specifically, he did not see that Hispanics in El Paso are not only very different from New York and Chicago but they are also very different from Hispanics in other parts of Texas. But his high success rate is founded on another essential lesson from Chapter 2 for dealing with the CDS: Business today is becoming less about the business defining the individual and more about the individual defining the business.

"We never bet on an industry; we bet on individuals," Fernandez says. "The individual is the one who can make a business." And when he doesn't understand the individuals? He educates himself *and* finds partners to help him who already have that understanding. That's how Fernandez and Magic Johnson ended up partnering in a business that served HIV-positive patients, of which Magic is one. The partners may seem like an unlikely pairing, but despite their different upbringings, races, professional experience, and politics, they appreciate those differences and see power in respecting them to create another thriving entity under Fernandez's company umbrella. Their first action at the HIV health-care company? Staff the business mostly with HIV patients and people who know or are related to them. "The same way someone from South Dakota cannot understand me being from Cuba, I had to learn to understand HIV patients. When we acquired Simply Healthcare in 2011, it had $38 million in revenues. Four years later, [it is] a $1.2 billion company without a single acquisition—all organically grown, all from bringing in the right people and aligning them with the patients."

Like Magic Johnson, Fernandez is also exceptional, but unlike Magic he didn't start that way. He used the innovation mentality to solve for the gaps in his industry and make more money for himself and his people that most of us will never see in a lifetime. But because marketplaces are changing so fast, it is becoming increasingly difficult to prioritize which opportunity gaps to solve for and how to go about solving for them. I've talked to hundreds of executives throughout the country, and most are uncertain about how to approach the CDS and make the right investments. That's because they are uncertain how to best measure the return on investment *and* determine the metrics for optimal performance and outcomes.

Before I get to the how, I'll answer the first question leaders and businesses should be asking about opportunity gaps in general: *What gaps should I be solving for?*

What You Should Be Solving For

The CDS is driving the fastest-growing part of our U.S. workforce, and shift populations represent the largest segments of America's potential purchasing power. But they also represent some of the fastest-growing demographics of business owners in the U.S. You want them to be your customers, but they are also fast becoming your *competitors*. Shift populations, like immigrants, have been compelled to use the innovation mentality to see opportunity and embrace an entrepreneurial spirit. This is part of the reason why black women are the fastest-growing group of entrepreneurs in the U.S. (up more than 322 percent from 1997 to 2015 according to the "2015 State of Women-Owned Businesses Report" commissioned by American Express Open) and why the number of Hispanic-owned businesses grew 15 *times* faster than other U.S. businesses (or at a rate of 7.5 percent from 2012 to 2015, according to a study by the consulting firm Geoscape and the U.S. Hispanic Chamber of Commerce). Those shift population businesses present opportunities to reach the populations a business does not have the talent internally to connect with. That's how we come up with the three most visible areas where the CDS has created immediate and obvious opportunities for growth (see Figure 4.2):

- Workplace/workforce
- External partnerships
- Marketplace/consumers

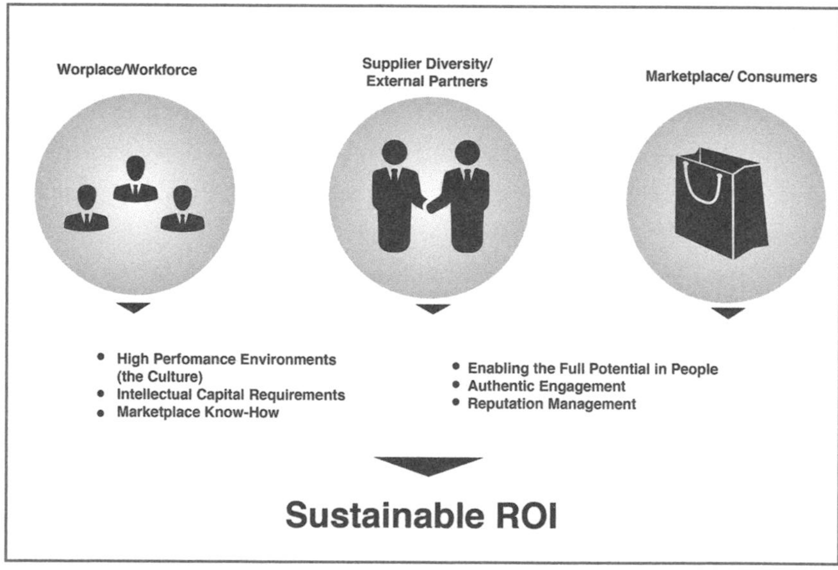

Figure 4.2—What Should You Be Solving For?

Solve for the gaps in these three areas using the six characteristics of the innovation mentality and you solve for high-performance teams through diversity of thought; authentic workplace cultures whose values are defined by individuals who are encouraged to breed continuous innovation; and intellectual capital and know-how previously unseen that enables the full potential in people. All this results in an intimate engagement that maximizes the full potential of people who are your employees and your customers. That's sustainable ROI!

So, ask yourself: "Does your workplace culture support demographic, cultural, and experiential differences and leverage them in these three areas?" Probably not. Most current leadership in the U.S. is woefully unprepared or unwilling to see the opportunity gaps, let alone invest in them. Unfortunately, American corporations see all this activity as an initiative (cost center) and will see the CDS as the last remaining true growth opportunity (profit center) only when Latin America and other international regions begin seizing the previously unseen opportunities because they had the vision to see it first.

Solving for Workplace/Workforce

This is the question we have attacked most frequently in the book so far: Do you celebrate differences and individuality in your workplace? Or are you like the hundreds of companies I have worked with that have done something similar to the financial services company in Chapter 3—the one that ignored the Colombian couple in its workforce or said something similar to what senior executives from a major investment-banking firm told me: "Today, we are afraid for the future of our business because our employees don't relate with our emerging global client base. Many of our new competitors are now owned and operated by Indians, Asians, African-Americans, and Hispanics. We continue to lose key diverse members of our workforce to these same competitors because we lack the cultural intelligence to keep them."

Remember, you cannot develop this cultural intelligence, let alone define your platform, unless you have leaders who own the experiences and influence their cultures can bring to how they think, act, and are motivated to perform. This is part of their leadership identity. That's why we spent so much time defining personal brand value propositions and leadership identities. When you are in evolution mode, you have to create your own platforms. Otherwise you just keep substituting, which is exactly what workplace programs like Employee Resource Groups do. ERGs are growing initiatives in corporations as the CDS has required new, diverse talent in management, director level, and senior executive management roles. I used to think ERGs could play this role and have a purpose beyond events, social aspects, and focus groups that usually define what they do at most companies—in a strictly voluntary capacity, mind you. But I realized today that they almost always have no real strategic value. They are just initiatives. Even when they have hundreds of members, only a small percentage of ERGs are active. It is difficult to recruit new members when these volunteer groups are not incentivized or properly invested in. And why should people participate when no one in senior leadership is active or sees any real strategic value in them, other than as initiatives that exist solely to check off another box on the "compliance" list.

That's irresponsible. ERGs and workplace groups like them have value only if they matter and have quantitative influence—and that happens at such a small percentage of companies it is almost statistically irrelevant. Until then, ERGs will likely make an organization *more* divisive until that organization can recognize the value that comes from different types of people. Which is why, like job descriptions, I believe they should be eliminated until organizations clearly define what their ERGs are solving for. Before it makes sense to reinstitute ERGs, organizations should view these groups as profit centers not cost centers, pay active members a small bonus to remain active, and quantifiably contribute to business growth. Without that, ERGs will continue to play the role of "diversity check-boxes" that unknowingly create more tension and widen engagement gaps among their members.

So what's the solution? Instead of large groups of inactive members, I'd rather see small "idea labs" led by subject matter experts who serve as examples of how their unique differences cultivate innovation and initiative. You can't come into the group unless you are a subject matter expert or have a desire to be one, because as experts, you know what you can solve for, see the opportunity gaps, and identify them quickly to build a plan around them. This group and its plan then serve as examples of how their unique differences cultivate tangible change and growth that impact the bottom line.

That's how ERGs become smarter about defining what they are ultimately trying to accomplish for themselves and the business and then create a metric to enforce accountability to assure their objectives are being measured and attained. ERGs must view themselves as formidable advancement platforms for talent and market development activity. They must be focused on defining a value proposition that is more strategically aligned to seeing and seizing business innovation and growth opportunities that are directly related to a person's cultural, gender, sexual-orientation, and societal identity. They must be more forceful and encourage different points of view and perspectives that translate into solutions to meet corporate growth objectives and initiatives across channels, brands, and business units. Until then, they will do little to alleviate the fact that the changing face of America is being met with tremendous resistance. That's how and why the "old guard" remains uncomfortable with the CDS; it still represents uncertainty and change for those who are uninformed about what diversity means to enabling business growth, which brings us to external partnerships.

Solving for External Partnerships

Do you, your leadership, and your business strive to establish trust with the people and businesses that offer your company the greatest growth opportunities, or do you use total market strategies that often fall flat and come across as inauthentic? After all, how are you differentiating the target audience from the total market approach if all you do is swap in the "Wong family" or "Garcia family" for the "O'Brien family" in the same new car ad? That may affect some of the target audience fleetingly by playing the status symbol card: They got a new car; they must be like everyone else! But do you think that is a long-term evolved strategy that reads as genuine to Chinese-Americans, Hispanics, or any population that is not the same as the O'Briens? It looks inclusive and, in some senses it is, but it's a superficial approach at best. Here's what nonwhite families think when they see that: Are you trying to cut costs because you don't care what our community represents to you? Do you not value us enough to engage with us the right way?

Recognizing the distinction between what the Garcia or Wong family looks like and what makes them special is what needs to be understood to connect with them or any shift population. We need to recognize the role they play as they become the face of America, understand their family values, and capture them in a genuine way to elevate and strengthen our value proposition to them. Yet companies are at a loss to do it any other way. Thus, while it may seem heartening that advertising outlays in Hispanic markets are growing by 12 percent, according to *Ad Age*—which is more than double overall U.S. major media ad spending—it doesn't mean much if it involves superficial approaches like Photoshopping different ethnicities in car ads. If you start with a baseline of the majority and try to engage the minority with that same approach, you are fundamentally flawed. That's not evolution, that's substitution. You need to build new perspectives. As Caroline Wanga, vice president corporate social responsibility at Target Corp., explained to the audience at my CDS summit, "The problem dealing with the Cultural Demographic Shift is we're using a Caucasian baseline and applying a colored filter. African-Americans are not brown white people. We need to change the baseline. That's an uncomfortable thing to say to some people, but having those intrusive insights and conversations that make people uncomfortable call out the real problem."

External partnerships can help you do this. Their goals should be similar to mine when I work with a company internally: strengthen an organization's solve—mitigate flaws, prevent them from happening, and give leaders and their businesses the right intellectual capital to strengthen their business models when they don't have the time and resources to own it themselves. But this works only if the leaders and businesses are engaged and aligned. This goes back to characteristic four: Live with an entrepreneurial spirit. It is not just the workplace that must become more entrepreneurial—our external partnerships must be so as well.

We need to re-evaluate our external partnerships and establish new ground rules for the role they play: what you should expect from them and what they help you solve for. They should evolve with you!

This applies to nonprofit organizations that big and small companies cut checks to as well. Who says these organizations are enlightened or evolving just because they serve populations represented by the CDS? I'm not talking about only nonprofits that are unethical but those that are stuck substituting instead of evolving, just like the companies they are trying to help. If you hired that ad agency that Photshopped the Wongs for the O'Briens and your only interaction was to cut them a check, you effectively abdicated responsibility and handed them the keys to your company instead of working with them to identify the intellectual property that allows you to drive and lead better. You need to stop paying people for their platforms and create ones that can be managed by your partners as if it was your own.

Of course, that's exactly what many companies do: take short cuts—even illegal ones—to satisfy Wall Street's quarterly earnings metrics rather than designing robust strategies for change. That's what happened when GE Retail Capital Bank (now Synchrony) found itself on the wrong end of the largest discrimination lawsuit in federal government history—to the tune of $169 million in June 2014. For several years, the company excluded tens of thousands of Spanish-speaking credit card customers from a debt-reduction program. That's the biggest consequence on record. Smaller ones happen every day as leaders erode trust in their brands by complacently and willfully discriminating against the very groups that offer them the greatest opportunities for future growth.

This is why Dell became the largest publicly traded company to revert to being privately held. It wanted to break free from the proverbial chains of Wall Street and regain its competitive advantage by taking new risks and trying new business models that were not beholden to shareholders. After a two-year hiatus, Dell has roared back with some new thinking about partnership through acquisition, moving to acquire storage giant EMC and spinning off its cyber-security division.

We need more companies like Dell that allow risk to become their best friend and who are willing to take personal accountability in how they wield the power and influence that comes with their role and responsibilities. Simply put, the external partners that you decide to align your business with can either positively or negatively impact your short-and long-term success. They can either lift your business up to reach greater levels of significance or pull your business down, elevating your risk profile, and guiding you down a path of ineffective decision making. Relationships with external partners (vendors, consultants, advisors, strategic industry partners, nonprofit organizations, etc.) can either make you stronger and wiser about your future, or they can weaken you and blind you to the opportunities perhaps right in front of you. More often than not, it is the latter as the partnerships grow complacent, opportunity gaps widen, and it becomes more difficult for the relationships—and the business—to evolve.

That's the situation one of my clients found itself in. I asked one of the senior leaders, "Why do you continue to conduct business with this particular external partner? Is it out of loyalty? Do you believe you owe them something? Are they adding any real value to your business needs? What are they helping you solve for to enable your business to evolve? Could it be that the relationship is being taken for granted?" What did this leader say? "We have supported the organization for more than ten years. They are a legacy relationship. We pay them $50,000 a year to provide us market research and attend their annual conference. Since they don't have much financial impact on the business, we continue to support them." But a year later, my client informed me he had courageously considered the questions again and ended the relationship: "We stopped taking the relationship for granted and realized that for $50,000 a year they were not adding value to our business. The quality of their research began to wane and was no longer relevant to our current business needs. They were not evolving, and the relationship was growing complacent. Attending their conference was costing us more as they were expecting us to contribute more time, resources, and money. The relationship had become an unnecessary expense, no longer an investment, but one in which they were hurting our business, not helping us grow."

Robert W. Stone, president and CEO of City of Hope, a California-based health-care provider and biomedical research and treatment institution focused on eliminating cancer and diabetes, echoes the importance of that leader's realization and shows just how complex these external partnerships have become and need to be in the changing landscape of American health care: "The way we deliver care has changed. For example, cancer care involves many disciplines: medical oncology; surgery; radiation . . . In many hospitals, however, a patient navigates making an appointment with a medical oncologist, then a separate appointment with a radiation oncologist, and yet another with a surgeon. There is no coordination of care; no taking care of the patient's entire spectrum of needs. City of Hope is far more patient-focused, and the industry is catching up in the understanding that the traditional way of doing things just won't get us there. We absolutely can and need to address our patients' other concerns, which means we have to partner with community hospitals, other doctors, and research institutions, which exacerbates the complexity for leaders. I admit I didn't initially fully appreciate the changing landscape—the degree to which partnerships are really part of the future—that we can't just recreate everything but have to partner with others. In 2011, we were a single-site of care institution and now we have 15 sites. We are on the verge of opening others, and many are done through partnerships. They are done through finding like-minded people who want to serve their communities and partner, whether it is in health care or communities and schools."

We need more leaders like Stone who see this and think courageously to take more ownership to reinvent themselves and their industries and truly innovate their processes for change management. That brings us to market intelligence: To ensure your organization continues to evolve and grow wiser through your external partnerships, ask these six questions influenced by and based on the six characteristics of the innovation mentality to evaluate your relationships with those partners:

1. *Do they broaden your perspectives?* Think of external partners as an extension of your organization's leadership that broadens the landscape of opportunities previously unseen for your business.
2. *Do they keep you on your toes?* It is not a strategic business relationship unless your external partners hold you accountable to anticipate the unexpected.
3. *Do they make you more courageous?* Business relationships that make you more courageous to take action and help you effectively maximize the full potential of the opportunities that are right in front are the ones that generate measureable ROI and mitigate risk.
4. *Do they help leverage existing assets and resources?* Do they help you cultivate greater strategic focus and connect the dots of intellectual

capital to create and strengthen ecosystems to make your business smarter and wiser?

5. *Do they have your best interests at the forefront?* Business relationships that have your best interests at heart are those that will always have your back and share the harvest of the momentum it should be fueling organically for the betterment of a healthier whole.
6. *Do they strengthen your significance to sustain your success?* Business relationships are sustained when shared values are continuously reciprocated. They recognize that success comes most to those who are surrounded by people who want their success to continue.

Solving for the Marketplace

Think back to that car ad I mentioned: Recognizing the distinction between what the Wong and Garcia family looks like and what makes them special is what needs to be understood to connect with them or any shift population. Does your organization know how to answer these four fundamental questions about your employees and customers, which directly connect to the six characteristics of the innovation mentality?

1. How does cultural upbringing (i.e., heritage) shape their mindset? (Characteristics 1 and 2: See opportunity in everything; anticipate the unexpected.)
2. What strengths and capabilities fuel their desires? (Characteristic 3: Unleash your passionate pursuits.)
3. What are their ultimate goals and ambitions (i.e., what matters most to them)? (Characteristic 4: Live with an entrepreneurial spirit.)
4. How do their core values and beliefs (i.e., what they stand for) affect their lifestyle choices? (Characteristics 5 and 6: Work with a generous purpose; Lead to leave a legacy.)

If the health-care example that started this chapter wasn't enough to prove that having diverse customers does *not* mean that you embraced diversity of thought, the innovation mentality, and the CDS, consider this: A Fortune 50 retailer serves more than 80 percent of Hispanic households, yet they have a $26 *billion* opportunity gap from failing to support the right product assortment, merchandising strategies, end caps, point of sale colors, and in-store employees. That's what happens when brands don't have the right strategy for investing in intellectual capital: They lose marketplace opportunity and fail to grow. Anyone who thinks they can make up this gap by hiring shift populations and then supporting them only through programs like ERGs and underfunded multicultural marketing programs will quickly find out the limitation of those groups.

An executive at a major beverage company told me proudly that he uses his ERGs "in focus groups to sell to African-Americans, Hispanics, and other groups they represent." That's great, but it's not the right metric. That's not something they individually influence to help the company evolve. Moreover, there is a good chance that the feedback they provided may not have even been authentic, because they may not have wanted you to know how they really felt. "If I tell you the real truth," they think, "something bad is going to happen to me." For example, I know from deep personal and professional experience that Hispanics do not share enough, even though they were raised to share; they don't want to be at risk of losing their jobs. That's how they are wired to think. They have learned for so many years that their unique differences have been devalued.

What *is* going to lead them to believe that they are being valued?

More than ever, organizations have been forced to redefine their leadership roles, growth objectives, brand identities, and relationships with their clients and customers. These activities have impacted the workplace and have led toward a massive transformation in the ways we think, act, and innovate. As a result, there is a looming sense of uncertainty, and people are seeking new methods for managing change and how to thrive in the workplace once again in order for the organization to evolve. Today's changing workplace requires a strategy that every employee, external partner, client, and customer can embrace. Workplace transformation must account for the impact of change both inside (employees) and outside (clients/customers) the organization. The strategy should represent the betterment of a healthy whole, because if I haven't said it enough already:

> *Remember, without strategy, change is merely substitution not evolution.*

We keep substituting, because we are treating symptoms, not solving problems.

Simply put, we need the wisdom to connect to the people and cultures that don't look and act like us *without* undermining who and what we are and stand for. That's what many of our corporate values tell us we *should* be doing, but we really don't. That would require leading with diversity of thought and the six characteristics of the innovation mentality, which allow for the evolution for our businesses. For example, anybody in a service or sales business in any industry is responsible for managing and maximizing opportunity with clients. They can take the first steps by asking these questions: How do you greet people (employees, external partners, clients/customers) that don't look like you? How do you make them feel important? How do you set expectations? Generate leads? Deliver reports and evaluations? How do you get them to come back again?

The objective should be to stop unknowingly creating tension when we ask these questions and start strengthening the people who can help build momentum to answer them in bigger and better ways. They can help us make the right investments that will capture new market share using the six characteristics. And as I said before, if you don't act to do it *and keep doing it*, some other company will—domestically *and* internationally. This is already happening. Look at the "American" beer companies Budweiser and Miller; they are no longer owned by Americans. We're losing control of our marketplaces, because we are not managing the shift. Even Warren Buffett, one of the country's most famous businessmen, turned to the Brazilian investment firm 3G Capital Partners LP for the merger of Kraft and Heinz (which 3G had bought a year before the merger). Seven months earlier, the partners combined on Burger King's $11.4 billion takeover of Canadian chain Tim Hortons. And how did *The Wall Street Journal* say 3G became one of the world's biggest acquisition firms? "Relentless ambition and big-name connections." In other words, they see opportunity in everything (innovation mentality characteristic one) and live with an entrepreneurial spirit (characteristic four).

Look at the auto industry. The South Korean company Hyundai came in and revolutionized the automobile industry simply by breaking with traditional approaches and valuing, understanding, and going after cost-

and warranty-conscious buyers that other car companies could not figure out how to sell to. Playing on this desire for value and stability, it reinvented the way cars are sold, especially to the large and underserved Hispanic market, and became the fourth-largest car company in the world. That's the innovation mentality! Soon other brands began to rethink what they were doing too. They saw that what the auto industry calls "multicultural sales" made up 27 percent of overall business, led by Hispanics with 14 percent overall. In fact, according to *Automotive News*, Hispanic consumers could be the auto industry's leading growth engine for the next 20 to 30 years. In 2014, Hispanic buyers delivered 96 percent of Ford and Chevrolet's combined year-over-year retail sales growth, 33 percent of Nissan's, 35 percent of Toyota's, and 100 percent of Honda's, according to IHS Automotive's Polk market data unit.

By ignoring the Cultural Demographic Shift, you lose your relevancy in the marketplace and are susceptible to new competitors.

How are they doing it? By embracing the innovation mentality and differences to form genuine connections. In terms of the Hispanic market, this extends from dealers and executives who speak Spanish to the leadership identities at the top. Toyota, Nissan, Honda, you name it; there are senior leaders valuing difference as a profit center, not a cost center, and helping the industry evolve. These leaders have, in turn, affected the work of their external partners that connect directly to Hispanic or any nondiverse populations and identities. For example, Toyota, the leading brand in the Hispanic market, has undone some of the external partnership damage I described earlier by working with ad agencies that have direct cultural connections with Hispanic markets. Its "*Más Que un Auto*" campaign, which plays on the Hispanic penchant for giving everyone a nickname and allowed Toyota owners to order a free badge with the unique names they gave their cars, was not only beloved but also won national awards.

At least some of this can be attributed to the brand hiring strategy executive Pat Pineda, a Mexican-American, who, as reported in *Automotive News*, does many of the things Magic Johnson did to build his brands and establish trust in urban America. Tactics include talking to the customers and *listening* to them to reaching out to communities and conferences, often with Toyota's dealers in tow. Toyota has even used its diversity of thought to create programs that recognize diversity within the nondiverse communities, noting that younger Hispanic buyers don't want to be categorized the same way as their parents. As a result, Toyota is now the top brand among Hispanics. That's quite an evolution from Toyota's recall crisis of 2009–2010 when the company didn't have anyone who spoke Spanish to talk to the Spanish media.

Does that mean everything Toyota or others in the industry are doing is now authentic? No, but these are steps in the right direction to move beyond compliance to commitment—from substitution to evolution. Consider what Fred Diaz, Vice President and General Manager, North America Trucks and Light Commercial Vehicles, Nissan North America, Inc., told me when he offered this admonition to anyone who can't see value in all parts of the CDS: "You have to live under a rock to not know that if you are not going after the multicultural consumer and you have any connection of sales and marketing, then shame on you." In fact, Nissan has made this one of their passionate pursuits (the third characteristic of the innovation mentality) by making sure everyone in the company knows how important the shift is to the company: 38 percent of its sales are to people of multicultural descent, which in 2015 represented 90 percent year-over-year growth. That doesn't surprise Diaz, though, "If you embraced [the shift] long ago, you should be experiencing these kinds of numbers. Multicultural is not a flavor of the month. We embraced it by being aware, adapting to changing mores, aggressively executing, and being authentic. Now, I realize that is easy to say, but if we did it half-heartedly, if we did not do the research and what it takes to reach that level of authenticity, they will see right through you."

In other words, Nissan has reached the finish line in winning those markets: They have achieved diversity of thought and converted cultural sensitivities into authentic relationships. As a result, Nissan has moved to second place among Hispanic buyers in America behind Toyota. It is first among black women and second overall in the black market. There is even expressed permission and encouragement for LGBT employees to go out and speak to their community. Does all this come at a cost? Of course!

Nissan increased its already substantial multicultural marketing budget by 15 percent in 2015, far more than other areas, and does substantial and ongoing market research. Diaz considers anything under 25 percent of a company's total budget that's designated for the shift as being underfunded. That's a lot if you still think of any work with shift populations as diversity training. But it's not a lot when you consider the shift a profit center and its populations as trendsetters, redefining how consumers buy and think and the way America operates and leads.

Yet there is still work to be done. I still see ads that are designed for the general market and someone simply translated it into a Spanish spot with a Spanish voice-over. That is the most disrespectful, inauthentic thing you can do to this audience. Why does it still happen then? The reality is, according to surveys done by my company, 78 percent of leaders have difficulty understanding the consequences and effectively articulating the requirements to thrive in these rapidly changing workplaces and marketplaces. They make excuses for inaction instead of leading through diversity of thought and creating new best practices and protocols. Why?

- They are afraid of losing control.
- They lack the courage to challenge the status quo.
- The change management required challenges them.
- Playing it safe is their security; they fear the unknown and are unwilling to take ownership.
- Supporting silos allows them to sustain negative disruption, which allows their irrelevant thinking to be perceived as relevant.

All these reasons fly in the face of the innovation mentality. Leaders can't become more afraid of making decisions at a time when we need them to step up their game as opportunity gaps widen and the emergence of new competitors abound. We need them to be more vulnerable. These gaps are like plate tectonics—the rigid outermost shell of our planet that moves naturally and inevitably. These gaps will exist whether or not Americans have prepared for the shift.

But there is hope: Talking to Diaz and others like him gives me faith that change is coming *if we can sustain it.* At Nissan, investment started with buy-in from the top on a daily basis. That mentality was driven through the leadership teams and peer groups down to the front desk and to the person who comes in to empty the trash. Outside, the attitude extended into social media, relationships with TV networks like BET and Univision, and, of course, the staff hired at the dealerships to make sure they reflect the markets they serve in order to earn their trust.

When you move from seeing to sowing, you can still get stuck in sowing because success is alluring—numbers don't lie, right? Pat yourself on the back.

Now, the hard work begins: Companies must continue to evolve, sustain, and keep driving change in the face of success. Leadership must work with a generous purpose, lead to leave a legacy, and embrace the long-sightedness of diversity of thought and the innovation mentality instead of the short-sightedness of more sowing. If a company sees a 33 percent increase in sales from embracing and investing in the CDS in one year or perhaps a 1 percent increase in shift populations, how many are going to increase their investment again the following year to build engagement and how many will expect similar increases the following year using the same tactics and budget? This circles back to what I said in the introduction: When diversity and inclusion initiatives are weak, one-off tactical approaches without strategy or follow-up and little depth, the result is some initial success followed by an immediate flat line or regression. The work may have started with the best intentions—valuing individual listening to the unique needs of shift populations—but once they see success, it's not about *inclusion* anymore. It's about just getting out there to sell, sell, sell (or rather sow, sow, sow). It's working! The brief reign of the individual is over. The transaction becomes king again. Forget about the empathy and seeing what got you there.

This is substitutional thinking at its finest and does not produce sustainable results. Substitution activities often go unnoticed when the business is making money and growing. It hides underneath the act of winning, and as a result leaders are solving for the wrong things more often than you might think. This is when leaders in the workplace lack the strategic focus to identify the opportunities of greatest potential (growing) and spend too much time doing things (sowing), which leads to unproductive substitution activities. This only becomes glaringly noticeable when an organization begins to lose their competitive advantage.

Evolution is at a premium when the business is losing ground in the marketplace. At those moments, leaders who embrace evolution become change agents who demand high-performance *and* critical thinking, and who filter out those who slow down the process. Evolution happens when leaders embrace risk as the new normal, live with an entrepreneurial attitude, and unleash their passionate pursuits to maximize the full potential of the people and organizations they serve. When leaders apply strategic focus with the mindset of evolution, they are in constant survival, renewal, and reinvention mode. Their sheer will to make things better, invest in relationships, and cultivate an environment of transparency and reciprocity—where diversity of thought is valued—allows them to lead to leave a legacy.

Sustainability is a product of inclusion, not diversity. It's about shared beliefs, values, and a culture whose impact and influence grows stronger over time.

When we take this step to see opportunities in the right way and drive that through the four skills of opportunity management (see, sow, grow, share) and the six characteristics of the innovation mentality, we can then use this success to resow opportunities. That leads to genuine sustainability and inclusion. But until we do that, we will continue to give away our innovation mentality to competitors that already have it. Hyundai learned this when its Japanese competitors in the U.S. seized the opportunity to take over the Hispanic market, and as America is fast finding out, many competitors also come from beyond our borders. Other countries have seized our opportunity gaps to gain market share.

Put aside concerns about the diversity of our own citizenship for a moment. More and more countries, such as China, India, Brazil, South Korea, and Indonesia, are growing fast and turning into entrepreneurs that want nothing more than to sell to America, the largest economy in the world.

Where is this new wave of entrepreneurs studying in preparation for competing here? According to *The Wall Street Journal,* more than 1.1

million foreign students attended American universities in 2014, up 50 percent from 2010. In the next five years, it won't be just our own shift populations who become our competitors, it will be people from other countries that have sent their top talent to the U.S. and built a pipeline for personal and professional development. These graduates return to train people in their mother countries on how to best see and seize opportunities in America. In other words, they come here and invest in our system, then teach what they've learned to their own countries so they can compete against us. Despite having no intention of immigrating, they are using America's "immigrant perspective" against us by embracing its six characteristics. Coincidentally, they have the innovation mentality and wonder why we don't.

It doesn't matter where I travel—Scandinavia, South Korea, Mexico—everywhere I hear the same thing: Why, given the strength of its corporations and educational institutions, do Americans seem to be getting *weaker* in their thinking? Until I heard objective audiences saying that, I hadn't noticed how much we're losing our edge.

At a time when innovation is at a premium, we need enlightened leaders to take ownership for the business, the people they lead, and the customers they serve. They must frequently reinvent themselves and have the mindset of always having a strategy for change that is focused on constant evolution with this end game in mind. Leadership must be seen as a privilege and duty to ensure we are continuously investing in people and that we are always adding value to make our people better and drive growth for our businesses through them. The more people who can see beyond the obvious and anticipate the unexpected, the more they become the business's most valuable asset against those who are slow to make decisions and take action. I know leaders *say* things like this in their speeches and companies tout this ability in advertisements and annual reports, but very few are acting upon those words. If they were, traditional thinking about "diversity" in its most corporate sense would no longer exist—and we'd be solving for the right things.

Knowing the power of these six characteristics is to see how they guide you to understand the difference between substitution and evolution. We need to get away from all the noise that compels us toward substitution.

It is our job to lead others and show them how to evolve department to department, leader to leader, person to person. It's our job to advance our needs by serving others. That's how we become better at sharing. We're still not good at it because we're too focused on our own agendas, rather than on how to enable a healthier whole by leading others to be able to see what we should be collectively seeing and solving for together.

It's not that companies don't recognize that they must create strategies for change. They just don't take enough time to define those strategies, since this is the basis for accountability. We have an unprecedented opportunity to impact the bottom line with innovative products and services, brands, and initiatives that empower our differences and create a heightened awareness of the value that they can bring. Yet few business leaders are implementing new models that reflect that value. I'm not referring to the results of employee surveys or consumer focus groups. I am talking about the knowledge that the organization has about their workforce and their consumers because they take the time to understand them as people and thus connect to them. Let's not forget Sam Walton not only wanted to shake the janitor's hands at every store he visited, but he also wanted the janitor to shake his.

The CDS shows us the importance of embracing diversity of thought, exploring developing markets domestically and globally, and retaining and developing the leaders and talent of the future using the innovation mentality. Every time companies ignore or don't take the time to use the six characteristics of the innovation mentality to understand and capitalize on the gaps created by the shift, they are creating tension with the communities of people that are at the forefront of that change—your employees, clients, and customers. Leaders are growing up in multigenerational and in increasingly diverse environments with manufacturing, supply chains, and partners in foreign countries that don't have any connectivity to the company's past.

All this should bring with it challenges but also new opportunities and ideas, but leaders don't see them because their mentalities are stuck connecting to the old ways. This is why to be truly inclusive and sustain success we need to "evolve the solve" from the inside out—not just for our leadership identities but for our corporate ones.

CHAPTER 5

EVOLVE THE SOLVE USING THE INNOVATION MENTALITY

As part of my work, I am often asked to review and present my thoughts on companies' diversity and inclusion plans for women, organizational development, corporate strategy, emerging markets, and multicultural groups or shift populations. The vast majority of these plans focus on three things: recruitment, reputation management, and sales. That makes them limited but does not make them bad. I am glad these plans even exist—at least companies are thinking about diversifying their workforce. On paper, the plans even look great: They are usually organized, well designed graphically, and use many of the right words. So why would the vast majority of these plans prove ineffective or fail within a year or two? Start talking to the people who put them together, and more often than not you realize that the details and depth of thinking behind them is as thin as the paper the plan is printed on.

I reviewed a diversity and inclusion plan for a company that believed its implementation would make them a better company inside and a more competitive company outside. I had no reason to doubt these words and still don't. They believed it, and that's what a proper diversity and inclusion plan should do. I appreciated the excitement of the people behind the plan who saw it as seizing an opportunity and a need, especially the executive behind the strategy whom I had some questions for. But I was having trouble mustering the same enthusiasm for it as a growth strategy.

"Can you help me understand what your plan's value proposition is for shift populations in five words or less?" Much like that executive in Chapter 2 who struggled to define his brand value proposition when confronted by me, this executive went on and on, struggling to find the words. I stopped her: "Maybe that was a tough question. You said this plan fills an opportunity and a need. Why do people need it, and what is the opportunity they are solving for in two words, please?"

She was flustered. She didn't know what to say. Would you? When you can't, you have no idea how wide the opportunity gaps are and little understanding of what needs to be solved for first, which out of the gate leads to plans like these solving for the wrong things at the wrong time.

I don't blame this executive for her struggles. If anything, the fault lies with her supervisor who put her in that situation and never bothered to engage it himself. He couldn't answer the questions either without making it sound like just another way to make money, not build something better, and couching it in business language gobbledygook that mimicked countless other plans you find on the internet peddled by consultants. He didn't know who, what, or how shift populations think, act, or are motivated to buy and perform, and he wasn't courageous, vulnerable, or wise enough to find out, and thus neither were the people who answered to him. For that reason, the plan became another desperate attempt by a company at "cultural competency." Don't get me wrong: Cultural competency is important. But it's substitutional thinking—it's not the solve we need to evolve. That solve is for representation and compliance. That's a tactical approach. The goal is to take the diversity and inclusion conversations from the fringe of the organization and move it to the center so that shift populations along with women, LGBT, military, and other groups pushed to the fringe of the organization become part of the ongoing and long-term strategic initiatives for growth. And that requires us to operationalize the innovation mentality.

Operationalizing means viewing the CDS not through compliance (outdated tactical templates and siloed departments) but through commitment (cross-functional and cross-pollinated departments that create an ecosystem that builds on the required intellectual capital and know-how to serve shift populations). This commitment becomes an internal ecosystem that expands outside the organization through the formation of strategic alliances and external partnerships that further strengthen and support the implementation of the CDS in both the workplace and marketplace as a strategy for growth (profit center). What this means is an organization must create and build on the required intel to serve all unique populations in support of the organization's goals. They can't mimic what other organizations are doing or repeat what has been done in the past because that wouldn't authentically support their current organization's goals.

As I always remind executives: Fail to operationalize the right strategies and run the risk of losing your competitive advantage. Only when we operationalize the innovation mentality to solve for the opportunity gaps between what our businesses have been doing and what the CDS and the six characteristics solve for can we achieve:

- Authentic Engagement
- Embracing Diversity of Thought
- Strategic Implications
- Creating Distinction
- Enabling Sustainable Growth
- Change Management (that allows the organization to evolve)

We must operationalize our innovation mentalities as a profit center—an ecosystem focused on strategic long-term growth.

Unfortunately, that's not what we do. As you now know, most businesses, if not entire industries, are stuck in the silo mentality in which people, groups, and departments lack the intellectual capital and know-how, which makes those businesses inefficient and ineffective when it comes to the CDS. They hear terms such as "diversity and inclusion" and default into compliance mode rather than seeing the broader opportunity to evolve with shift populations. What they are then solving for is reputation management—to avoid being negatively impacted when a client, customer, or the media calls them out on their workplace/workforce shift population numbers. Again, the intention may have been good, but the thinking was incomplete, because most diversity and inclusion plans do not apply all six characteristics. Do they see things others don't? No. Anticipate the unexpected? Yeah, I'll give them that in the narrowest of senses. Passionate pursuits of endless possibilities? No. (They don't define possibilities but competitive advantage.) Entrepreneurial spirit? A little by getting bodies in the door, but do they know what those people are solving for? Generous purpose? Possibly, but that requires you to be transparent and continually have each other's backs (not the business's), and few plans do. Lead to leave a legacy? I don't think they could conceivably think these plans are contributing to the legacy of the brand; not one of them mention long-term goals. That's why the good intentions of these proposals lead to unknowingly creating tension. They lead to false promises that in the short term kill hope and enthusiasm.

The message is: We recognize the importance of the individual, but we will continue to do only the most superficial things that look good but actually devalue the individual before our mission even begins because our plans don't go far enough.

Only companies that have the right intellectual capital and best practices inside the organization to "operationalize" and lead through the CDS will win the war for diverse talent, help strengthen overall decision making to best serve shift populations, create new private/public partnerships, and develop new revenue streams in the process. Companies and their leaders who see this paradigm shift for what it is (a strategy for growth) must then create new plans that respect the economic and societal implications of the CDS. They must compel leadership across the business to break free from their identity crisis and have the courage and vulnerability to shift their mindsets and view diversity and inclusion as a profit center, not as a cost center or a threat to their job security.

To lead and drive sustainable growth through the CDS organization, you cannot play it safe with lifeless diversity and inclusion plans that view the CDS as just another expense. Plans must be developed for identity-crisis-free leadership that's innovative and courageous enough to evolve and invest in the shift; redefine their business models; and take ownership for closing the growing opportunity gaps within the three pillars of the workplace/workforce, external partnerships, and the all-important marketplace/consumer.

To do this requires a deep and detailed plan for moving diversity and inclusion from the outside of the organization to the inside.

Diversity and Inclusion from the Inside Out

In 1979, Jorge Caballero was one of a few minorities when he started his accounting career. In 2015, he told me two-thirds of the new hires the prior year at Deloitte were women and shift populations, and retention has been outstanding. According to Caballero, now a senior partner at the firm, "Deloitte saw diversity and inclusion as a business strategy driven by the needs of its clients and also the well-being of its own professionals and their opportunities to find success. That means fostering an environment of authenticity and openness—a place where people feel comfortable having a dialog not just about their similarities but about their differences and the uniqueness they bring to the table." Caballero cites evidence that shows how much more effective well-integrated diverse teams are than nondiverse ones, but he knows from simply looking around the firm and listening that the teams that perform best are the ones that are open with one another—where each individual feels valued enough to bring their authentic and unique selves to the dynamics of the team. Developing this type of inclusive culture is important for any organization but particularly for those whose business depends on selling the expertise and capabilities of their professionals. And because their client service teams are so diverse, they can include individuals from similar backgrounds and cultural perspectives as the clients and who speak languages other than English, giving them a deep understanding of what is important to the clients in developing a relationship.

Simply put, Deloitte embraced the innovation mentality and saw diversity and inclusion as an ongoing business strategy and made it a change management imperative. The firm went beyond diversity to apply diversity of thought. That's how it—and we—finally start to close the right opportunity gaps that until now have been widening at an accelerating pace in today's economy. Thriving in this economy depends on committing yourself to the six characteristics and attributes and creating what WorldBlu, a global network of organizations committed to practicing freedom and democracy in the workplace, calls an "organizational democracy" or organizations designed to "amplify the possibilities of human potential and the organization as a whole."

Nothing makes Vineet Nayar more passionate than the idea of organizational democracy. Nayar, former CEO of HCL Technologies in India, a $22 billion global IT brand, is the author of the book, *Employees First, Customers Second*, which explores his transformational journey at HCL and the need to turn conventional management upside down. He told *The New York Times* that as CEO he wants to be "the guy obsessed with enabling employees to create value" and succeed at what they do well. He inspired a connection to the rank and file at his company by dancing on stage to a Bollywood song at a company-wide meeting even though he couldn't dance.

As Nayar told me in an exclusive interview, "Our workplace environment propels a 'we are in this together' mentality. Employees feel a deeper sense of accountability. They feel that they are making a direct impact on the business and that unleashes positive energy in the workplace. As a result, our people are motivated less with compensation and more with participation. Democratic organizations have a better way of approaching growth and problems because they are innately more collaborative. What I know is that growth in emerging markets and new business models bring innovation to the center of the table to solve problems to those on the outside looking in. CEOs from Fortune 100 companies are seeking advice, and they recognize that employee-centricity is a mechanism to solve their problems and grow faster. All revolutions start with dissatisfaction. The conventional management model brings with it dissatisfaction, and organizational democracy is a viable solution."

Figure 5.1 shows what that kind of organizational democracy looks like in the new workplace compared to the traditional workplace when it comes to diversity and inclusion and applying the innovation mentality effectively, strategically, and sustainably.

Notice that diversity and inclusion as well as employees and consumers have been moved to the center of the organization and all the functional departments are interconnected. For years, those departments have operated as silos. The CDS not only evolves traditional workplace models by creating interconnected ecosystems but also evolves traditional diversity and inclusion models by moving them to the core of an organization's growth strategy. By focusing the diversity and inclusion conversation around growth, shift populations become more influential and their value is elevated.

But until all parts of any workplace come together as boundaryless interconnected parts, people will continue to solve for the wrong things—and slowly, because they don't know anyone's leadership identity. When they do become interdependent on each other, you get closer to solving for the right things, because they begin to touch the business differently as your intellectual capital strengthens, which allows us to get wiser about

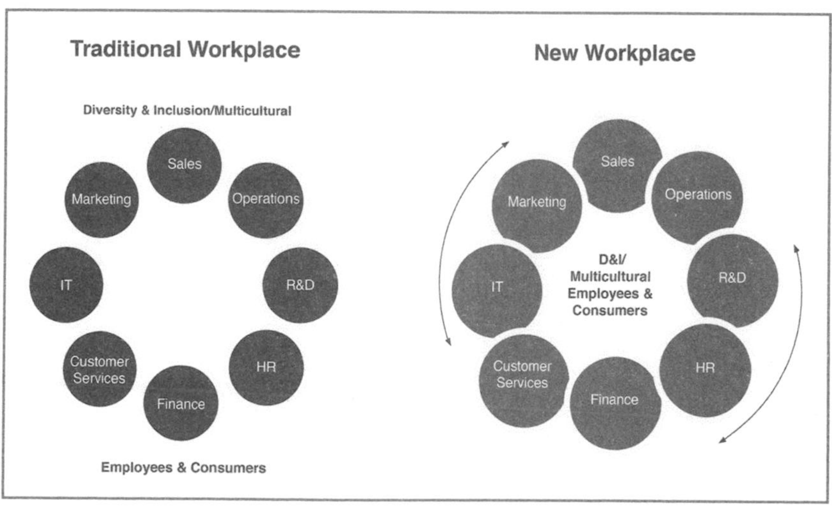

Figure 5.1—Moving the CDS to the Center of the Organization

what we should be solving for. Then when leadership and companies overlay its brand value proposition and promise on top of that, they can figure out how to solve for things much faster as all the key characteristics of the new workplace come together.

- Mission is defined by employees as individuals.
- Employees are defined by their personal brand value propositions and leadership identities.
- Departments are interconnected.
- Clients/consumers are more aligned part of the company, and business is client/community-led.
- Innovation becomes a mindset that can be measured.
- Maximizing potential is mandatory.
- Diversity of thought is a strategy for growth.

When diversity and inclusion is in the middle it gives employees the chance to be more vulnerable, including nondiverse leaders. Until they are vulnerable, diversity and inclusion will never allow the people to rise to their maximum potential. Every business has more shift populations coming in as employees and customers. How do you integrate them—through their voices or their perspectives? You need a fresh mindset. How are you going to do that when the mentality is sow, sow, sow, and diversity and inclusion are on the fringe? If diversity and inclusion falls on a single marginalized chief diversity officer, that practically gives the company license to ignore them because they hired someone to take care of them for the leaders who don't want to. That's not a mandate to invest, let alone understand. If we stay in siloed bubbles, we will never have empathy and see the opportunities that are right in front of us.

> *We need to move diversity and inclusion to the middle of our organizations' long-term strategies and see it as a profit center and a strategy for growth.*

Moreover, we will never have authenticity. Too many organizations spend time mimicking what they say other companies have done when it comes to diversity and inclusion in the age of the CDS, hire a consultant who tells them what they should do but leaves immediately afterward, or simply do what they think they should do, rather than understanding what fits to support their own needs and requirements without first asking their own employees—the very people whose potential they want to maximize. This is another example of how we unknowingly create tension. We are desperate for solutions but in rushing to find them we are creating chaos and confusion. As one mid-level Latina executive at a Fortune 100 company told me, "Why is it that when I have a great idea or sense of what the company needs to do or solve for, the company doesn't believe me, but then they go and spend millions of dollars on consultants?"

When organizations attempt to renew their values and reinvent themselves during times of uncertainty, they often hire consultants who survey only select leaders about employee satisfaction and then retain research firms to obtain customer insights before they make multimillion-dollar decisions. This describes the traditional outside-in approach of businesses defining the individual and can no longer carry much weight. Organizations must take a more balanced approach that engages their culturally diverse employees to be part of the solution rather than exacerbate perceptions that they are part of the problem. When employees are not an integral part of the reinvention process, it doesn't allow them to take ownership and they begin to disengage. When employees find themselves implementing a strategy they didn't influence, they don't fully buy in to the deployment process. If employees are the ones that are touching the business and are most mindful of the opportunity gaps and the requirements to close these gaps, why do they not have more influence? It's because their leaders stopped listening to them and respecting them, and they lost their identity in the process of change that was not supported by a strategy. Employees may do what they are told, but they lose their passionate pursuits in the process.

This disconnect is most stark when you look at companies that have employees working inside and outside the company offices (e.g., retail companies with brick-and-mortar stores and distribution/fulfillment centers; food franchises; health-care companies with clinics). Looking at the data from my "Workplace Serendipity Quiz" and "Workplace Culture Assessment," the employees in the field and most in touch with the marketplace tend to embrace the six characteristics far more than their corporate counterparts. In fact, my assessments show that in any industry and in any kind of corporate environment—from traditional offices to funky open-plan startups—people working outside the corporate environment score much higher on see, sow, grow, and share than those inside. They may not be proficient in growing and sharing yet, but they are when it comes to seeing with broadened observation and sowing extensive innovation.

Why? It all comes down to people: For example, in retail, the talent working outside the company headquarters in stores or warehouses is usually more diverse and almost always embraces diversity of thought in connecting with shift populations. In fact, it is usually a mandate—at the center of what they do every day. Thus, it should come as no surprise that those leaders and the people who work for them beyond the office environments see things others don't and are more adaptable and flexible in solving for opportunity gaps—they are all about serving others and being directed by others! Interestingly, the same is true about people who come from the outside to work inside a company's headquarters. According to my assessments, the longer you are at a company—any company—the less you see, grow, and share. In other words, employees start with so much hope, but as they rise in the traditional corporate hierarchy and spend a few years there, they are forced into "grow mode only," so they sow to grow, and growing without seeing and then sharing doesn't resow for the future. This is true in even the most seemingly supportive environments. Across the board, even when 80 percent of the people my organization assessed said that their workplace is supportive and treats people like family, only half of those people said that their manager, supervisor, or leader challenged them to find new opportunities in the workplace and marketplace and pursue their personal brand's value proposition.

This is exactly what Caroline Wanga had seen in her decade-plus as Target's director of diversity and inclusion. She told my CDS summit she is proud of her work as what she calls a "Cultural Architect" (her unique term for the work she does). But she knows, much as my mentor at Sunkist helped me understand long ago, that the ability to construct, deconstruct, and reconstruct cultures and deliver solutions and results are easier to see from the outside in. "The folks that lead teams and people in our field organizations are trained that the most important person in their ecosystem is the guest," says Wanga, "the person that's coming into our stores to engage and have a transaction. There is no room to exclude in the stores; everyone is all in. Movement is constant in the operational environments."

The customers in these environments represent the seismic Cultural Demographic Shift, and leaders have no choice but to engage a team that can engage that customer to maximize the relationship. They actually consider it to be a risk to not have a team that isn't reflective of the guest that walks into their stores. Are people told this same thing at the business's headquarters where chances are the people do not represent the CDS? Perhaps. But do they live it every day. No. They don't engage with the customers, just the data about them. They don't have the day-to-day interaction that leads to accountability, impacts the transaction, or changes somebody's life.

As one retail executive told me, "At headquarters everywhere, many people have been there 'forever,' and as a result, headquarters works and looks nothing like the stores. Everyone silos. If the business problems are at headquarters and your solution is far away, you will not be successful. You need to have relationship capital. How do you offer people more than you ask them for? This requires more than just courageous conversations. It requires courageous listening. This is why improved hiring and embracing of the six characteristics are happening outside headquarters, which continue to lag behind. There is much higher engagement, favorability, and approval outside the headquarters then there are inside. The cultures are healthier outside when it comes in contact with 'the real world.'"

You want ROI? You got it right there. Nik Modi, managing director at RBC Capital Markets, calls this investment strategy "courage arbitrage" and "the single best investments strategy for our time. Most companies lack the courage to do the right things. The result for today's CEOs in the S&P 500 and beyond, who complain about pressure from shareholders, the markets, and their ability to embrace the CDS, is a giant disconnect between what CEOs believe creates value versus what the markets say creates value. Companies must invest in their futures with the same approach taken by Jeff Bezos at Amazon or Elon Musk at Tesla—make no money and invest, invest, invest—only on the 'people level.'"

That's how we create massive value in the workplace and marketplace. In fact, taking that risk and creating relevancy and massive value also means companies may be around a little longer. Modi noted that while the average age of S&P 500 companies was once 67 years, in 2012 it was down to just fifteen years, which is part of the reason they get stuck in sowing—there is only so much time on the proverbial clock. "Corporations should understand that while most of the population growth will emanate from the Hispanic community, the seismic shift is essentially multicultural," says Modi. "The influence of Hispanics is often understated given their influence on other ethnicities. Unfortunately, CEOs remain so focused on their company's stock price performance and serve for such a short tenure that most avoid making the necessary and significant investments to truly understand this growing customer base and win their trust and loyalty. With pressure from shareholders, they'd rather kick the can to the next CEO, rather than take a hit on the next quarterly earnings report."

And if this sounds like a lot of touchy-feely stuff that everyone says matters when the proverbial cameras are rolling but doesn't affect the bottom line just look at what happened to one of the companies Mike Fernandez, chairman of MBF Healthcare Partners, sold to UnitedHealthcare for $525 million in 1983. "When we sold the business, we owned, managed, and controlled about 300 health-care facilities and saw about 400,000 patients," Fernandez recalls. "Each of these facilities had a small cafeteria. Those were 'the key' culturally for the Hispanic patients and were the differentiator from our competitors. Patients who came in the morning went to the cafeteria to be social. Hispanics like to be around others. They also served inexpensive sandwiches and coffee at a business that catered to a lower-income group. Lots of time they would eat a sandwich and take the other half home for dinner. When United took over, they shut the cafeterias down. 'We're not in the food business,' they said. That was the only substantial change they made. Flash-forward to 2002: The business we sold for $525 million, we bought back for $10 million. Two years later, we sold it to another health-care company for $525 million. The difference was not just what the cafeterias did—it is what they meant. The difference is in the thought process and the values. Unless you change to include the people and know their culture, you are missing the boat."

In Fernandez's case, a boat filled with hundreds of millions of dollars. How can a company like UnitedHealthcare make a mistake that big? They never asked the customers what they wanted. They saw no value in those cafeterias. They saw a cost center, not a growth strategy. So they shut it down, and as a result, they cost a large number of people something that affects us all: our health. Which is why the health of American enterprise is linked to and reflected in the health of our entire population.

A Matter of Life and Death—Literally

American businesses and leadership will be hearing the term "population health" more and more as it applies both to the health of the public as a whole and as a brand strategy to solve for inequities in the workplace and marketplace. There are now population health executives at Fortune 500 companies and beyond who are responsible for managing the health care, wellness, work/life balance, and other related needs of their employees and addressing similar needs in their businesses' consumer base. Companies are learning that wellness (healthy minds, bodies, and careers) among employees and customers is essential to sustained success in all part of their business, especially when it comes to shift population engagement and career advancement. But to succeed, these businesses must realize that real solutions in support of population health have to be based on the understanding that wellness and well-being—like business overall—is becoming less about the business defining the individual and more about the individual defining the business. This means we must all strengthen our intellectual capital and know-how around the distinct needs of the individuals within every population. In health care, like so many companies, it has been the opposite: The business and its leadership—namely physicians and large organizations—have been dictating the course of health for individuals for generations. Yet this is where the real opportunity for growth lies. It's where saving lives and generating ROI co-exist. We all will see embracing the CDS and diversity and inclusion as a game-changing strategy for growth in health care and beyond as profit centers, not cost centers, by driving new research and revenue—if we just have the courage to work from the inside out and have the wisdom and vulnerability to both solve for who we are and what we don't know.

For that to happen, each stakeholder in population health—hospitals, care providers, retail health-care operations, food and consumer brands, food services and facilities management, community influencers, big pharma, educational institutions, nonprofits, insurance providers and payers, and beyond—must know with clarity what the cultural shift means for their organization. After all, health—just like diversity—is something that for the most part happens outside of health-care facilities. Where it really takes root is within the families and communities of shift populations. Health cannot be placed in a silo off to the side of someone's life. Neither can diversity and inclusion.

But given the urgency, even when diversity and inclusion is put at the center of a strategy for growth, we cannot underestimate the power external partnerships have to help us evolve the solve. In population health, for example, businesses must also collaborate to heighten awareness across industries and the country, which will fuel diversity of thought, help solve for the talent gap faster, and bring attention to other opportunity gaps in the delivery of health and wellness to shift populations. This shift in mindset gets back to the health-care lesson for every leader in every industry: Every caregiver (not just doctors) and all organizations have the competencies to serve individual needs and that requires access to new and different resources, capabilities, and intellectual know-how that has not historically existed because there hasn't been a need for it to exist. As such, the health-care industry must broaden its observations to engage with external partners in new ways to design more cohesive solutions.

In the end, just like the CDS, no one organization has all the solutions for population health. Only together can we address the urgent need to more authentically serve and build loyalty and trust with shift population communities by creating the depository of intellectual capital. Only collectively can we promote proven preventive care methods and the need to close the health-care workforce development gap in culturally fluent ways. Only when this cultural fluency is achieved with brand strategies and partnerships that authentically lead, innovate, and engage with today's increasingly multicultural patients, workforce, and consumers will we have the ecosystems that truly make it about the individual defining the business.

Simply put, to truly succeed, a more focused, holistic approach is required among all stakeholders committed to solving for the health, wellness, and societal advancement of shift populations. For example, medical institutions need to become part of a solution ecosystem that leverages strengths and resources of external partners among retail health care, food and consumer brands, community influencers, pharma, food services and facilities management, educational institutions, and nonprofits. Historically, however, this collaboration and focus on the needs of individuals is exactly what the business templates of the past prevented them from achieving.

Know the power of strong ecosystems and when there is a need to build them using external partnerships.

As population health takes off and more and more organizations and medical institutions, pharmaceutical companies, retail health-care companies, and food and consumer brands all play roles in managing the overall health and wellness of those employees, an immense amount of work will be required. They all must effectively collaborate (internally and externally) to build strong intel and know-how ecosystems. This is much more than the subject matter expertise or personal brand value propositions any one business or organization can handle. To support population health, leaders must consider the strategic implications of cross-cultural intelligence and diversity of thought, along with the rapidly evolving insights and unique needs of the changing face of America's new workforce, patients, and consumers to influence the business of health both directly and indirectly.

Most of us see this playing out every day: As retail health care—CVS, Walgreens, Walmart, Target—continues to play a more defining role in the delivery of health-care services in the U.S. through their growth of in-store clinics, their responsibility to help solve for the widening talent gap in the health-care and biomedical fields among minorities, especially Hispanics,

Anticipating Shift Population Needs for Population Health

Robert W. Stone, president and CEO of City of Hope, a California-based health-care provider and biomedical research and treatment institution focused on eliminating cancer and diabetes, provides a fine example of how his institution has anticipated the needs of the patient population and how will they change for years in the future. Forty-six percent of City of Hope's catchment area is Hispanic, so City of Hope needs to understand and be able to communicate with that community as they seek medical care sooner and more often.

City of Hope wants to deliver on the promise to its Hispanic community and all shift populations in its catchment area to detect and treat diseases and conditions that are disproportionately higher among Hispanics than other populations earlier than in the past (which not only raises the bar for their overall health but also reduces costs for treatment). Doing this goes way beyond having a language translator at the facilities. Ideally, City of Hope wants its workforce to mirror the marketplace it is trying to serve. That's difficult in an industry where Hispanics are severely underrepresented among U.S. doctors, nurses, and pharmacists. Stone knows City of Hope must address not just how care is being offered but the pipeline: For example, City of Hope does a T.E.A.C.H. (Train, Educate, and Accelerate Careers in Healthcare) partnership, which provides students with the opportunity to gain college credit while still in high school by taking college-level classes at no cost. They also formed *El Concilio*, a Spanish-speaking version of their successful Patient Family Advisory Group, which is designed to build trust through increased engagement and a more positive patient and caregiver experience. As Stone says, "You have to start at the point when people are looking at career options. That starts really early. We believe we are not just a scientific organization or health-care provider but a member of our local community in which we reside and want to give back. That builds a foundation of trust within the community, especially that kid who comes in with his parent for care."

will heighten. Those businesses must join leaders from medical institutions that predominantly serve Hispanics—as well as other multicultural communities—where there is a need to attract, develop, and advance Hispanic talent to more effectively serve the unique needs of the growing Hispanic patient population.

Given the magnitude and multiple variables involved to solve for health inequities, external partnerships are critical, says Randy Martinez, director of strategic diversity management and pharmacy benefits management at CVS Health. "The many multicultural community partners we engage with help us define our message and tailor it to the communities where we operate as a retailer," says Martinez. "From an overall health-care perspective, external partnerships are a lifeline to our customers and patients. Our partners not only help us convey the message that puts people on the path to better health, but they help fit the message to the diverse communities we serve. At the center of all these discussions at CVS and beyond is the rapid growth of the U.S. Hispanic population, which is leading the charge for changing the business of health and business as a whole. You can see this most clearly in the urgent need for more culturally competent physician care and genetic research to serve those Hispanic populations and among Hispanics themselves in the call to action to become more educated about preventive care and self-advocacy.

Yet most in the health-care industry are lagging behind this key part of the cultural demographic shift, says Dr. Ricardo Martinez, former managing director at North Highland, a global management consulting firm. "When you reframe the conversation about public health and health-care disparities in terms of population health," says Martinez, "it becomes a different dialog—one about opportunities."

Adds Fletcher Lance, national healthcare lead at North Highland: "There's an emerging America coming to the forefront, and it's surprising how many people don't see it."

And if you don't see it, you can't seize the opportunity as a strategy for growth. But that's exactly what we are doing because we aren't thinking holistically about where population health fits in to any growth strategy. If you have been thinking that population health and its importance to growth is limited to serving shift populations in the health-care industry,

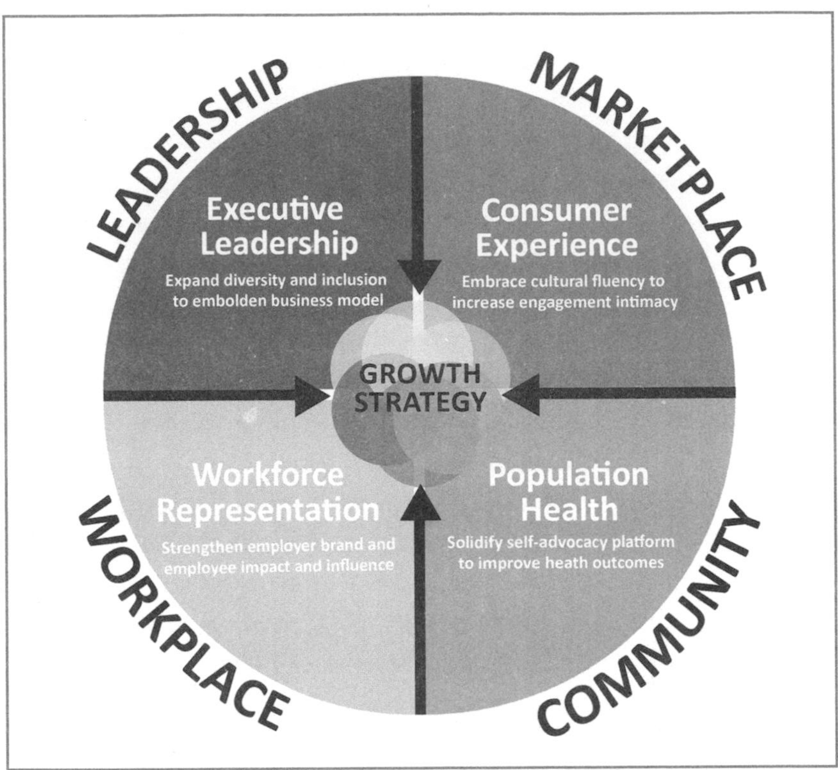

Figure 5.2—Four Pillars for Moving People to the Center of Your Growth Strategy

you are wrong. And so was I. Not about population health as an essential health-care issue but population health as just a CDS health-care issue.

Population health is about the overall state of health for businesses and all our populations in leadership, the workplace, and the marketplace. It is, in fact, the fourth and ultimate strategic pillar for moving people to the center of an organization's growth strategy (Figure 5.2).

For an organization to evolve and grow, all four of these pillars must evolve simultaneously to move people from the fringe of organizational development objectives to the center of their enterprise-wide strategy. That's when real growth/ROI happens. When they fail to evolve simultaneously, an organization will end up with shortsighted tactics and misinformed strategies that end up solving for the wrong things.

When I say this to clients, nine times out of ten the next words are: Where are the numbers to back up thinking? Where is the quantitative argument? And what I say is: Where are the numbers to back up the opposite approach—one that leans upon playing it safe as a cost center—that you have been following for decades? We have had more and more data around the topic of "people" for years just like we have had experience for years, and where has that led us? Flawed initiatives that keep creating silos, poor employee engagement, execution mindsets, tension . . .

The way we've been doing and measuring the impact and influence of people has been flawed. We need to reinvent the entire model—in particular the role that numbers and experience play—to operationalize the innovation mentality by investing in people and moving them to the center of our growth strategies.

CHAPTER 6

OPERATIONALIZE THE INNOVATION MENTALITY FOR ALL OF US

I was on a call with the senior leaders of a division of a major national food service company. The company had responded enthusiastically to my initial presentations and work with them, and this follow-up conversation had turned to "doing." Specifically, one of the leaders asked me, "What is the most immediate thing that our division can do to embrace the Cultural Demographic Shift, seize opportunity in the marketplace, and solve for the shift on multiple fronts?"

If I were a different kind of consultant, I might just have given them what they asked for. "Hey guys, that's great. Let's focus short term on what you can do now in the market . . ." But you've probably surmised that's not me.

Still, I found myself at a crossroads.

On the one hand, I wanted to push them and say: That may sound like a great question, but it isn't the right one—or rather it's not taking you in the right direction. You can't just go and "do" in the marketplace without first thinking about the individuals who work for you; you must make sure your talent and market development are connected. And what about the rest of the company? You're talking about one specific area of your business, but by getting out of your divisional silo and having the same conversation and asking the same question across departments, you could multiply the effects of any answers and ideas across your entire business. And what about you? Do your people know what your leadership stands for? Do your managers feel enabled and empowered to think, explore, and own what you need them to do? If you don't know what your leadership stands for and if your direct reports are not on board, how will your employees respond long term to any directives to "do"? How will the marketplace?

On the other hand, I thought I should shut up and not push them; I should let them discover they are just substituting one limited short-term strategy for another. Let them see that this approach will not solve their leadership identity crisis. Let them figure out that talking about an outreach strategy before fixing internal leadership problems will leave them unprepared to support that strategy in the workplace. Let them learn that using the innovation mentality to better serve clients and customers and seize opportunities for growth in the marketplace starts from the inside out. Let them realize the necessity of fostering interdepartmental ecosystems—across IT, sales, distribution, finance, customer service, marketing—and making sure every individual can "see, sow, grow, share" and feel empowered by, connected to, and aligned with the expectations to seize the opportunities. Eventually they would get there.

But I chose not to shut up.

And here's why: The other way might create short-term growth, but it would not embrace the six characteristics of the innovation mentality and lead to sustainable evolution and long-term "see, sow, grow, share" success. Eventually the same problems will return and much faster. Transformational change does not happen on one phone call or in one meeting. That just leads to more short-term sowing—doing without thinking. They were enlightened people who believed in what I said and wanted to do the right thing, but like too many people in business, they were thinking through the lens of the company. By continuing to manage by the old templates, they have been stripped of their identities and left insecure about who they are and how to face change. There are too many leaders out there who lack a refined leadership identity, simply because the company doesn't and hasn't allowed them to be themselves. They are doing the company's thinking and looking for quick results to comply with corporate scorecards. They want solutions without evolution.

We need to allow individuals to speak up as enablers of evolution without repercussion.

Even though people want to think and be valued more than ever before, leaders are too confined and restrained by past modalities, organizational operations, and personal insecurities. They are not ready for the individual to define the business and take the level of ownership required. Leaders are failing their people, themselves, their partners and customers—indeed failing our country—by not embracing diversity of thought or developing a long-term strategy, and then doing the work that the innovation mentality requires to evolve in the right way.

If you're stuck in the world of sowing, then it is only what is in your field of vision that matters, which is why sowing is such a powerful idea when it is connected to selling a vision or product as an immediate path to success. When we get stuck in sowing, we forget to step back and see all the opportunities before we sow. That's because we let others control our thinking too much. We've allowed the business to define the individual. But as we discussed in Chapter 1, business today is becoming less about the business defining the individual and more about the individual defining the business. That's how people feel they are making contributions and connecting to leaders and their companies—as individuals who create shared cultures that drive change and foster growth. You must have the wisdom and courage to lead through this. Unfortunately, the resulting leadership identity crisis has left leaders and companies uncertain about

We can't end up where we started—more sowing without seeing, growing, and sharing—substituting without evolving.

how to lead in a more diverse, multigenerational environment that requires them to embrace and then apply the six characteristics of the innovation mentality to themselves. As a result, leaders fail to see the potential opportunities for workplace and then marketplace success.

This is the case with well-meaning and smart leaders like the ones at that food services company or the executive who had recently started at a major health-care provider and asked me, “How do we really start serving the market because we are behind? I have about five direct reports and hundreds in my division. We are not doing a bad job, but we could be so much better.”

“OK,” I said turning the question inward to her. “Do those five direct reports know what to expect from your leadership? If I were to ask them, would they give me consistent answers?”

“No,” she said.

“Can you tell me what you expect from their leadership?” No.

“Do they know what you should be expecting from them?” No.

How was her problem a marketplace issue? This leader had to establish her leadership identity first. Fortunately, her tenure was still relatively new, so she had an advantage many leaders don’t: a clean slate. But there is a lesson in her story for all of us, whether we have been at a company five weeks or 15 years: The best way to transition your leadership is establishing the meaning of that leadership, making people feel comfortable about what they can expect from you. What better way to eliminate the uncertainty that rightly accompanies any leadership change or indeed any change in direction for the existing leadership at a company? Sure, morale will still get a jolt of energy like a sports team on a winning streak when it switches coaches during the season, but soon the old inefficiencies and problems will resurface if the leadership identity does not remain intact and everyone stays true to their personal brand value propositions. That’s the difference between a dynasty in sports and winning it once.

And it’s all because that leader had not evolved the solve. So I asked her, “What is less intimidating and more reflective of what you are trying to accomplish: change or evolution?”

“Evolution!” she said. “Evolving put the onus on myself to understand what others might expect from me and, over time, how I can begin to contribute." Then she told me that right before our meeting, she had had another meeting, and all the facilitator did was talk about "change" and how the company needed it. But there was no meaning or direction behind the word. It made everyone feel broken and even threatened.

"Great," I said. "So here's the question: How do you influence the evolution of the organization today?"

"I don't know."

I walked out of that meeting and wondered how many leaders would actually have this dialogue between themselves and their supervisors. Few, I imagined, which is why things stay in substitution mode until tensions rise, leadership changes again, and the cycle repeats.

This is how leaders (especially at the top of the organization) are complicit in creating tension, albeit unknowingly. Their lack of leadership maturity puts the people they serve in the workplace and marketplace off balance, creating chaos and confusion along the way. This leadership vacuum constrains rather than fosters opportunity and results not in ownership but in gamesmanship and politicking. High-potential employees and next-generation leaders, once expectant, hungry for direction, and hopeful for evolution give up not only hope but also their individuality. The environment restricts them to learn the right ways and evolve themselves. They can see no alternative to conforming to corporate templates without understanding what they mean; the traps and tension they unknowingly create; the wisdom to translate them into tangible, desired outcomes; or imagining how their own leadership identity can best support them. They soon lose any sense of empowerment and eventually commit. They begin to question their own long-term loyalty and career goals within the organization. That then trickles down to the people who work for them and eventually external partners, customers, and clients.

I have seen this happen at companies of all sizes in every industry. For example, after a presentation to a multinational food manufacturing company, a senior executive came up to me and said, "I am so disappointed in my company's leadership. You gave my top people every reason to engage, and I know why they did not. Your message was clear: We are a company that has been bogged down—hierarchical, traditional, and beholden to templates—and we don't have an environment where leaders at the top have to take ownership for changing this. Leaders at the top don't want to evolve. Leaders at the top want to keep helping their people drive whatever initiatives or objectives they have, and that's why we are at risk of just substituting as you called it. It's about the individual, but they don't want to take ownership of that. So when you ask them profound questions, they have no answers."

Scenarios like this are just as prevalent in high-tech industries as they are in businesses that existed at the turn of the 20th century. It is especially true in institutions and organizations that focus on marketing and sales at the expense of research and design. It is most interesting to see the conflict and resistance between new and old templates in industries like education and health care as some leaders try to transition their knowledge into wisdom while others fight them and unknowingly create tension by resisting any evolutionary change. But there is also opportunity there.

Break free of the thinking of the traditional workplace and retrain yourself on how to think; give yourself permission to think in ways you've been constrained from thinking for so long.

"If there's resistance, you have to understand the why behind it," says Paul Heredia, chief human resources officer of the Los Angeles–based Citrus Valley Health Partners. "Resistance is just a symptom; you've got to get at the root cause of why someone does not want to change and gain a comprehensive view of their perspective by bringing together stakeholders from across functional areas. That includes the naysayers; let them challenge you but also challenge them to bring some answers and solutions to the table too." Yes, Heredia told me, he gets pushback from physicians and others who might be resistant to change, but you've got to engage them in the process, coach them, and build connections with champions throughout the organization: "It's another case of suspending judgment and not forcing people to change but bringing them into the conversation. You have to explain and educate how the change will benefit them and their patient base, and back it up with actions that match your words and fact-based, data-driven supporting evidence."

The problem is when leaders become too comfortable with a one-size-fits-all approach to leadership, they conversely become uncomfortable with the uncertainty that more successful leaders embrace as part of the job. The most effective leaders are self-aware enough to know why they are successful in certain situations and transparent (and vulnerable) when they are not. They have the clarity to anticipate the unique needs of the business and the people they lead—and the wisdom to see opportunity in everything to meet those needs. They know what leadership role they play, when to play it, and when to let others play their role. Their ego and humility work in tandem.

That's how leaders evolve from their identity crisis and serve the changing needs of businesses and the people they serve in the workplace and marketplace in the age of the CDS. They understand the power of the six characteristics to drive seeing, sowing, growing, and sharing. Evolving while we are executing means we are seeing before we sow and then growing and sharing to resow more success.

See

1. See Opportunity in Everything
2. Anticipate the Unexpected

Sow

3. Unleash Your Passionate Pursuits

Grow

4. Live with an Entrepreneurial Spirit

Share

5. Work with a Generous Purpose
6. Lead to Leave a Legacy

But as I learned in my call to that food services company and so many other calls and discussions like it, there are huge disconnects between understanding and operationalizing these characteristics, which is why I keep repeating them again and again. This shouldn't be easy work, but it shouldn't be too confusing either. Solving with these characteristics is designed to simplify the ways we work and lead, not make it more complicated. That requires a lot of upfront work to evolve to that point, and too many leaders just don't want to (or have the directive to) get their hands dirty, changing the way things work, so they expect others to get dirty for them. Operationalizing these characteristics and transitioning from substitutional to evolutionary thinking requires leaders to broaden their capabilities, be more courageous, and enable those around them to think as much as do.

Operationalize and Move from "Sowing" to "Growing" and "Sharing"

Sustainable success does not come from abdicating responsibility in this way, and it surely does not come by accident. It's by design. Leaders who fail to see this do not deserve to serve in a leadership capacity, because they let the marketplace pass them by. They let their identity become too dependent on what their business card says or the artificial power their company lends them in its effort to define those leaders' identities and less about evolving in their ability to better lead and over-deliver for the organization they serve. Unfortunately, I've seen this pattern too many times. So we keep having meetings that go nowhere and cultures that don't come together, everything staying siloed while people lose trust and leaders lose influence. If your thinking changes, that's good. But could you actually put a plan together that people can act on knowing that they are collectively evolving as they execute? That's why so many meetings go nowhere. They are filled with energy and great ideas but . . . then what? How do you take it from substitution to evolution mode? What do you do with the thinking? How do you operationalize it? What do you do to make the thinking turn into revenue? Operationalize it.

I am intentionally repeating myself here, because the point is too great not to: Evolution in business is about the ability to operationalize and go from "doing" to "growing and sharing" beyond words on a PowerPoint presentation. Leaders must have the ability to design a plan that shows exactly how their thinking will be deployed throughout their team, department, and the entire organization. Only then will they help others understand how it impacts and empowers them. This is why 21st-century leaders must use the six characteristics to operationalize their thinking. They use it to ensure that their organization can be most successful and profitably apply it in the marketplace. But then we don't operationalize the innovation mentality, because we don't practice it. This is big game thinking, and no player—from the benchwarmers to the superstars—has ever won the big game in sports without showing up and practicing.

We don't know how to operationalize the innovation mentality, because we don't know how to go from doing to thinking to reality.

This is why it is so much easier to just "do" rather than think and evolve. Thinking requires a lot of work and changing a whole lot of things. It requires us to rewire our learned tendencies and get back to embracing our ideals. It requires taking the ideas from all those meetings, writing them down, and then sharing them across the company—getting them out of the conference room, away from the job titles and department silos. To go from idea to action requires leaders—not just the people who work from them—to identify the parts of the thinking that can be further involved and potentially resown across other parts of the organization. Otherwise, opportunity gaps will continue to be missed.

This goes beyond diversity straight to the bottom line. This is why, as discussed in Chapter 2, we need new metrics for success. Remember, this is about people who have felt conflicted in the ways they are thinking but not courageous enough to do anything about it. But we are not set up to do this. We have neither the action plan nor the trust, and we will never have it if we keep using the old templates.

To operationalize the innovation mentality, we need new metrics for success founded on the six characteristics.

What are the new ones? The six characteristics of the innovation mentality fueled by diversity of thought. Start by holding people accountable to their personal brand value propositions and what they solve for, not their job descriptions, and make the ability to embrace diversity of thought the driving factor of the company's best practices and key performance indicators, or KPIs. I hear a lot about the need for measuring the success and impact of my work through KPIs, which are metrics businesses, institutions, and even governments use to evaluate factors that are crucial to the success of an organization. They differ from institution to institution and department to department, but they share a common purpose: to use data as a gauge for success and progress against goals. So make what each person solves for that data. Leaders must know not only what their brand is but also every single person's on their teams and the people that they connect with. They should have a dashboard that defines that expertise and how they should use that expertise to define how they will influence the future of the business and whether or not they've contributed. That's how individuals define the business and how leaders define KPIs through the contributions of their people. That's how you will quickly learn that you will find greater contribution from people who come from a diverse background than those who do not. Because it comes naturally to them—they are just not enabled by the organization to evolve into this role.

When you keep operating under the old metrics that have been forcing us to substitute for years, not only do we not have the right metrics, but everyone gets completely confused and nothing gets done. So progress is slow. Evolution? Nonexistent. That's why most companies "manage by template." After all, it is so much easier to manage by template, when you have a predetermined approach where decisions are made based on past history rather than on being courageous enough to seize new types of opportunities, redefine the future, and become less dependent on the past. But when the template those companies have followed to drive growth for years begins to change, sustaining any competitive advantage becomes difficult and vulnerable to the changing marketplace. When leaders don't pace themselves to the rhythms of the marketplace or listen to their employees, they can't maximize the resources and human capital that lie within their own organizations and market share.

But wait a minute: That's not you anymore, is it?

You now see that a lack of diverse thinking makes companies less competitive in engaging developing markets domestically and globally and retaining and developing the leaders and talent of the future. You understand this extends beyond the CDS and shift populations like the 85 percent of women and Millennials, many of whom are represented by shift populations and, like them, also want more individualized, community-focused, and transparent workplaces. You know why all we have discussed goes well beyond corporate social responsibility programs or hiring mandates to increase, say, the number of blacks in our offices. You get why the CDS connects to any group that feels misrepresented and misunderstood—anyone who has felt the need to work ten times harder to get an opportunity and, when they find one, feel they must check their individuality at the door. These are the people who are most attuned to the innovation mentality and the leadership of the future. They can see beyond the traditional workplace that is hierarchical and departmental and operates in silos and fear-based cultures; their skill sets, capabilities, and know-how transcend these limitations. They thrive in environments of transparency, trust, and empowerment of individuals to think freely. Their experiences have taught them to embrace the six characteristics of the innovation mentality.

People not steeped in the way things have been learn to value in others what they lack to effect evolutionary and transformative change.

Find Like-Mindedness in People through Their Differences

The old ways of doing things don't apply any more. Maybe they never did, but today's employees want more from the workplace. They need their leaders to have their backs (work with a generous purpose). But too many leaders are operating in survival mode and thus don't share enough themselves to protect their own domain. Without leaders to sponsor and mentor high-potential employees, many are reckoning with the changing terrain on their own, which puts their organizations at risk. Remember what those executives at the major investment banking firm from Chapter 4 told me: "Today, we are afraid for the future of our business because our employees don't relate to our emerging global client base. We continue to lose key diverse members of our workforce to our competitors because we lack the cultural intelligence to keep them."

This is why when brands don't invest in and retain the right people intelligence, they lose marketplace opportunity. With a workplace and a marketplace that are becoming younger, more diverse, technologically savvy, and globally connected, leaders should become more intent on seeing what lies around, beneath, and beyond what they seek for their businesses as a growth strategy. But just like leaders at that wine and spirits company at which I started my career, too many leaders today don't create workplaces that value diversity of thought. Millennials, women, and other diverse populations are more inclined to see, show, grow, and share—and value them all—but cannot manage in the wrong types of environments that don't allow them to be more of themselves. We can see this in the demands Millennials are making on the companies that they are willing to work for—and the kinds of companies that they are creating. They want transparency. They want community environments that give back. They want a new kind of trust based on clarity, consistency, and contact rather than hierarchy and authority. They want to agree to devote their talents to a particular organization for as long as it allows their personal brand and its value proposition to develop and remain relevant. And when they can't get what they require, they move on just like I did years ago from that wine and spirits company.

In today's fast-paced, talent-based, trust-demanding world of work, remaining competitive requires alignment around a set of values, beliefs, and behaviors. These values must then become part of and define a company's culture beyond words in training manuals and annual reports. Culture must be a conscious choice and created by design, not by accident. Without shared values that everyone can embrace and act on, corporate cultures harbor contradictions and conflicts, creating environments where leadership agendas abound and disengaged employees lack the right mindset to perform at their best. By contrast, the shared values that cultivate the best corporate cultures serve as the ultimate platforms to drive growth, innovation, and opportunity.

Shared values in the workplace translate into marketplace performance and sustainability.

Nurturing shared corporate values to support and protect long-term success requires vigilance and constant attention from leadership at all levels. In a world of rapid change, increasing transparency, and competition for the best talent, leaders who fail to commit to who they are as individuals and what the company stands for as a whole will put their companies and their people at great risk as they fail to connect internally and externally to consumers. At the same time, they face corporate "values" that confuse employees and consumers alike, making it difficult for leaders already struggling with their own identity crises (as described in Chapter 2) to solve for the right things and creating confusion for how the brand can authentically solve for the unique needs of people. Thus, it takes great leadership to keep these corporate cultures on the right path and continuously improving. The values they propagate within their organizations should be explicit, thoughtful, and authentic as they focus on what everyone should be solving for simultaneously—the opportunity gaps in the workplace/workforce, among external partners, and within marketplace/consumers—so they continue to evolve and grow stronger. That's how we create high-performance environments that enable the full potential in the people our leadership and businesses touch.

Leaders, regardless of hierarchy or rank, must be held accountable to communicate, illustrate, and reinforce the values that will help the company achieve its missions, goals, and objectives. Effective corporate cultures support high-performance through both diversity of thought and like-mindedness in approach, style, and attitude. Strong corporate cultures blend the strengths of people while celebrating their individuality and authenticity in support of an organization's vision and mission, goals, and objectives. But for this to happen, the culture must become automatic and repetitive—part of leadership "muscle memory." Leadership for the most part is learned behavior that becomes subconscious and instinctive over time. At the speed of business today, leaders must act like coaches in professional sports, making important decisions often under immense pressure in the time it takes most people to understand the problem.

It's time for corporations to showcase their executives' leadership identities and personal brand value propositions to grow better together—to be more open-minded and embrace new perspectives previously unseen, regardless of hierarchy or rank. These are the lifters and leaders of the future—if we let them define the business. To do that, they must learn to deploy circular vision rather than the traditional linear approaches that limit their vision to only what is in front of them. Many executives only see the problem but not the solution. They need to change. We need to change. Yet according to my company's surveys of thousands of leaders, only 32 percent of leaders identify themselves as change agents to reinvent the way their businesses work, but they are being held back by the status quo and refuse to fight. Which is exactly how we ended up with the leadership identity crisis in Chapter 2 that prevents us from being innovative and embracing the innovation mentality.

Be a change agent. Reinvent and embrace diversity of thought—be vulnerable.

Leaders need the resiliency the innovation mentality gives them to constantly move people (not just bottom lines) forward and avoid falling into complacency traps. They must use diversity of thought to make sure that everyone is contributing and embracing their personal brands and adding value—value that is measurable and sustainable. They apply the six characteristics of the innovation mentality to break free from templates and create organizations led by those personal brands and their value propositions, not job titles or descriptions. Instead, we all must be led by our identities that maximize our full potential and value everyone as individuals and extend that to the marketplace. You can't focus on one without understanding the impact of the other. In traditional companies, talent development is optional, because they can always find more people to fill positions. It's not about the individual; it's individuals learning to conform to a company's way of doing things. They learn to check their best selves at the door as they walk in each morning. In this kind of organization, you can be whatever you want to be, as long as the company already has a slot for it. Individuality? Your whole self? Showcasing your personal brand? Forget it. Not going to happen. This no longer acceptable—not in diversity and corporate social responsibility programs. Not anywhere.

Instead, the six characteristics of the innovation mentality empowers all of us to:

- Share our identities. Be proud of who you are. Our differences are our strengths. (See Opportunity in Everything)
- Own our development. Invest in yourself. Anything is possible. (Anticipate the Unexpected, Unleash Your Passionate Pursuits)
- Bring others along. Invest in the development and advancement of others. Make dreams come true. (Live with an Entrepreneurial Spirit, Work with a Generous Purpose)
- Define our future. Improve the experience for everyone. (Lead to Leave a Legacy)

The days of taking a one-size-fits-all approach are over, never to exist again. Our goal as leaders is to convert the melting pot of differences into a mosaic that fuels strategies for growth, innovation, and opportunity to maximize the full potential of people, brands, and businesses. Simply put, the CDS is about understanding your identity and the identities of all people—not just Hispanics, Asian/Pacific Islanders, blacks, LGBT, or women. Through the innovation mentality, we embrace the transparency, trust, individuality, risk, social responsibility, entrepreneurial mindset, passion, and promise to be a community-minded leader in the workplace, and much, much more.

Workplaces must adapt to the strengths of their people and their whole selves in everything they do. We must be courageous enough to challenge the status quo and our leaders'/company's thinking to avoid solving for potentially the wrong things. We must define and apply new metrics for leadership and performance that aren't tied to the same ones our great-grandparents used. We need to hit the pause button on helping people understand "identities" and instead help everyone turn their identities into results—and then talk about how our diversity of thought that is influenced by our culture led to unique outcomes. We must also hit pause on selling and start leading! To do this, we must apply the six characteristics of the innovation mentality to be much more people intelligent and learn to convert that intelligence into areas for innovation and growth in the workplace and marketplace.

All business today is about "people intelligence." Regardless of functional responsibility, leaders must become "chief people officers" who evolve and allow their staffs to confidently renew, reinvent, and refresh their departments. This means having a purposeful intention to become more aware and engage with the differences of the people and more effective at connecting the dots of opportunity embedded within these differences and then translating them into business outcomes. When business is about people intelligence, wisdom is the new growth currency. You discover and develop your personal brand to fit best. You broaden your perspectives and those of your team, enable creativity, and strengthen teamwork and the value we place on one another. You create new best practices and improve output. You problem solve, plan, and execute more effectively. And you propel innovation and seize opportunities previously unseen.

So, how do we get going in the right direction? How do you get started? Ask your employees. If you give them the safe space free from judgment, they will tell you. They will unleash their passionate pursuits if you are courageous and vulnerable enough to listen to them, and advance them into roles of influence as a strategy for growth. And when you do ask them, ask uncomfortable questions. Not just tough questions, uncomfortable ones.

It's easy to embrace the six characteristics, but embracing them is not enough to fully break free from our leadership identity crises.

David Casey, CVS Health's chief diversity officer, offers an easy way to start answering these questions: Ask yourself, "If I were in charge I would . . ." and fill in the blank. This gets away from blame and toward personal accountability that you are willing to evolve the solve and act to make the changes to your leadership identity. That's what the second part of this book is about: mastering the six characteristics to effect change in today's fiercely competitive global marketplace by helping you develop and practice the skills and conscious thought, action, and practices you and your company need, knowing when to apply them and when not to, and when to bring others in to help.

To help guide you, Part II shares insights and frontline experiences from myself; leaders of the roundtables at my executive summits, the companies I have worked for and with; and workers at those companies and beyond. Together, they will provide you and your organization with tangible ways to change the conversation and use the innovation mentality to drive growth, generate greater clarity, and create some real discomfort.

Yes, discomfort. I'm done with what's comfortable and what it has done to us.

Let's accept diversity of thought as inevitable, evolutionary, and essential to our future success! Evolving and operationalizing go hand and hand. We must operationalize evolution to give it significance—operationalize by owning leadership identity and then staying within the ecosystem of the six characteristics. Let's master the characteristics and truly develop a strategy that focuses on evolution not substitution.

PART II

MASTERING THE SIX CHARACTERISTICS OF THE INNOVATION MENTALITY

CHAPTER 7

USING THE INNOVATION MENTALITY TO INFLUENCE BUSINESS EVOLUTION

This second part of the book guides you through the first steps to influencing evolution of your organization the right way, ensuring people know what to expect from it and your leadership so they can evolve as well. It shows you that the more you put value into individuality and diversity of thought and broaden your observations of opportunities previously unseen, the more that influence can be shared to generate results in both the short and long term. It breaks free from the old templates by asking and helping you answer the questions:

- What should you be you solving for—how do you evolve your solve?
- How do you know which characteristics to use and how best to apply them based on what you are solving for?
- How will (you/your team/your company) apply and operationalize the six characteristics of the innovation mentality and diversity of thought to seize opportunity gaps and evolve?

In other words, it's time to get your hands dirty. The substitution party is over.

If this sounds like foundational thinking that you've heard before, good . . . and true. As I said in the introduction, the principles of the innovation mentality are a return to the immigrant perspective that established America's greatness. Foundational thinking has gotten so lost in substitutional thinking that we have difficulty identifying it, let alone evolving from it. Leaders give me backhanded compliments all the time, saying they have heard these concepts before and my version was just a good take on them. My first thought is, "Then why did you hire me? And why can't you articulate the lessons learned?" Truth is, most leaders can't answer this last question. They hide from reality—fearing the chance of being exposed in front of their peers and subordinates—and actually *won't* answer it. They can't answer this one either: When was the last time you had a meaningful conversation around questions like these? If the answer is anything but "recently and continuously" then you're not evolving, you're substituting. Enabling evolved leadership and business evolution through the innovation mentality is about retaining all the good things you did before, eviscerating all the things you were knowingly or unknowingly doing to create tension, and rediscovering what we have been missing out on. This explains why leaders forgot how to lead. So why are you not applying this foundational thinking?

I understand if you are skeptical. I welcome healthy doses of skepticism and encourage you to do the same. Those who use their skepticism to engage, question, and gain the clarity they need to reach their goals often end up seizing the greatest opportunities. Leaders need to have the courage, vulnerability, and wisdom to view and empower evolution through the foundational thinking of the six characteristics at their companies. I'd rather have you courageous enough to be skeptical, uncomfortable, and engaged, developing the self-trust you need to apply them when the moment calls than just nodding your head "yes" to everything I am saying without taking any real ownership. When you reach the stage of ownership, you are ready to assume responsibility and take the leap of faith you have longed for in search of how to reach your full leadership potential. The leader that embraces evolution understands that success comes most to those who are surrounded by people who want their success to continue. These types of leaders find respect by making wise decisions and casting a clear vision. They work to ensure the organization is foundationally strong to withstand the demands of organic growth in the workplace, the marketplace, and among its external partners.

How Will You Influence the Evolution of Your Business?

This is the question I asked the leaders I just mentioned and at every company I have presented to and worked with from Fortune 10 companies on down. (A version of the exercise I use to ask it can be found in the Appendix.) The question is an essential one to ask and applies to every business from mom-and-pop stores to global brands. The basic answer is of course "you operationalize evolution," which simply means to start working on it—to put it into operation or use. "But how do you do that?" I ask those leaders. "How do you move from ideas to strategies for change? What role will your leadership identity play in influencing the way you think and work for the evolution of the business? How do you influence the evolution of your business?"

The answers start coming then: Be more accountable! Embrace differences! Engage! Connect! Develop! Take action!

Maybe you thought the same thing, and they are great answers—just wrong. They may *sound* great, but those words are not strategies for evolution. They are about substitution and what got us stuck here in the first place.

Not that any of those words are *negative*. It's not like engagement, connection, or professional development are bad; they are just legacies of substitution—words that *limit* leaders and institutions from seeing opportunities and staying in substitution mode. To answer the defining questions of Part II and take those first steps to influencing evolution of your organization, we need a new set of words. *Engagement* means nothing without *intimacy*. *Connection* goes only so far without *aligning* of corporate *and* individual goals. *Professional development*? Is that beholden to a corporate scorecard and job description, or does it actually *maximize potential?*

This is about huge semantic differences that go well beyond words through language matters, because it can help us break free from old substitutional templates. Think of it this way: Substitution is the caterpillar; evolution is the butterfly. You probably already have an "unevolved solves" in places throughout your business under the guise of objectives and goals linked to corporate values. But as I said in Part I, none of these companies, from the Fortune 10 on down, were fully stimulating and incentivizing diversity of thought through those values—even those companies that had statements like "respect individuals," "our people are our point of difference," or "value our and all people" as part of their mission statements. Why? Because those *corporate values* did not reflect the *shared beliefs* of its leaders, employees, and customers, just what the company wanted them to believe.

Does that mean having objectives, goals, and corporate values linked to substitution are bad things? Of course not. Only that they are unevolved. For example, most objectives are easy to use to measure specific results that leaders and companies want to achieve in a specific time frame. You will often hear those objectives linked to SMART (Specific, Measurable, Attainable, Relevant, and Timely) goals, which are neat and easy replaced by new SMART goals and objectives once they are achieved. Objectives like that may be important, but most of the time they are about sowing, not seeing, growing, or sharing. Influence requires leaders to solve through seeing, sowing, growing, and sharing to create real solutions for big problems. These solutions can be messy, as well as complicated (at least at first), disruptive, challenging, and slow to evolve as they involve actual thinking before they settle into success. Objectives can and should be part of those solutions but not as means to a limited end. *That's about substitution, not evolution.*

Now, here's the good news: Just by reading Part I and accepting that you must evolve as a leader to embrace the innovation mentality, you have started to master the words that inform the six characteristics of the innovation mentality and evolve the solve (Figure 7.1 on page 173).

In the remainder of Part II we will put you on the path to true mastery by confronting the ten most common and thus most glaring substitution words I hear from leaders when I ask how they will influence the evolution of their businesses (Figure 7.2 on page 173). These are the words every

Substitution Words	Evolution Words
Accountability	Anticipate the Unexpected
Attitude	Mindset
Business	Individual
Compliance	Commitment
Differences	Distinction
Diversity	Diverse Thinking
Job Title	Brand Value Proposition
Melting Pot	Mosaic
Personal Brand	Leadership Identity
Recognition	Respect

Figure 7.1—Substitution versus Evolution Words in Part I

Substitution Words	Evolution Words
Connection	Alignment
Control	Influence
Corporate Values	Shared Beliefs
Professional Development	Maximize Potential
Engagement	Intimacy
Ideation	Exploration
Managing	Relationship
Progress	Momentum
Responsibility	Expectation
Success	Significance

Figure 7.2—Substitution versus Evolution Words in Part II

leader and business must confront and understand to operationalize and master the innovation mentality and have true influence.

Like the words from Part I (and there is some overlap), the objective in Part II for each pair is recognizing:

- The *differences and similarities* between the substituted and evolved words
- Whether or not the substituted word is *a complementary part of and incorporated into* the evolved word or in conflict
- How to apply the six characteristics—*as lead and supporting characteristics*—to move from the substituted word or expression to the evolved one

That's how you start to operationalize the innovation mentality. Remember, just by reading Part I, you have laid a foundation within yourself to do this. Refer back to Chapter 1 in which we first laid out those six characteristics in detail along with their associated behaviors and questions to ask your company in detail. We've asked and answered many of that chapter's questions about *you* already. Now, it's time to drive the questions for your company through the end of this book. Remember, as I said in Chapter 5, just like people don't lack all of these characteristics, you do not need every characteristic to confront every substitution and evolve every solve; you just need a mindful and balanced proficiency. Balance allows you to apply the appropriate characteristics on your way to mastering them long term.

I have one question for you before we get started: Will you be a vulnerable and courageous leader when the moment calls for you to evolve your solve (see, grow, and share) and not just act (sow)? I hope so, because this question contains a bonus set of substituted and evolved words to get you started:

Substitution Words	Evolution Words
Taking Action	Being Courageous

Lead Characteristic: Work with a Generous Purpose

Supporting Characteristic: Lead to Leave a Legacy

On December 4, 2015, Mike Fernandez, chairman of MBF Healthcare Partners and the top donor to Jeb Bush's Republican presidential campaign, made two startling announcements. First, the *Miami Herald* reported Fernandez saying, "If I have a choice—and you can put it in bold—if I have a choice between [Donald] Trump and Hillary Clinton, I'm choosing Hillary . . . She's the lesser of two evils." Later that day, an email with the subject line "BULLYonaire? We deserve better" was sent to me and an undisclosed list of recipients and later reprinted by the website Politico. He wrote, "We live at a time when decisions are influenced by the press and how they slant our words. Yet all we do [is complain]. You can also take action. We can do more. We can use the press by printing our own views; yes, it's expensive, but how much do you value your opinion and how much is it worth? Consider having your voice be heard." Fernandez then put his money where his e-mouth is and self-financed the placement of several full-page newspaper ads on December 14 in Des Moines, Iowa; Las Vegas, Nevada; and Miami, Florida, to counter the ideas and ideals of Donald Trump.

As he wrote in his email, "I do this as an individual. Not a Republican, not a Jeb fan. I do this because I can. I do this because I owe it to our future. I hope that if one of you feels in a similar way that you follow your own path."

All this was long before the primary season was over, Trump secured the nomination, and dozens of Republicans echoed Mike's words. But at the time, Mike's words and actions stuck with me as perfect examples of rising to the challenge of personal accountability and responsibility to be courageous in our actions.

Are you a courageous leader? Are you vulnerable enough to truly be courageous? That's really the question that underlies Part II and what the innovation mentality is all about. Leadership is a constant fight for what you stand for and what you seek to achieve for the betterment of yourself and the healthier whole. Leaders must be vulnerable to have influence and for their organizations to evolve. How would your people rank your vulnerability as it relates to leadership style and approach?

Do you have the self-trust to endure the journey? A belief in yourself that can't be derailed by others who may doubt your intentions? The preparedness to stay the course or course-correct—and not lose faith, focus, and hope along the way?

Leaders must be courageous to be vulnerable and vulnerable to be courageous.

Leadership is about knowing how much you can stretch your thinking and that of your colleagues, challenging your core beliefs during times of uncertainty, and staying true to yourself when the pressure seems insurmountable. It's about having the wisdom to know what your experiences have taught you and trusting yourself to be brave enough to stand by them or create new experiences to confront new opportunities and deal with any resistance and obstacles when you do. It's about fighting to be yourself as you evolve and authenticity is constantly challenged. It's about your mental toughness and ability to get rattled to the point where you may be tempted to pivot away from what makes you unique and different and choose to conform to what everyone else wants you to be or the way things have always been.

These are defining moments that measure your ability to practice courageous leadership. Do you have the endurance to stay the course in support of diversity of thought and what you believe in? To be a courageous leader, you must desire to be relevant. Being relevant means making unpopular decisions, challenging the status quo, and taking the calculated risks that others won't. Where others may be afraid to challenge conventional wisdom, the courageous leader has the awareness and experience to know what people are thinking but not saying, and will not be afraid to speak up for them.

As I said at the start of Part II, this is why most leaders are short-sighted and choose to pick only what is commonly referred to as low-hanging fruit to achieve short-term results. They are afraid to fight, be accountable, and take ownership of anything more. They lack the courage to break free from the fear that is holding them back from reaching their full potential and helping others reach theirs.

Courageous leaders intuitively know that the accumulation of wisdom gained through experience and acquired from others that have been there before you is what will define your eventual success. Wisdom especially comes from the failures and lessons learned along the way. The word failure scares most people, but the courageous ones know that leadership is a journey upon which you must welcome failure, change, and uncertainty to grow, evolve, and become wiser. Anyone who doubts how this resonates today and with generations before need only see the movie *Creed*, which is essentially the seventh chapter in the four-decade-old *Rocky* series and an epic retelling of the first film. In *Creed*, Rocky Balboa mentors Adonis Johnson, son of his old rival and friend, Apollo Creed. Rocky's most salient piece of advice to his protégé is one for every leader: "One step at a time. One punch at a time. One round at a time."

Courageous leaders live by the notion that you must not be afraid to fight, fall down, and get back up with the determination to fight on. How much hardship—rounds of the fight—can you endure as a leader and still keep moving forward? Not until you have put yourself in a position to test your ideas and ideals will you truly know what makes you unique and gives your leadership distinction. Most leaders don't know what they solve for and how their leadership influences the evolution of the organization and people they serve—and this is the primary reason leaders are failing in the 21st century. Courageous leaders do not allow the marketplace to pass them by. They never stop fighting for themselves and those that would benefit from their acts of courage. They take their courage to the next level and are mature enough to be vulnerable and comfortable enough to be uncomfortable. Like one former NBA player told me when he transformed his shot to start hitting three-pointers: "You fight through the strange. Don't worry if that fight feels weird. When I changed the form of the jump shot I had taken for years, it was uncomfortable. It felt awkward, until it became natural."

How will you influence the next generation that represents tomorrow's leaders and the evolution of legacies past? Your courage as a leader is measured not only by the path you create for yourself but also by the wisdom you share to benefit others. Leadership is about teaching others how to be courageous themselves—to fight through the uncertainties in business and life with perspectives they can relate to from the past and that will see them through to reach the end game.

It's not just about what people perceive about your leadership but the realities you create that shape how others grow. What you are capable of achieving does not stop with you but ultimately can advance the unique needs and desires of others.

Not everybody wants to be courageous, and I understand that's why leaders may be skeptical of what I say or maybe they just don't want to work anymore than they have to. But it's a lack of leadership courage that pushes people out of our workplaces and into other companies, and customers to other brands in the marketplace. In this way, being courageous ties into all six characteristics: to see beyond the obvious to avoid complacency; to anticipate the unexpected to ensure that circumstances don't force their hand; to explore endless possibilities in search of previously unseen opportunities; to invest in relationships and maximize the utilization of resources to be more strategic and efficient; to strengthen the organization's intellectual capital and momentum; and to lead to leave a legacy of significance.

But it really comes down to the last two: How will you influence the next generation that represents tomorrow's leaders and the evolution of legacies past? You must have the intellectual curiosity to know the truth of what you are going to lead people through. You have to know in your head and your heart that you are willing to back up what you throw out there. You're willing to take it all the way through to the end. You need an incredible amount of mental toughness knowing you're going to withstand a lot of negativity. You're going to have to be prepared to execute and mindful of what this is going to mean to others. You have to be certain that you're going to create a lasting impact.

Being courageous has been the story of my life. I've not lived my life by what others think I should do. I always felt the responsibility to pull or push people out of complacency. It takes guts to do that. It will take the same guts for you to attack the substitutional thinking that makes organizations complacent and impedes evolution to master the six characteristics of the innovation mentality.

CHAPTER 8

APPLY THE INNOVATION MENTALITY TO MOVE FROM SUBSTITUTION TO EVOLUTION

Time to put all your 21st-century leadership skills to the test. Let's evolve the solve and drive diversity of thought through your organization. Operationalizing that evolution to seize opportunities for growth will require not only you but people across your company to own their leadership identities. You all must work together to drive thinking that is big and bold enough to undo the legacy of decades, perhaps even centuries of substitutional thinking—thinking that may lie at the very foundation of your business.

To get you where you need to be, I've taken ten of the most common substituted words from Chapter 7 and evolved them using the six characteristics of the innovation mentality. There could be dozens of other pairs that might be important to your specific company. I won't pretend these are the only pairs you need to wrestle with. That would violate the very spirit of individual identity my work promotes. I never expect such sameness in readers or leaders I work with, which is why

I customize all my in-person work. But starting with these ten pairs will hone your skills and set you up to address your individualized company culture.

Your leadership legacy should evolve by design, not by accident.

The goal of this chapter is first to show you how to apply the six characteristics to more universal pairs of words like we did in the last chapter with "taking action" and "being courageous" so you have the clarity and understanding to apply them to the needs and problems affecting your business and industry. (A list of what the six characteristics solve for as well as a longer list of substituted and evolved words appears at the end of this book.)

To make this exploration easier to understand and navigate through the six characteristics, the substituted words (before the arrows) and evolved words (after the arrows) are designed to be read as a progression:

- Corporate Values → Shared Beliefs
- Connection → Alignment
- Ideation → Exploration
- Progress → Momentum
- Responsibility → Expectation
- Managing → Relationship
- Engagement → Intimacy
- Control → Influence
- Professional Development → Maximize Potential
- Success → Significance

For each pair, I have selected one lead (primary) and one supporting (secondary) characteristic of the innovation mentality to help you move your company from substitution to evolution. (You might want to review Chapter 1 before continuing.) Does that mean the other characteristics are not needed to evolve each solve? Not necessarily. There are no perfect answers. One size does not fit all. By definition alone you can associate a characteristic with a word, phrase, intention, or goal, but your personal brand and its value proposition and leadership identity influence how you interpret the words and also the characteristics. It's just that some characteristics are going to get you to the solve faster. For example, you may see a word and say "see opportunity" while I say "entrepreneurial spirit" and "passionate pursuits," and you would not be wrong. If you were to start with see opportunity, you would eventually have to use entrepreneurial spirit to evolve the solve. So, don't feel that you have to pick a certain characteristic to support a specific term because if that is the case then I would be in violation of one of my core principles: promoting that my business defines you as an individual. I want the following pages to give you room to recognize your brand value proposition has distinction based on your enduring idea, primary differentiator and experience, and what you serve and solve for in these characteristics. But I will also guide you in how I use a lead and support characteristic to solve for a particular word or need based on my leadership identity.

What I hope you will discover is staying within the ecosystem of the six characteristics (Figure 8.1) allows you to get to the right solve regardless of

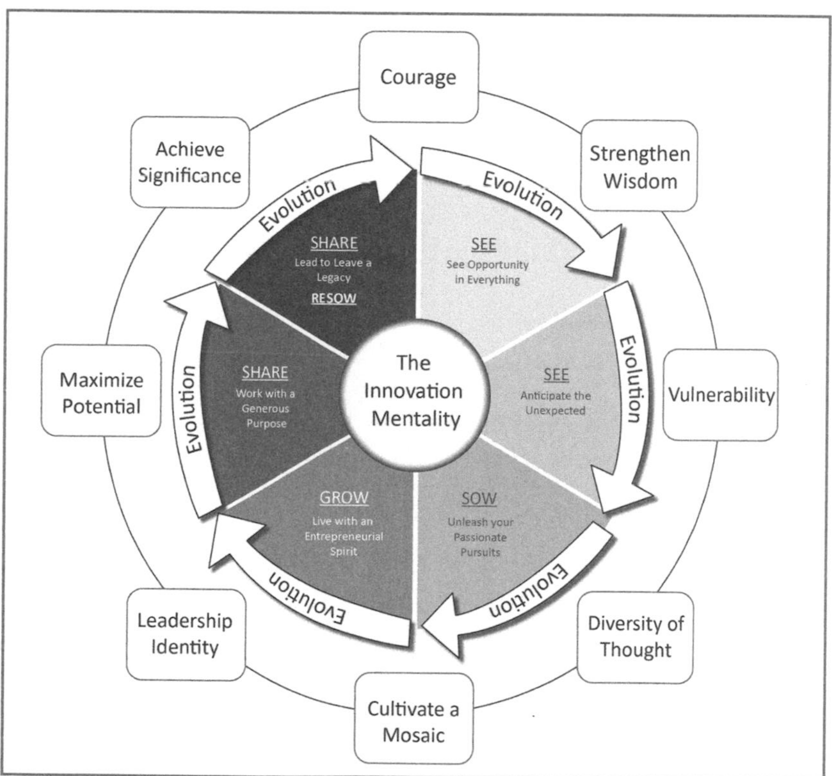

Figure 8.1—The Six Characteristics Ecosystem

the way you got there and that evolution was authentic to your leadership identity. That's why you as a leader might have as a particular sequence for the characteristics that is different to mine. As long as we stay within the ecosystem and everybody's brand is being activated and supported to realize its full potential, we are going to get to the evolution end game. You are going to accomplish and solve for the right things, because the characteristics pull us back to the ecosystem.

Do this for those ten pairs, and you will have the foundation to evolve by design, not change by accident, by understanding how to:

- Best apply the characteristic(s) you will use for other scenarios you face in the workplace and marketplace
- Identify the opportunities evolving each solve presents with great clarity and understanding
- Achieve desired outcomes
- Live your leadership identity

Got it? OK, let's start the final steps in gaining balanced proficiency on your way to mastering the six characteristics of the innovation mentality and begin to influence business outcomes by evolving these solves.

Turn Corporate Values into Shared Beliefs

Substitution Words	Evolution Words
Corporate Values	Shared Beliefs

Lead Characteristic: Work with a Generous Purpose

Supporting Characteristic: See Opportunity in Everything

As I said at the end of Part I, nurturing shared corporate values to support and protect long-term success requires vigilance and constant attention from leadership at all levels. Reading the corporate values and mission statements of countless organizations—which often say things like "we respect individuals" or "our people and our customers are our point of difference" or "we value and strive for diversity and inclusion"—you would think their leadership gets this. But my research shows otherwise. The very individuals these businesses supposedly respect—and whose diversity companies want to value—often don't share belief in those stated corporate values and missions.

This sense of alienation is especially felt among Millennials and those shift populations represented by the CDS. According to my organization's study of Hispanic leadership, only 20 percent of the workplace and corporate values that matter most to Hispanics are represented, authentically applied, and lived in Fortune 500 companies. According to a 2015 Gallup Poll of more than 80,000 U.S. employees, more than two-thirds reported being disengaged or actively disengaged (i.e., not "involved in, enthusiastic about, and committed to their work and workplace") with Millennials being the least engaged demographic group (only a quarter of them report being engaged) and "traditionalist" executives being the most. *Harvard Business Review* estimates the annual cost of this disengagement is at least $450 billion.

And it's not like companies haven't noticed: Disconnect between the values and missions on paper and the reality experienced in the workplace is of utmost concern at the companies I work with. For example, I consulted with a Fortune 500 company that wanted to get back on track with Latino populations outside the U.S. It felt it had "lost mindset" with those populations and needed a change. Looking at its corporate values, you would not have thought this possible: Everything about this company on paper screamed, "Evolved!" Reading through its mission statement and supporting materials, I thought this company's leaders had gotten a copy of my manuscript and drawn on the six characteristics the way they used the word "innovative," talked about winning mindset, and expressed willingness to engage and embrace failure and learning in its leadership. It is unbelievable how organizations are thinking this way . . . at least on paper. But what happens beyond the words of your corporate values? What would happen if your people were empowered to challenge them and encouraged to influence them?

This is why corporate values are usually about substitution. Simply substituting more inclusive and evolved words every few years and never challenging anyone to do the evolved thinking needed to live those values does not lead to evolution. It leads to more substituting with more evolved window dressing. In fact, despite sounding evolved, the values of that company I just mentioned were not new. They were written well over a decade ago for a workplace and marketplace that has experienced much change and evolution just in terms of technology and global competition as well as people. No wonder the workplace was disengaged and the marketplace had passed the company by. Few at the company shared in the beliefs that defined those values, including its leadership! The uncourageous, unevolved traditionalist executives doing what they are told, leading by old templates, and thus suffering from leadership identity crises may be writing the corporate values and mission statements, but they are still hugely disengaged from them. According to Gallup, those traditionalist executives may be the most engaged demographic group, but only 42 percent report being engaged in the workplace.

This is not *a* problem. It is a *huge* problem.

When was the last time your corporate values were challenged? How and how often are they revised? What is the revision process? Have you discussed, listened to, and thought about what your corporate values mean to individuals in the workplace and marketplace, and how they will live them? Probably not. So many companies struggle to live their values internally and externally despite all the wonderful words used to create them. Those corporate values are just words without shared meaning.

Corporate values are about attitude; shared beliefs are about mindset. It is the difference between doing (sowing) and thinking. Mindset is about refusing to be bound by legacies and seeing the opportunity to make the brand stronger. Mindset is about sharing to gain buy-in across departments and colleagues that alter the mentality of how we are engaged and motivated to perform and, in turn, get our customers to buy. That's why this Fortune 500 company I just described was right about "losing mindset with Latino populations." It just didn't see that the lost mindset could be traced back to lost opportunity in its workplace. Its seemingly enlightened corporate values were just an attitude captured on paper, not integrated with a generous purpose into shared beliefs in the work its people were doing. It had failed to achieve this mindset and lost sight of its amazing values for the reasons stated in Chapter 7: Senior leadership fought the evolution out of fear it would expose their insecurities about how little they understood what needed to be done and their inability to lead through change.

To succeed fully and for the long term, your organization must do the thinking and have the mindset to *see opportunity* in evolving its *corporate values* and *working with a generous purpose* to turn them into *shared beliefs*.

To bring these values to life and evolve them into shared beliefs, you must get past the fear, as well as hierarchy, ego, envy, and politicking, to see the opportunity that the values represent for the business and the situation at hand. That's how an organization truly understands where the gaps exist in each stated corporate value and takes the initial steps to provide greater clarity and understanding for every individual. Only then will individuals truly see themselves in the values and thus see opportunities previously unseen. Only then can they stop sowing and start seeing first!

> *Value diversity of thought by finding the like-mindedness in people* within *their differences.*

If you lead by old templates and force people to work by them, they will see only what you tell them to without any circular vision. And if you think that isn't possible, you need to see the experiment (www.theinvisiblegorilla.com/gorilla_experiment.html) Dr. Christopher Chabris and Dr. Daniel Simons did on selective attention that inspired their book, *The Invisible Gorilla*. "Imagine you are asked to watch a short video in which six people—three in white shirts and three in black shirts—pass basketballs around," the authors say. "While you watch, you must keep a silent count of the number of passes made by the people in white shirts. At some point, a gorilla strolls into the middle of the action, faces the camera and thumps its chest, and then leaves, spending nine seconds on screen. Would you see the gorilla? Almost everyone answers 'Yes, of course, I would.' How could something so obvious go completely unnoticed? But when we did this experiment at Harvard University . . . we found that half the people who watched the video and counted the passes missed the gorilla. It was as though the gorilla was invisible."

Don't make people invisible by letting them see only what the company tells them to. To have people evolve, see opportunity, and truly take ownership of these values, you must break free of "gorilla psychology." You must work with a generous purpose and promote the spirit of giving and sharing and compel individuals to see what they are missing. That means having the best interests of your people at heart. Move away from making people see the values that define the organization as inherently valuable and automatically shared. This is circular reasoning (not to be confused with circular vision), and your thinking can't evolve if it simply goes round and round.

Cultures fail when people do not evolve together.

Instead re-educate yourself by valuing your people as individuals as often as possible. Establish trust and transparency by re-educating the team about the role that the values play and where they are created. Use your generous purpose to create pathways for others to express their points of view so that in the end their shared beliefs bring the fires of empowerment to life in an authentic way. Shared beliefs belong to everyone, and a truly inclusive process is the best way to have an authentically inclusive outcome from bottom to top—from the people in the stores and the cubicles on the ground floor to the corner offices at the top. Let everyone shape those values to share in their beliefs.

No group wants this more than Millennials—the largest generation in human history and the next generation of leaders in the workplace. But you must do it authentically. Nationwide, across race, gender, and ethnicity, Millennials are all about authenticity. They want things that feel and are real and align with what they believe. They want to live their goals and values through their work so you must have the goals and values of your company aligned with theirs. Traditional corporate values don't do this. They are one-way streets. Shared beliefs are two-way streets that place a premium on commitment, not just compliance.

This need for alignment is where the next pair comes in.

Create Alignment

Substitution Word	Evolution Word
Connection	Alignment

Lead Characteristic: Live with an Entrepreneurial Spirit
Supporting Characteristic: Lead to Leave a Legacy

A Fortune 500 company, one of the largest manufacturers of its kind in the world, hired me to enhance the overall engagement of its increasingly diverse workforce. The goal was clear: Maximize workplace performance to drive measurable business and marketplace growth. This company was specifically interested in developing the leadership team of Millennials and shift populations it had and recruiting new talent from those groups who would see the company as a place for career advancement and business development. It wanted to evolve its workplace from a "melting pot" to a "mosaic"—to break down misconceived stereotypes and the silos that devalue individuality and slow productivity. This evolution would embrace individuality in an effort to build a higher-performance work environment united around shared beliefs. By continually searching for innovative ways to develop and leverage each employee's brand value proposition and individual strengths, it would effectively strengthen its overall competitive advantage and market position.

That's quite a mission—a courageous one, too—and this Fortune 500 company seemed poised to accept it. They wanted a strategy to build leadership for their employees and to disseminate it throughout the organization's culture, brand, and external partnerships. In a word: alignment.

Companies use the word alignment without knowing what it really means or how it differs from connection and why connection is a substitution word. Connection puts people together, like in a room, bound by a cause or employment. But it doesn't necessarily guarantee or create meaningful synergy. Alignment carries greater weight because it implies reciprocity. If you're able to align the goals of individuals and the company, you encourage employees to look beyond job descriptions. You get them thinking as individuals about what your company's shared beliefs mean. Yet most companies don't see the importance or difference. I surveyed more than 10,000 leaders at Fortune 500 companies and asked what was most important to them as leaders to effectively serve their employees and customers; 37 percent said alignment and 63 percent said connection.

Your organization must have the courage and wisdom to *align* its people and let them *live with an entrepreneurial spirit* to embrace the differences this reciprocity requires and then *lead to leave a legacy* to create a sustainable ecosystem based on that reciprocity.

The Fortune 500 company I just mentioned believed that embracing differences was their greatest asset. As such, they will seek to build organizational ecosystems based on the six characteristics that will support collaboration across departments and functional areas. Confident in the belief that success comes to those who are surrounded by people who want their success to continue, this company genuinely wanted its employees be courageous enough to reach their full potential—to live with an entrepreneurial spirit to make things better. This is why many companies are trying to have as many of its employees as possible be more entrepreneurial and refine their performance by staying true to their values.

Sounds great, right? But creating this kind of ecosystem requires that we accept a degree of difference that is almost unprecedented in traditional workplaces. It requires employees to actively share their ideas and ideals. It requires the creation of a workplace culture that embraces difference in those employees as part of encouraging an entrepreneurial mindset in their work in order to grow. Which is not something I see often in my work. Consider what happens at my workshops and consultations when I ask groups of leaders to rank their senior leadership by how they live their organization's corporate values every day in the order that they personally feel most aligned with them. Of course, the rankings should be all over the place not only because no one lives each value every day, but also because different people value different things. But the rankings aren't all over the place. They are living those values the same way, meaning the company is defining them as individuals and they are just doing what they are told and trying to get through the day. As one manager told me after my presentation, "I have the attitude that they are paying me to get trained so that's what I'm going to do."

Most of them come by this belief honestly. We all do. Our entire school system hasn't evolved much in a century and is extremely resistant to change. Sure there are new technologies, but do they change the paradigm of learning to focus on the individual or just substitute more standardization through a laptop or iPad? There is little sensitivity to student differences and what they may be interested in or how varied their backgrounds may be. It is about a "Common Core." That's education defining the individual, which evolves to the business defining the individual and which is at odds with everything we have discussed so far. No wonder, according to the World Economic Forum report "New Vision for Education: Fostering Social and Emotional Learning through Technology," "The gap between the skills people learn and the skills people need is becoming more obvious, as traditional learning falls short of equipping students with the knowledge they need to thrive."

How can a company evolve beyond this standardization we all grew up with, so it has people who align with those values differently? How do you create that ecosystem? What is a company's responsibility? Tony Hsieh at Zappos got rid of corporate hierarchy and moved to a system of self-management. HCL Technologies, a rapidly growing multibillion-dollar Indian global IT services company, created a program called LeadGen, in which every employee can record and bring forward ideas on how to improve what the company does, which has led to more than $500 million in new ideas. I'm not asking for anything quite as radical when I ask those questions to executives at the companies I work with. But I still mostly get silence, because too few are willing to publicly embrace the diversity of thought needed to truly own what other people think, feel, and desire differently, and that difference can be a powerful driver for growth. The company must accept that each person may live this entrepreneurial spirit differently to help define the business. Only then will each employee be given the resources and tools to thrive and be challenged to improve outcomes.

Most employees feel their individual goals are not respected—let alone feel safe to express them—and thus their goals do not authentically align with the company's.

We don't need to embrace our similarities; we need to align the differences around shared values and beliefs. During this process, leaders must embrace diversity of thought to ensure that their thinking is in alignment with each individual so they can optimally deploy it through their leadership identity. That's how we build on the trust we established by having those shared beliefs in the first place.

Our approaches may be different, but our intentions can be aligned—that's the true value of shared beliefs. They help evolve everyone's personal brand value propositions to their leadership identities and move together toward a common company goal.

Remember what we covered in Chapter 2: The evolution of your personal brand and brand value proposition (you are what your personal brand solves for) ultimately defines your leadership identity (who you influence and how you influence business evolution). Your brand value proposition is what you are accountable to solve for. When you define that value proposition, you become a subject matter expert, the go-to knowledge resource, and growth strategies guide and can provide the best implementation recommendations. Your wisdom shapes your thinking. You go beyond evolving your personal brand value proposition—you evolve to reclaim your leadership identity. That's what happens when you have alignment, not just connection.

To take the first steps, answer the following questions about what it takes for each employee to live with an entrepreneurial spirit:

- What are the resource requirements to own these values? Do we have them?
- Have we built the right relationships?
- Are we making the right investments in people to be able to align and live their values and ours?

Of course, the CDS makes accepting difference and alignment more difficult but also more powerful when you create a culture in which all employees can step up as who they are. Before authentically seeking this alignment, you were asking shift populations to buy into values that they did not align with—asking them to own something they don't comprehend because they don't understand their own identities in the workplace. How do you bridge that gap beyond just embracing the evolution to shared beliefs and align what these shift populations need? You need to understand what they feel about the issues being discussed so you can begin to solve for them.

This is where leading to leave a legacy comes in. Everyone has a team first/collaboration/reciprocity mentality, operates with respect before recognition, and protects what others stand for. As we discussed in Chapter 2, the workplace and marketplace are demanding leaders who are connected with individuality and value diverse thinking, who understand that people domestically and globally think differently and want to be accepted and respected for who they are: diverse thinkers who are courageous enough to invest in closing the growing business opportunity gaps between themselves and the company and people who don't look, sound, act, or live like them or lead in support of a healthier, collective whole. That's how leaders and businesses will ultimately make the decision to deliver on their cultural promise to support workplace cultures and the marketplace—their entire six characteristics ecosystem—in everything they do and how they act.

Don't get me wrong, once companies show a willingness to do this with their traditional leadership and corporate values, employees must show a willingness to align what they are doing as well. As we discussed in Chapter 2, too many diverse leaders and employees are complicit in creating tension in the workplace, albeit unknowingly, through their words and actions. Instead of trying to explain how their heritage and cultural values provide them distinction, which gives them a competitive advantage at work, they must identify and measure what their diverse thinking has done to affect and add real value to the bottom line. In other words, as they seek opportunities to contribute and discover their talent, these diverse leaders and employees must shift their approach and evolve in alignment with the company.

> Everyone—*not just nondiverse leaders—must be held accountable to evolve and align their goals with their leaders' and company's goals.*

Do your employees believe that their jobs are not just jobs but opportunities to shape their legacies? Do your customers, clients, and partners believe that you do? Being able to answer this question with a resounding, "Yes!" is to evolve from connection to alignment in your organization's workplace by leading to leave a legacy. Building strong ecosystems where collaboration and diversity of thought are embraced as opportunities is essential to building strong legacies.

Remember, the marketplace is telling us that it is becoming less about the business defining the individual customer and much more about the individual customer defining the business.

As such, it is important to create an environment of inclusivity that promotes greater awareness, clarity, and understanding people's authentic identities to connect to the individuals in the marketplace. When you also include the role that your heritage plays, you can fully realize the tangible benefits that diversity of thought can bring to influence the evolution of the business for the long term.

This need for alignment through living with an entrepreneurial spirit and leading to leave a legacy in the workplace and marketplace is exactly what keeps Robert W. Stone, president and CEO of City of Hope, up at night. A cancer and diabetes research and treatment institution with a 212-bed hospital and outpatient services in 15 locations in California, City of Hope is by all measures successful. Founded in 1913, it is still growing with more than $1.8 billion dollars in revenue and more than 4,000 employees. But as we learned in Chapter 4, the changing nature of health care has tested City of Hope to evolve and align the needs of its rapidly changing marketplace (shift populations make up 66 percent of their catchment area) and a workplace that has been treating patients the same way for years. As a result, Stone has had to evolve his thinking, not just act.

"I looked at the passage of the Affordable Care Act, the potential of narrowing networks, and the move to population health," Stone told me, "and saw potential challenges to our ability to provide the care in the future in the manner that we had previously. We had a fundamental question of 'Where does City of Hope fit in that future?' I now see it as an opportunity to make a contribution on a far larger scale than we have contemplated in the past. Our hospital is 103 years old, and our motto has always been that there is no profit in curing the body if in the process we destroy the soul. Think about how that motto applies to the new health environment. I firmly believe City of Hope has an obligation to fill a gap in healthcare, or as a society, we run the risk of health care becoming commoditized and purely a low-price question with people having to wait months and months to see a doctor. City of Hope has an obligation to serve our community. Talent, culture, and planning drive that conversation."

So what about that keeps Stone up at night more than anything else? Aligning new and existing leadership around these evolved shared values. "Leadership demands are just different," he says. "We spend a lot of time identifying leaders who can lead in the future we are envisioning, recruiting them, retaining them, onboarding them, and supporting them. We talk constantly about community and sponsorship of our leaders, and it takes a lot of our time so they can ask and answer the questions that support the vision of our organization: How do we best serve humanity? What am I supposed to deliver as a leader? What are my strategic contributions? We also spend a lot of time focused on our culture with our leaders, navigating it, shaping it, and preserving what is good about it. How are we special and unique? How do we preserve that as the organization undergoes dramatic change?"

Stone's biggest concern when it comes to that culture is a mistake any company wants to avoid: growing to make the impact it wants but losing the specialness that differentiated the company. When you move quickly, leaders run the risk that for all the positive evolution, the culture changes in ways that are not productive and intentional. In fact, similar concerns were my impetus for this book. The good news is Stone is asking all the right questions. Building a culture of sustainability and reciprocity is essential to leading to leave a legacy. How is that possible in an age when, as one educator told me, business degrees have a relevancy shelf life of about a year before what they were taught no longer applies in the marketplace? This is where the next group of substituted and evolved words comes in.

Encourage Exploration

Substitution Word	Evolution Word
Ideation	Exploration

Lead Characteristic: See Opportunity in Everything

Supporting Characteristic: Unleash Your Passionate Pursuits

A few years after his Magic Johnson Theatres became a thriving chain, Magic turned his attention to another retail opportunity for underserved urban communities: Starbucks. In his presentation at my summit, "Preparing U.S. Leadership for the Seismic Cultural Demographic Shift," Magic told the audience that despite his success with Sony, he got nothing but resistance from Starbucks as he made his "urban coffee opportunities" pitch. Minority urban customers, they said, didn't drink coffee, and those that did would never pay $3 for a cup of coffee. But Magic knew his customers and refused to give in to the accepted knowledge. Being Magic, Johnson was able to make his case all the way to the top. And Starbucks's CEO Howard Schultz told him . . . "No."

It wasn't just that Schultz didn't see opportunity for growth in exploring urban America. (This was back in 1998 when Starbucks had 1,886 stores; today it has almost ten times as many worldwide.) And Magic or not, Schultz said Starbucks did not (and still does not) franchise. Magic told Schultz he wasn't interested in a single franchise; he wanted a partnership to set up stores in urban centers nationwide to better serve their shift populations. Determined to show Schultz what he was missing and why, Magic invited him to come to the Magic Johnson Theatre in the Crenshaw neighborhood of South Los Angeles. Magic explained, "You can't 'do' urban America from an office in the sky or suburbs."

Here's what Magic told us happened next: "Howard came in and saw all the people in the theater and in line for hot dogs and sodas. Whitney Houston's first movie was out, and there were thousands of African-American and Latino women in the lobby and concession stands greeting one another and talking. The concession stand was ringing. Howard is just amazed. Then we walk inside the theater. The movie had just started and Whitney's character is having a problem with her man, and every woman in the theater starts talking to the screen: 'Girl, why you still with him?' 'You should dump him!' 'If I was you, I wouldn't take that!' Twenty minutes into the movie, Howard grabs me, takes me outside, and says, 'Magic, I've never had a movie-going experience quite like this. You got the deal.'"

That deal was for 125 stores, and Schultz told Magic that Starbucks would change anything necessary for them to be successful. But Magic sensed his partner was still believing what he read, not what he saw, and thus not seeing the full opportunity. An article in the *Los Angeles Times* about their deal repeated the refrain that minorities would not pay $3 for a cup of coffee. But Magic told Schultz they were wrong. Yes, tailoring offerings for the communities would be essential for the stores' success, but he didn't want Starbucks to change what defined its brand or coffee. That was not the point, not good business, and could even be interpreted as condescending.

"I knew we'd pay $3 for a cup of coffee," Magic said he told Schultz. "We just don't know what the hell scones are. So we do have to tweak the desserts. Take the scones out and put in sweet potato pie, pound cake—things that resonate with the urban consumer. Then we took out the music they played in suburban stores and put in Lionel Ritchie and Earth Wind & Fire—music urban consumers knew so they would feel welcome, come back, and be loyal."

Was he right? Absolutely. In the decade that followed, few of those Starbucks closed because of poor sales. In fact, 105 of the stores overall were still in business in 2010 when, as part of a broader redistribution of his business interests, Magic sold his 50 percent interest back to the company for $27 million. That's a lot of $3 cups of coffee. All because Starbucks was willing to evolve from ideation to exploration and see opportunities in what Magic Johnson offered them.

Leaders need to see that opportunities are everywhere, every day, and they need to make the most of those that cross their paths: Forward-thinking and visionary leaders move from *ideation* to *exploration* by having the courage to *unleash their passionate pursuits* and *seeing opportunity in everything* to drive diversity of thought for their companies and propel initiative and innovation.

Even in 1998, Starbucks was known as a great place to work, one of the most progressive companies when it came to retail ideas, employee benefits, and community sponsorship. But Magic saw a company that in spite of its rapid expansion had been doing things the same way for too long. Moving quickly, Starbucks got stuck in ideation instead of evolving to exploration. Ideation is about the here and now; exploration is what lies ahead. Ideation leads to the same action and results, when companies and leaders don't open their minds enough to see with broadened observation. It's more like a fresh coat of paint on the same wall you've been looking at for years, even decades: You might fix a crack now and then before painting, but basically you are substituting one color for another. There's nothing wrong with that on a basic level, but what's beyond those walls?

Ideation is about the present; exploration is about the future.

Exploration grows out of ideation but forces us to be mindful and courageous enough to see and operationalize the new opportunities beyond the walls. This is why companies bring people like Magic or even me in—to compel them to see all the opportunities they can create and be more courageous about exploring them. They just don't hear the right words on the inside, because no one is saying them out loud, which is why external partnerships have the power to shake us from getting stuck in ideation and too complacent about sowing and force us to think about how to operationalize. Someone might say that "ideation" is about the future. But it's not until you begin to explore the opportunities within the outcomes of an ideation session that you begin to operationalize and truly think about the capability requirements to put into action.

Other times when people work with us they say, "You know I thought about that, but I just didn't know how to do it." That's the point; you don't need to explore what you think you already know. Starbucks needed Magic's external partnership and perspective to get out of ideation, see new ways of doing things, and answer "yes!" to a fundamental question about exploring opportunities. Do your external partners understand your business well enough to help you see and explore previously unseen opportunities?

Magic understood Starbucks' business, but he also needed to deliver the customers he promised and make sure they explored the opportunities Starbucks offered—in the workplace and marketplace. He had a larger goal for the success of their "urban coffee opportunities" partnership: Create economic opportunity and a stronger sense of community in the neighborhoods they served. Sustainable success goes well beyond the availability of sweet potato pie and satisfying pent-up demand for Frappuccino. That work required Magic and his company to develop external partnerships as well. He may have understood and connected with the customers in urban areas, but Starbucks didn't touch them every day. So, just like Magic did with Sony, he engaged the community and its trusted leaders through churches, neighborhood councils, and community groups to explain why Starbucks was coming and the opportunities it provided. In other words, it wasn't "magic." He simply answered another fundamental question about seeing opportunities and exploring them: Are your customers empowered enough to contribute and be heard?

Of course, for those customers to be heard in the marketplace, Magic knew his team needed to be ready and empowered to be heard to explore as well. They were, and so are yours if you've worked to achieve the evolutionary steps of alignment and shared beliefs we just completed. The importance of community outreach and the relationships that result cannot be underestimated. For example, medical institutions can't assume that diverse patient populations want to be healthier; they must start educating them to get healthier so they are able to achieve their best and contribute most effectively at their jobs, for their families, and in society at large. To form these relationships, what happens outside the hospital or doctor's office walls are increasingly important. This means reaching out into communities, connecting with them, and breaking down barriers, whether they are ones of awareness or access, communication or cultural know-how. Embrace differences in people to drive new ways of thinking that propel creativity, innovation, and initiative.

What are new ways to design community benefit and social responsibility outreach strategies? What roles should community influencers, nonprofit advocacy groups, and government leaders play?

Without at least considering these questions, leaders and employees don't just paint walls of ideation instead of exploration; they build them. On the one hand, companies get complacent about success. On the other hand, they hide behind real policies (Starbucks doesn't franchise) and imagined obstacles (minorities won't pay $3 for a cup of coffee) to dismiss opportunities.

I believe people want to be lifted. They want to be extended. They want their minds to be stretched. But you have to communicate, lead, and guide them to evolve beyond expectations. The simplest way to build confidence is to develop clear measures.

How will you, your people, and the people you report to know whether new explorations have proved beneficial? What outcomes do you seek? What metrics will let you know whether you are moving toward them? Clearly lay out the needs and benefits of pursuing any exploration and indeed any movement from substitution to evolution:

- Understand how much time it will take.
- Map out potential outcomes.
- Help everyone in the organization see how they are connected to the opportunity, what they will experience, and how it will benefit them.
- Define how success will be measured for these grassroots activities that impact business strategies, using Key Performance Indicators (or KPI, as discussed in Chapter 6—not everything is as easy to measure as the number of $3 cups of coffee sold).

But then, when you are hitting all your metrics and your KPIs that you need to, turn around and say, "What could we be doing to make it even better? How do we blow things up?" Now your business isn't just exploring opportunities, it is conquering them. This is when you unleash your passionate pursuits and become a potent pioneer, breaking down barriers, and pursuing opportunities all the way to the end, which doesn't mean more sowing but growing and sharing.

Wait! Didn't I say that unleashing your passionate pursuits is about sowing? Yes! But just because you are sowing doesn't mean you are living the innovation mentality and using diversity of thought. Remember the role sowing plays in the ecosystem of the six characteristics: Sowing is the linchpin between seeing opportunities and then growing and sharing them—and then resowing them. That's what Magic did after Sony; that's what Starbucks did after Magic. That's why the "urban coffee opportunities" partnership between Magic and Starbucks strove to create economic growth and a stronger sense of community in the neighborhoods they served. In fact, when the partnership was dissolved, the millions earned by both sides was not the sole measurement of success. Schultz made special note of how the store in New York City's Harlem played a part in the neighborhood's redevelopment, and nationwide how "the partnership helped create jobs with health benefits, build community gathering places where they're most needed, and empower change makers to innovate and take action in their communities." This is why Magic, with no financial interest in the company, still assists Starbucks with its community development projects in urban areas.

As a result, the partnership didn't just make progress; it generated momentum.

Generate Momentum

Substitution Word	Evolution Word
Progress	Momentum

Lead Characteristic: Anticipate the Unexpected

Supporting Characteristic: Unleash Your Passionate Pursuits

My father used to tell me, "Progress is good, but if the process of creating progress doesn't convert into momentum, then you don't have the right amount of strategic focus to help it become something more evolutionary!" Progress gets stuck in substitution if all you're doing is sowing. It becomes momentous when you start growing because quite simply *you cannot build momentum without growing.* You might think you are growing by one measure—sowing—but you do *not* have sustainable momentum.

You cannot build and sustain momentum in an organization without being able to see the next opportunities of greatest potential, sow them, grow them, share them, and then resow them into new opportunities. That can never happen successfully without anticipating the unexpected. You must identify competitive threats that could come from companies in and *beyond* your marketplace—and understand how all this connects to the people who work for you as well as your customers.

To move beyond just making *progress* and evolve to *generate momentum*, people across the company must *anticipate the unexpected* by practicing circular vision and embracing risk as the new normal. This requires that leadership not only take actions for the betterment of the workplace and marketplace but also *unleash the passionate pursuits* of those people so they want to embrace that risk with you.

Robert W. Stone has taken steps to anticipate the needs of the patient population and how will they change for *years* in the future through programs like its T.E.A.C.H. (Train, Educate, and Accelerate Careers in Healthcare) partnership and *El Concilio* (discussed in Chapter 5). That's the kind of circular vision you need to operationalize momentum. Remember, circular vision provides you with a healthy skepticism and prevents you from getting too comfortable even in times of great success, because someone else is always looking to get the advantage over you. This is not being negative; it is a way of being cautious and strategic and to avoid being blindsided. But to truly anticipate the unexpected and evolve from making progress to generating momentum, you need to ask two important questions: *Do our people do the same things? How can we make sure they do?*

If you fail to ask these questions consistently and constantly, the competition will seize the opportunities while your company focuses only on what is in front of you. I learned this firsthand in 1997 when, after serving as a corporate officer in the food and beverage industry, I decided to start my own company with business partners in San Miguel de Allende in Guanajuato, Mexico. Back then, the U.S. market didn't understand or value the strengths and capabilities of food manufacturers from Mexico. We prepared our partners in San Miguel to commit to (not just comply with) U.S. manufacturing standards and found ourselves selling millions of dollars worth of products to Costco Wholesale and more than 6,000 national retail grocery stores throughout the country. We began to cross-pollinate insights and best practices between the U.S. and Mexico and successfully started a licensing operation that not only expanded the importing of goods into America, but also exported American brands to Mexico.

It was this experience that made me realize that the CDS first took place outside the U.S., creating new forms of competition among suppliers. Today that shift is evolving within the U.S. to create new forms of competition among brands and organizations for top talent and consumers. After years of processing the wisdom shared by my father, I realized what I then called the immigrant perspective started by seeing the opportunities through a new mentality for success that extend outside our borders.

Today, direct foreign investments from privately held companies are changing the template and blindsiding U.S. companies that have grown complacent (as Wall Street slows them down). Mexican-brand Bimbo has acquired several U.S. brands and now has headquarters in the U.S. Fabuloso Cleaning Products, another Mexican brand, outperforms Colgate's Pine-Sol in Hispanic markets because it more authentically connects with Hispanic lifestyles through the packing, scent, colors, etc. Peru is using technology as a competitive advantage: Drip-irrigation to turn deserts into farms and food exports to the U.S. Then there is Gruma, the global leader of corn and flour tortilla production worldwide. It has built 17 plants in the U.S. and is bringing its proprietary technologies with it as well as hiring unemployed American Hispanics. I'm not saying this to be alarmist. I'm saying this because it's not just the Mike Fernandezes and Magic Johnsons who are minding the gaps in the CDS from within our borders. There are global brands that have embraced the innovation mentality and have the diversity of thought to compete for the opportunities too. As the senior executive from what I consider the most forward-thinking grocery retailer in the U.S. told me, "Doing business with people in Latin America requires you to be nimble, understanding, and patient. But their entrepreneurial spirit and willingness to learn and adapt far exceeds that of their U.S. competitors. They bring far better intelligence about the Hispanic consumer, which reflects in our sales. We invest in companies throughout the world and encourage direct foreign investment in Texas as it makes our supply chain much more efficient. We can't always wait for domestic supplies to act."

This requires more than just evolved alignment in the goals of your company, yourself, and your people; it requires *belief in* yourself and your leadership identity, your people, and your partners and customers to see the opportunities and keep moving ahead by anticipating the unexpected (for better or worse). It requires continuous growth and development and a willingness to invest in people. In other words, help your people work together to anticipate the unexpected.

Unleashing your passionate pursuits is how you resow success again after seeing, sowing, growing, and sharing. To pursue your passions in times of prosperity and explore possibilities for the next big thing, you need don't just need to go with your gut—you need guts. You need to unleash your passionate pursuits to shake people out of their complacency and pursue their own passions. Let's stop sowing the seeds in front of us. Instead, let's use the power of our passionate pursuits to compel those around us to start growing them with an entrepreneurial spirit, working with a generous purpose, and leading to leave a legacy. Then let's start it all over again by seeing opportunities in everything! That's when we break free from conformity and stop playing it safe—when leaders are willing to put themselves at risk and stay uncomfortable to keep the momentum going and then drive that evolutionary thinking through the workplace and into the marketplace. Being comfortable and conformity go hand in hand and lead to substitution not evolution.

Sowing without passionate pursuits leads to immediate, short-term results, not better exploration or momentum.

Think back to when we first discussed the characteristic of unleashing your passionate pursuits and how my father urged me to keep going. He wanted me to own what I did and maximize my influence through my passionate pursuits. He wanted me to be a "natural explorer" for the betterment of a healthier whole. So, are you taking ownership? Are you using your ability to be a "natural explorer" to unleash your passionate pursuits and evolve from ideation and progress to exploration and momentum. My father's point was if you keep going, you not only grow and share the opportunities in front of you but you generate the momentum needed to see unseen and new opportunities more clearly, explore them, and seize them—not just for yourself but for others.

Then make sure you fuel the passion of the people who you work for and with you. They must own what they do and strive to explore endless possibilities. Your people need to know that if they see something with potential for growth, they can say something despite any real or imagined obstacles and break free from ideation and progress.

Remember, what shift populations want most is to have a safe space to speak up free from judgment. If your people have the courage to see something that can create more momentum, then that's another huge step in helping them and you act as individual agents of change and evolve from the silos and traditional workplace limitations. You have now lifted your people up and pulled them in new directions and toward opportunities that maybe they never saw. This begins their journey of being able to influence the evolution of the business they serve.

Of course, you could get met with suspicion because people want to know what it means to them, how much more they are going to have to do, and how much money or resources it will take from the company and partners. Sometimes even when you lay out the needs and expectations clearly they will still resist. But remember what I said about skeptics' potential to be your greatest opportunities. Keep pushing to give them the clarity to commit to evolution, and they will commit.

Those that do will also understand that they don't just have a *responsibility to sow*. They should have an *expectation to grow and share.*

Exceed Expectations

Substitution Word	Evolution Word
Responsibility	Expectation

Lead Characteristic: Anticipate the Unexpected

Supporting Characteristic: Lead to Leave a Legacy

Recall what my Sunkist mentor helped me understand: *constructing, deconstructing, and reconstructing cultures and delivering solutions and results are easier to see from the outside in.* Leaders and employees at the store level are trained that the most important person in their ecosystem is the customer or client, and they strive to have a team that is reflective of the guests who walk into their stores. But even when they aren't reflective of that guest, they can evolve to see their job as more than just a *responsibility* to do what needs to be done and instead have the *expectation* to get their hands dirty and help.

Consider how a few Target team members went above and beyond to help one customer in its stores. The story serves as a lesson on expectation to leadership and employees at any level of any business.

Yasir Moore, a 15-year-old boy from Raleigh, North Carolina, had landed an interview at a Chick-fil-A for his first job. His mom told him to wear a tie, but he didn't know how to tie one. So he went to Target to find a clip-on and couldn't find one. That's when a team member on the floor, Cathy Scott, spotted him. She walked over and asked Yasir if he needed help. Yasir said he needed a clip-on tie, and Cathy explained they didn't have any. At that point, Cathy's basic responsibility to the guest ended. She could have just said, "I'm sorry, can I be of any other assistance?" and walked away if Yasir said, "No." But Cathy had an expectation to do more. She said, "We don't have any clip-on ties, but what do you need a tie for?" Yasir told her about his first job interview and that neither he nor his mom knew how to tie a tie. Enter Dennis Roberts, another floor team member. Dennis, the father of four grown sons, had plenty of experience teaching teens to tie ties. He proceeded to show Yasir how to do it and stayed with him until he could do it on his own.

The story does not end there. As Yasir worked on his knot, Cathy and Dennis gave him interview advice: Talk slowly, sit up, have a firm handshake. Dennis told him, "It's time for you to raise the roof, tell these people exactly who you are, what you are made of, and that you are the right person for the job." Yasir listened and nailed the interview. He was called back a second time and got the job.

Maybe you've heard this story. You may have. I learned all this not through Target, but from CNN and ABC News. ABC even made Dennis, Cathy, and Yasir their "People of the Week." But it wasn't because Target pitched them. There were no cameras rolling in the store that day. In fact, the only reason anyone learned about this was a Target customer, Audrey Marsh, who saw Yasir, Dennis, and Cathy from across the store, thought it was a terrific moment, and snapped a candid picture on her phone. She never spoke to any of them. Later, she posted it to her Facebook page and tagged Target, which picked it up. It had more than 60,000 likes by that evening and the story went viral from there.

When asked why she took and posted the picture, Marsh told ABC, "You certainly don't expect that to happen. Certainly not in a big-box store. Certainly not down aisle 11."

Do *you* expect that? You don't expect that if you just feel *responsibility* to your job description and what you are told to do. You do expect that if you have an *expectation* of accountability to do more—to do what your gut tells you and act. That's how you *anticipate the unexpected* and *lead to leave a legacy* to move from responsibility to expectation.

> *Responsibility is substitution, but expectation is evolution.*

Expectation is about getting your hands dirty and taking a greater level of ownership. This just does not happen enough in our workplaces when we are detached from the day-to-day of the marketplace.

As Caroline Wanga, vice president corporate social responsibility at Target Corp., explained to me when we discussed the story of Yasir, Dennis, and Cathy, "Headquarters works nothing like the stores. We don't have the day-to-day interaction that impacts the transaction or changes somebody's life. But that's the environment the people at the store level live every single day. It didn't matter that the workers were white and the customer was black. And I'm willing to bet that there wasn't some big conversation about it before they approached about how do we get along? It started with, 'This kid needs help with a tie.' At headquarters we would overanalyze that to death: 'Well, what if he doesn't want help with this tie?' or 'What if it is offensive?' or 'Will the kid be threatened because the worker is a white male?' But at store level they are at the center of the Cultural Demographic Shift and have an expectation to be accountable to much more. They do not get to opt out."

Exactly! So why are these stories newsworthy? Because most of us are stuck in responsibility and are touched by these human interest stories. I just wish that more leaders took interest in the humans in our workplaces and marketplaces and helped everyone be accountable to the expectation of doing more in operationalizing the power of the individual defining the business at all levels of business.

This is exactly what a health-care provider senior executive, the head of a division that employs more than 300 people, faced when she started her new job. Her predecessor had different philosophical views and a leadership style and approach that created silos within and across departments. She wanted to transform the division by guiding its leaders and teams to evolve their thinking, attitudes, and overall approach. She believed that success comes to those who are surrounded by people who want their success to continue. So, she opted to act and led the transformation.

In this pursuit, she desired to create an environment that fuels clarity and understanding, and demands direct and honest feedback. One of her priorities was to be more intentional about defining and communicating the expectations for her own leadership—and encouraging her immediate direct reports to do the same. She wanted to create an operating culture that promotes collaboration so they could build ecosystems of intellectual capital that organically propel innovation and initiative. Leadership expected her and her team to achieve measurable results in six months (as reflected in operating best practices that translate into tangible positive outcomes for the business, its patients, and the communities they serve).

To succeed by that measure, this leader needed every characteristic in her innovation mentality arsenal *and* needed her direct reports to take greater levels of ownership—to be courageous enough to move from responsibility to expectation and anticipate the unexpected to avoid any problems that would affect their timeline. They all needed to become masters at that while also leading to leave a legacy. Because when you have expectations there is a level of reciprocity that goes beyond responsibility. It's not just "what you can expect for me" but "now that you know what to expect from my leadership, you should be able to define what I can expect from you." That's very different from a top-down job description laying out an employee's responsibility as the sole definition of responsibility.

Leading through the lens of expectation puts the onus of evolution on individuals, not on the business. That's how you establish that team-first mentality and collaborative environment. That's how you eliminate silos and replace them with communication and feedback across teams, departments, and the entire company. That's leading to leave a legacy by keeping your promise to your people, customers, and clients. That's why external partners should be centered on being community-minded and accountable for the advancement of yourself and others.

- What is the legacy that your promise has created for those around you?
- Do your customers, clients, and partners feel that the workplace is an environment where everyone treats each other like family?
- Do your employees believe that their jobs are opportunities to shape the legacies of themselves and everyone they touch?
- Do your customers, clients, and partners believe that you do?

Yasir Moore does. The ABC cameras were actually rolling at his second interview, hidden until he got the job he interviewed for. Who was waiting to congratulate him when he did? Dennis and Cathy from Target.

As Yasir said, "It is more than just a tie."

Know the Power of Relationships

Substitution Word	Evolution Word
Managing	Relationship

Lead Characteristic: Live with an Entrepreneurial Spirit

Supporting Characteristics: Lead to Leave a Legacy and Work with a Generous Purpose

The wealth created through authentic relationships stimulates growth and innovation, advances commerce, and benefits all. Relationships sustain more than momentum—they create and sustain *relevancy.* But these high-level relationships take time to cultivate. By valuing relationships, maximizing the utilization of resources, investing in your people, and always looking for ways to improve strategic-resource sharing, your business sustains momentum. The key word? *Relationships.*

To seize the opportunities great *relationships* create, leaders must evolve from *managing* and *live with an entrepreneurial spirit* that values relationships and invests in people, including themselves. Then they must deploy two supporting characteristics: first, *lead to leave a legacy*, which holistically supports better relationships through reciprocity; and second, *work with a generous purpose*, which requires a commitment to collaboration, sharing, and giving to grow.

I shouldn't need to tell leaders another story about the importance of evolving from managing to relationship. Hundreds of studies of Millennials and shift populations show your employees, partners, and customers want to have relationships with you, one another, your business, and your brand. Wouldn't you rather have a relationship than to just be managed? Which makes you feel more empowered? Just watch Robert Waldinger's popular 2015 TED Talk, "What makes a good life? Lessons from the longest study on happiness" (www.ted.com/speakers/robert_waldinger). Waldinger is a clinical professor of psychiatry at Harvard Medical School and the director of the Harvard Study of Adult Development, which recently completed a 75-year study that tracked annually the lives of 724 men of varying economic statuses. The ultimate finding? "Good relationships keep us happier and healthier. Period."

I can't think of better foundational or fiscal reasons—happiness and health, not to mention growth and innovation—for building great relationships. So, why aren't you building them? Because you, like most leaders and businesses, are still stuck in the substitutional role of managing your leadership identity crisis and the templates of business past. You lack the ability to see that building these relationships doesn't start with *others;* it starts with you. Which is why *you* must continuously invest in yourself to sustain your relevancy. This investment will not be driven by money alone. In fact, it will require you to find the right people who can further guide you and teach you to invest in yourself. It requires you to answer a foundational question of living with an entrepreneurial spirit: How can I nurture and develop a relationship that invests in mutual success for the future rather than what I need now?

Only after answering this question can leaders truly value relationships in the broader workplace and marketplace and encourage entrepreneurial mindsets in others.

I have this relationship with my good friend Walter, who perfectly summed up the way management and leadership are often confused and the need to evolve through relationships: "Leadership development has been around forever. Leaders really need to learn relationship development. I have several situations where my clients are confusing management and leadership. Management is about process. Leadership is about people."

Does this mean management is bad? Absolutely not. This is a clear case where the substituted word must be incorporated into—not simply replaced by—the evolved word! You can't have leadership, let alone a successful business, without strong management of and thus accountability to processes and systems. But as a result, management is necessarily restrictive, because those processes and systems tell you what and how to do things. Management is important for saving time and completing the most mundane tasks, as well as for knowing what steps to take when you need to put out fires. Managing people, however, is not the same and cannot be done by templates, accountability to job descriptions, and letting the business define the individual. Relationships must be mutually rewarding and beneficial. They value individuality, allowing that individuality to prosper, multiply, and add value to others. They are about giving not getting and creating that mutual success. They are about sharing and taking business to the next level so you can grow.

Managing is a transactional relationship. It is about getting results. Relationships transcend transaction. They are about giving and reciprocity.

Of course, you can't operationalize relationships without good management, which Walter also helped me realize: "I frequently see managers that use their leadership skills—their relationships with workers—to substitute for a lack of management or organizational skills and capability. This actually describes me. I'm not a very good manager, but I am good at developing relationships so I can overcome my lack of management skill with strong leadership. But it is really a weakness. When people can't automatically provide me with information—numbers, data, materials—they need, that's a management problem, because I have not provided the tools they need to manage it or manage the people the information comes from. I can help those people deal with this management issue through my relationship with them and by coaching them to have a better relationship with others. But the real solution is to have a management process in place that demands the information so no one needs to rely on a personal relationship to ensure that things are done properly. The management process should do that and then 'Leadership à la Relationship' can take things to the next level."

That *next level* is what it means to move from just sowing to sharing and growing by creating a culture of reciprocity in relationships through leading to leave a legacy and working with a generous purpose of giving.

First, you ask the legacy questions:

- What is the legacy that your promise has created for those around you?
- Do our employees believe that their jobs are not just jobs—they are opportunities to shape their legacies? Do our customers, clients, and partners believe that we do?

Then, you ask the generous purpose questions:

- How do I give back to my people?
- How can I share my expertise beyond my everyday work?
- Do our people, customers/clients, and external partners believe that our company promotes sharing among and giving back to our people and the communities and causes they and the company embrace?

Why lead to leave a legacy when generous purpose seems to be all about people first and thus relationships? Because relationships represent the embodiment of resowing. And much like we have lost that ability to resow in our businesses, we have lost it in our relationships, not just in business but in life in general. Relationships should always be reciprocal. Unfortunately, they have become too much about getting without giving. Real relationships can't be about something that exists for our own benefit or getting a return on an agreement to work together in any capacity, be it a mentorship or a contractual agreement. They are about perpetuating the momentum that each person brings to the relationship. Without leading to leave a legacy, that relationship will disappear and reappear based on when you need to get something out of them, and that's selfish.

To reinvent the way we work, lead, and live our lives, our relationships must evolve.

Mark DeBellis was my manager at Sunkist when I started there in 1993. It has evolved into a relationship decades later. We may come and go in each other's life, as we have gone on to different careers and industries, but we never let go or disappeared. I know our relationship is strong, because DeBellis always has a pulse on my career and how he can continue to add value. But just as he has invested in me, he has allowed me to invest in him. We are accountable to each other, and our relationship has become selfless, not selfish. He is vulnerable with me, and I am vulnerable with him. He may be ten years my senior, but DeBellis believes I add value to him as much as he adds to me.

The same must be true in leadership: It should never be one-sided, nor should the leader always be the one generating the ideas or making the decisions. Leadership means actively listening and advancing the ideas of others (and injecting recommendations along the way to further strengthen or add value to them). If you are the type of leader that needs all the attention, you will not seek to cultivate wisdom in others.

Reciprocity within the leader-employee relationship is critical to embracing diversity of thought, inspiring independent thinking, and stimulating new ways of doing things.

Reciprocity is key; cultivating wisdom requires being in touch with what matters most to your employees and giving them the room to express their opinions and put their ideas to the test. The more you can gauge and unleash the passionate pursuits of your employees, the more effective you will be in challenging them to stretch their thinking and expand their endless possibilities to resow.

Once you have answered these questions, share your success stories. Discuss the best practices they helped you create and the impact they had on employee morale. Perhaps examine a new client relationship and lay out the new ways you approached and set forth the standard for building relationships, and the role they play to fuel the growth of your business. That's how other opportunities are created as you resow the core relationships into other opportunities in the business. That's how your people start to add value back to you and the company beyond just doing what they are told—you give and share and then get giving and sharing back. That's how the resulting relationships allow your people to feel they can share back—from pointing out mistakes and creating new systems to taking on new responsibilities and making the workplace a more fun environment. That's the foundation for sustainable momentum.

Sure, sometimes just managing and holding people accountable for their actions can lead to evolution beyond sowing, but it is usually slower and riskier without the mutuality and reciprocity of great relationships. In truth, we seek relationships in the marketplace with companies by seeking out the stories behind the products and seeing our stories in them. In this way, the marketplace influences the workplace. Of course leaders might say, "Of course, the marketplace dictates everything." But this is beyond the transaction.

Relationships in the marketplace now must go beyond the transaction—to evolve beyond the sale. Because what influences the marketplace? The individual—much more than ever before. Because we have shifted to individuality in the marketplace, customers are looking well beyond a brand's products and are measuring a brand by intimacy and relationships with them as they make their selections. Customers want to share how great and authentic the story is behind what they consume. If all you have is a transactional relationship, then as soon as another brand offers a better deal, they are gone. A relationship based in generous purpose means it's not all about the money. So why can't businesses truly find that in their talent too? Talent should be all about fit, feel, and alignment—growing by working with a generous purpose. Leaders who work with a generous purpose know the wisdom behind having

Evolving from managing to relationship means evolving from a "getting" mindset to a "giving" one to share success and grow opportunity.

a culture that joins everyone's best interests and takes them to heart, regardless of hierarchy or rank.

Fred Diaz, Vice President and General Manager, North America Trucks and Light Commercial Vehicles, Nissan North America, Inc., told me that this generous purpose informs his work at Nissan. According to Diaz, to ensure Nissan builds relationships with multicultural employee and consumer populations represented by the CDS, the same way the auto industry has for a century with nondiverse populations, the company practices four qualities— awareness, ability to adapt, execution, and authenticity—all of which have propelled it from also-ran to an established leader in those markets.

- They are *aware* of the opportunities these populations represent on a daily basis. He and his team are evangelists for multicultural marketing so the message permeates the company. Everyone embraces the strategy and works together to move the company in the direction it needs to go. Diaz explains, "We take our marketing intelligence very seriously, dissect it and digest it so that when we speak to our consumers—whether it's the Hispanic, African American, Asian, or the LGBT community—we have brand research in our back pocket that reflects what they want and need from an automotive company."
- They *adapt* to changes and do it quickly when it comes to their multicultural consumers. This is not simply found in increased marketing budgets but increased diversity in the workplace so that dealership networks and in-house staff mirror their markets and can communicate with customers on their terms—from language to shared culture.
- They *execute* and seize the opportunity, leveraging the relationships of their external partners. That means engaging with media agencies that know and understand how critical the multicultural market is to the company's strategic business plan. This includes minority-owned agencies with strong relationships with media giants, such as BET and Univision. Diaz notes, "Minority groups and Hispanics, in particular, consume their media digitally via

mobile and social media. Knowing this is an opportunity to reach consumers where and how they want to be reached. It's not about them coming to us but about us going to them on their turf—and speaking to them on their terms."

- They are *authentic*. Any company can say it wants to do multicultural marketing, but if it doesn't do the research and take these consumers seriously, lack of authenticity will be evident. Worst-case scenario: They risk being inappropriate and even offensive. This is often the case with those companies who take advertising spots made for the general market and simply translate them into Spanish for the Hispanic market.

Why don't we all do these things to create great relationships? As Diaz's rules for the road demonstrate, they require hard work to do and maintain. If Nissan can sustain these words, invest in them, stay authentic, and not get stuck in sowing, they could own the shift population market. But for Nissan and any company with a similar approach, it won't just be complacency about their success that gets in the way of that first. It will be if they lose not only the connection that comes with great relationships but also the intimacy.

Have Intimacy

Substitution Word	Evolution Word
Engagement	Intimacy

Lead Characteristic: Work with a Generous Purpose

Supporting Characteristic: Unleash Your Passionate Pursuits

At a dinner after a presentation to a multinational consumer packaged goods company, a group of midlevel executives inquired about my work with other businesses. They wanted to know what the trends were, the common threads I saw, and especially what leaders needed to be more focused on. As I started to talk about the pillars of see, sow, grow, and share, I stopped and realized they weren't asking for clarification of what they had heard me say. They were looking for deeper connection to what they were doing and from their leaders. They weren't looking for a way *out*;

they were looking for a way *in*. And their leader was not providing that. He engaged them to do their work but didn't care enough to evolve and do more for one simple reason: He feared the level of accountability that intimacy might bring.

The days of mere *engagement* are over. Operationalizing *intimacy* requires leaders to sustain a level of alignment that never ends—to continue to develop relationships with a *generous purpose* and touch the business every day to create a workplace centered on sharing, standing for something, and advancing by serving others. Then, leaders can *unleash everyone's passionate pursuits* in support of that intimacy and empower themselves and others to bring their whole selves to work every day.

Think back to our work on your personal brand value propositions in Chapter 2 and how they shape your leadership identity. Now answer the same question I ask the leaders in my workshops: Are you living these qualities every day to influence the evolution of you, your people, and your business? Most leaders aren't because they are engaged but lack intimacy. Intimacy is what Magic Johnson meant when he said you can't do urban America from the corporate offices—you can't engage it on a spreadsheet; you need to go to the movie theater. Intimacy guaranteed that 15-year-old Yasir Moore left Target with much more than a tie. Intimacy empowers Fred Diaz to go beyond engagement to caring—evolving. Intimacy enables Nissan to build relationships with multicultural populations. Intimacy is why Mike Fernandez, for all the billions of dollars he is worth, still listens to customer service calls every single week.

> *Engagement has become the equivalent of an "initiative," meaning something that starts and stops.*

Engagement is not bad; it's just not enough. How does engagement get you stuck in substitution? Because it doesn't necessarily mean that you have to take ownership; it simply means you have to comply and be involved. Intimacy is more like a best practice. Intimacy is what the workplace and marketplace craves. Intimacy is about connection; it gives our relationships energy through its implied investment in understanding and valuing differences. Engaged leaders might attend a meeting, add input to the conversation, leave, and wait for a report on where any of the discussions might go. That's like using the meeting equivalent of hand sanitizer after each meeting. Leaders who are intimate would leave the meeting and "stay dirty," exposing themselves to what's going around. "Sanitized" leaders are disconnected, unable to quickly and nimbly deploy resources or people to seize and close the opportunity gaps.

Leaders who use the word *engagement* are more often than not trying to make others *feel* as if leadership is in tune with what is going on and that they do actually care. Leaders who are intimate never need to say they care, because intimacy supports constant caring. They understand what my mentor at Sunkist taught me: The moment you stop touching the business is the moment you stop understanding it.

Intimacy means you are in it and touching the business every day. Are you?

- How many of your friends, colleagues, coworkers, customers, and clients know what you stand for? Can they articulate it in three words? Can you?
- Do your people, customers, clients, and external partners believe that your company promotes sharing among and giving back to your people and the communities and causes they and the company embrace?

These questions are more important than ever, because the marketplace is changing so quickly. Engagement works well enough when things are predictable. Intimacy helps prepare for and deal with uncertainty. (And when in recent memory has there been a time when there wasn't uncertainty?) Intimacy is about finding meaning and relevance for you and the company. And yet engagement is the word we find in most corporate value statements and in encouragements from the stage, books, and blogs.

Intimacy is something that Hispanics, the largest shift population, embrace deeply. I was talking to a group of senior Hispanic leaders at a Fortune 500 company who told me they understood the need for intimacy and wanted to immerse themselves in their work. But as one of them said, "We are controlled by a U.S.-based company. They hear a word like 'intimacy' and they think it is 'soft.' But when we talk about it and you talk about it in your presentations, it comes from a position of strength and courage and being bold enough to do more."

Remember the stat from Chapter 3 about how Hispanics only work at 40 percent of their potential? You now have another reason why: lack of intimacy. And Hispanics aren't alone. We see the ill effects of this intimacy deficit in other multicultural populations and in the generation gap between Millennials and non-Millennials: People have been penalized for being themselves and have been told to shut down the passionate pursuits that need to be reawakened and unleashed!

- Are your employees empowered to bring their whole selves to work every day—their cultures, personal perspectives, and passions?
- Do they own what they do and strive to explore endless possibilities?

Answering these questions requires not just courage to explore but vulnerability to listen intimately. Do you and your company have the courage and vulnerability to care about the individual and displaying kindness and concern for others? That kind of caring requires genuine giving of one's self to support the passions of others. The process is never neat, but the results are often transformational. In fact, intimacy is often the only reason we change our positions on anything. We get to know someone and their passionate pursuit of their beliefs. Do you have any intimacy with people on the other side of your position? Do you truly know someone who is a Muslim? Evangelical Christian? Conservative Republican? Gay? Gun owner? Transgender? If you don't, you lack *intimacy* with the other side. The same is true in business: If you lack intimacy with differences and diversity of thought, you will keep *control* of your position, but you will limit your *influence* over others and your ability to help the business evolve.

Influence Individuality

Substitution Word	Evolution Word
Control	Influence

Shared Lead Characteristics: Work with a Generous Purpose, Lead to Leave a Legacy

After a new business meeting with a team from a company I respect immensely, I debriefed with my team and our attention turned to one of the company's executives. "Did you notice how he would seemingly agree with what we were saying about the importance of leadership influencing the evolution of the business? Then he would say, 'Well, yeah but . . .' and 'I guess I think . . . .'" My team nodded. "You know why he said that? Because he had no leverage. He was new to the company and the industry. He wanted to impress, which made him even more afraid to show that he really didn't understand the business and industry as well as everyone else in the room. What he should have said was, 'Listen, I am still learning and really appreciate your helping me better understand this.' And then he could have asked, 'Can you help me understand why this is done this way?' Instead he tried a power play to make himself sound important and only revealed that he didn't have a clue."

On an even deeper level, this meeting also revealed how much that leader needed to keep control of every situation. Control is not necessarily a negative, but it doesn't lead to influence. Instead, control restricts momentum. It completely represses and devalues individuality for what is in the best interests of the business short term. Control might be essential if you are a Navy SEAL on a mission or the TSA performing an inspection checklist, but in most other situations, being vulnerable and courageous enough to give up some control and allowing individuals to feel valued *increases* your influence. In business and in life, loosening your grip on control benefits you, your people, and the business. It leads to reciprocity and increases relevancy. That influence enriches and broadens your relationships, leads to more intimacy, and finally has a resowing effect and leads to seeing more opportunities (resetting the cycle of see-sow-grow-share).

So, where does *influence* come from, and how do you evolve from *control* to have it? By *leading to leave a legacy* and *working with a generous purpose*—the two characteristics that create sharing in business.

That sharing extends to the characteristics themselves in this pair of words. While these characteristics interconnect to support each other, sometimes you need to be wise and bold to create cognitive harmony in giving them equal weight.

With *influence*, leaders are truly leading to leave a legacy. They see the value in treating people in their workplace and marketplace like family and protecting what they stand for as essential to a successful future. They believe in respect for others before self-recognition, believing that success comes to those who are surrounded by people who want their success to continue. This is where generous purpose comes in: When employees at all levels know the leadership authentically cares for and values relationships and intimacy, they feel those leaders have their backs and want to reciprocate; they want to have influence too.

Representation without influence is like engagement without intimacy· a zero-sum game.

Leaders who allow their people to have that influence generate trust and transparency at the highest levels, all because they had the wisdom and courage to see influence in being vulnerable. That's exactly what was missing from the leader we debriefed about that day: vulnerability, as if opening up to respect others, appreciating what they know, and thinking with nuance is a weakness and something to be feared. But all that fear leads to in the workplace is judgment, envy, greed, and fierce protection of territory through a siloed approach, not fierce protection of your people. In other words, rather than a respect for others that earns influence, it leads to a belief in self-promotion and a deep desire for recognition. Unfortunately, an unwillingness to make yourself vulnerable leads to unforeseen vulnerabilities that can weaken your company.

I gave a keynote speech to a group of Fortune 500 executives, which included midlevel directors to top senior executives. All the leaders had expressed interest in advance in finding new ways to evolve their business both internally and externally. But it was the midlevel leaders—the directors and senior directors—who embraced my core message about how business is becoming less about the company defining the individual and more about the individual defining the company, and for their businesses to evolve, leaders must take greater ownership and accountability for evolving themselves. I knew this was the case long before I received feedback from the post-workshop evaluations. After the keynote, a group of directors approached me and all nodded when one of them said, "Mr. Llopis, did you notice that the majority of the reactions and questions came from us and not many VPs and EVPs? We are deeply concerned, because we heard what you said. Our leadership is not ready to change in order for the business to evolve. They are not willing to be vulnerable at a time when we must all have each other's backs if we are to grow together as a team."

What a lesson! Lower and midlevels of leadership notice when those above them refuse to evolve through vulnerability. Leaders above them must see how vulnerability earns them influence with these direct reports who need this message the most, not hiding their insecurities behind their titles and tenure in an attempt to stay in control and play it safe. Breaking free from their leadership identity crises is essential to their evolving to achieve that influence. They can't expect others to take personal stock on this level if they won't. When leaders don't have the courage to be vulnerable and lead by example, they unknowingly disappoint those they lead to the point they begin to lose respect. Self-promotion undermines influence. The workplace and marketplace are demanding a new type of thinking to influence the evolution of the business. Today's leaders must welcome change, and that means seeing strength in vulnerability. Regardless of hierarchy or rank, they must be mature enough to evaluate their own performance and the consequences of their actions and inactions. Their ability to sustain long-term relevancy demands it.

When you live in a culture fueled by identity crises and power plays, people leave. Sure, new people will come in and be excited about the opportunity to work at the company. That's why many leaders see talent development as optional, because they can always find other people who will be excited at the outset. But that hopefulness will fade as their replacements find themselves in the same situation. When the controls kick in, the excitement fades. I have seen this happen at all levels, from smaller businesses to Fortune 500 companies. I have seen it in my assessments, which after ten years show a major decrease among leaders in the belief in growing and sharing. When that environment stifles people after several years because the leader is not vulnerable or the leader's negative influence makes them feel like they can't be intimate, so there is no value in having a relationship, people will either get stuck in substitution mode and do only what they are told, or leave, creating perpetual inefficiency.

How do you begin the move away from control and operationalize influence? Accept that the old ways of doing things just don't apply as much anymore.

At a roundtable on preparing for the CDS, Victor Crawford, chief operating officer at Aramark Corp., offered an example of operationalizing influence from his company's work at hospitals that serve large groups from shift populations. Aramark provides uniforms, food, and services to companies and buildings as well as institutions like schools and prisons. As such, its connection to people in the workplace and marketplace is huge. (Aramark is a Fortune 250 company and, as of 2015, the 23rd largest private employer in the U.S.) For example, at hospitals they provide pretty much everything that the doctors and other caregivers don't, including repair and maintenance of biomedical equipment, environmental and dietary services, infection prevention and control, and food and uniforms. Focusing on one aspect of his business, Crawford revealed that Aramark is one of the largest employers of dieticians (approximately 800 of them) in the country. These dieticians have a tremendous influence because they work with a generous purpose and lead to leave a legacy.

"We deliver an experience of what we call enriched and nourished lives," Crawford says. "With every patient who comes through the door, we sit them down with a dietitian, because with a lot of chronic illnesses, you will typically find other issues, such as obesity, high cholesterol levels, and high blood pressure. For many multicultural groups, we've got to educate them that the way they've been eating in the past is not the way they should be eating going forward."

Among the solutions Aramark has developed with its dieticians is a proprietary community engagement program called Healthy for Life® 20 By 20, which is designed improve the diet and health of millions of Americans by 20 percent by the year 2020. They partnered with the American Heart Association to launch the program in Philadelphia, Chicago, and Houston. It also has partnerships with other health organizations centered on getting people to eat a healthier diet. In hospitals, where 85 percent of patients are on some form of restricted diet, Aramark dieticians help design the menu, often going back to the culinary lab to make sure that the food not only tastes good but is good for you. "There's a lot of innovation that has to happen with hospital food when you start taking the fat, sugar, and sodium out in terms of adding healthy ingredients and seasoning to bring the taste back to multicultural diets," Crawford says.

There's another important element to driving patient satisfaction too, he adds: "You want to look at things from a health and wellness perspective, but you also want to be very mindful in terms of how you do that. In our case, the patient doesn't necessarily know it's an Aramark employee and not hospital staff cleaning their room or delivering their meals. But that doesn't mean you can just walk in and drop off a tray. There's a hospitality aspect to the job and you've got to connect with the patient on a human level, perhaps culturally, perhaps from a language perspective. Oftentimes, if you're delivering meals to a patient three times a day, you're going to be seeing them more than even their doctor does."

Crawford understands the power of earning and operationalizing influence. Unfortunately, I've seen the reverse too many times. My challenge to you: Throw your titles out the door. Be courageous enough to own the responsibility and earn what the title truly represents to your people and customers. Powerful things happen when a leader is vulnerable enough to do this. Transparency leads to trust, respect is earned and multiplied, the workplace becomes fun again, and the leader—once at risk of becoming extinct—starts to evolve, along with the organization they serve. At that point, there is no limit to how far you can evolve to maximize potential and significance and truly operationalize all six characteristics of the innovation mentality.

Maximize Potential

Substitution Word	Evolution Words
Professional Development	Maximize Potential

Lead Characteristic: Live with an Entrepreneurial Spirit

Supporting Characteristic: See Opportunity in Everything

When I worked at American Seafoods, I pushed the company to start a more upscale "Bayside Bistro" brand, but my bosses did not see how it fit with the company's product lines and direction. Problem was, that direction was the same one it had been going in for too long. We lacked diversity of thought. We followed the existing paths and remained complacent about success; comfort with past accomplishments prevented us from being intellectually curious, sharing ideas regularly, and seeing unseen opportunities. I preferred the uncomfortable. In this case, I was the skeptic and leveraged the goodwill I had through the relationships and influence I had built. I pushed my leaders and the company to break free from complacency and evolve to seize this opportunity gap. I wasn't trying to be disrespectful; I wanted to maximize my potential in the workplace and my company's in the marketplace.

After I left American Seafoods, I did the same thing when I started my food business with partners in Mexico, and I launched the Luna Rossa brand in the U.S. One of my first targets was redefining the processed artichokes category. And if that makes you think, "Why in the hell would anyone spend time doing that?" you pretty much sound like everyone I say and said that to. Sure, artichokes already had a legacy in the food business that seemed static, but that was the point: I was curious enough to see an opportunity for growth that others did not. Everyone else was just servicing that legacy. Eventually, I managed to leverage opportunities with Costco because they saw an opportunity with smaller companies to get the distinctive products they knew their customers wanted at the value they expected. Most large brands were not willing to budge with elevating quality or changing ingredients and packaging. My business was.

In the end, Bayside Bistro took off and so did my processed artichokes. In fact, with Luna Rossa, I expanded the brand into roasted red peppers and other gourmet vegetables, and then into licensing agreements that included salad dressings and pasta sauces I sold to warehouse club and retails stores. I multiplied distribution (the growth opportunity) of the same product in different categories. Luna Rossa soon built a brand that originated in Mexico and expanded by seizing opportunity in the U.S. Typically, it had been the other way around: The brand came from the U.S. and was then licensed and expanded internationally.

All because I lived with an *entrepreneurial spirit* and *saw the opportunity* to resow past accomplishments into something greater—not just *develop* them but *maximize their potential.*

That we are talking about artichokes is more fitting than you might know: Baby artichokes are not, in fact, "newborns" but the little ones left behind in the plant's final days. In other words, they are a seed of an idea—an opportunity that grows at the end of a productive life. Maximizing potential in the workplace and marketplace requires the same thing. Don't "veg out." Encourage your people to use their brainpower to innovate and create—to think and see opportunities that turn that thinking into new marketplace realities.

How will you use your improved relationships, deeper intimacy, and increased influence to lead tomorrow's leaders today and evolve your business from past legacies?

Maximizing potential gets away from professional development by template. It moves beyond job descriptions, hierarchies, scorecards, and advancing the company's goals and objectives at the expense of individuality. But you have to take responsibility for maximizing your own potential before you do the same for your company. Your potential starts with taking responsibility for you and evaluating your own performance, actions, and ability to evolve and then drive that through your team and the company. To do this, you must lead by example and:

- Have the intellectual curiosity and belief in the truth of the idea.
- Know in your head *and* your heart that you are willing to back up your people and the idea to see it through to the end.
- Demonstrate the mental toughness to withstand a lot of negativity and be mindful of where that negativity comes from. Connect your idea to the best practices of the business, its values, and its performance metrics. Don't dismiss them or any compliance requirements simply because they are about substitution.
- Be certain you're going to leave a legacy. Don't just present a block of clay to the people you want to convince; give them a sense of what the end result will be because completing the evolution is

highly dependent on those people breaking free from their silos to collaborate with your team and other department leaders to push the idea forward.

That last point is one too often underserved by leaders—maximizing others' potential must be the goal of maximizing yours. Without that, we fail to connect maximizing potential to a key word: *purpose.*

Maximizing potential requires you to invest in what matters to your people and you as a rule, and thus is deeply connected to our first words for operationalizing evolution: shared beliefs and alignment. Connecting them all means that when new opportunities are seized, your people have ownership from the start and take responsibility for looking for and sharing new ones. There is no path to greater relevancy for a leader and a company.

Maximizing potential also maximizes purpose.

This is especially true when it comes to the 75-plus million Millennials who are fast becoming the driving force in our workplaces and marketplaces. Millennials pride themselves on individuality and want to maximize every moment doing the things that they enjoy doing. But survey after survey shows that those same Millennials have serious doubts about the future. A little doubt can be healthy, but too often it creates create crises of confidence. Maximizing Millennials' potential can help avert these crises. When a company maximizes its employees' potential at work, they find self-satisfaction in what they can achieve and what they are capable of achieving well beyond the obvious. It allows them to define at least some of their own objectives beyond their current role and responsibilities to benefit the business. In other words, they find purpose in what they are doing.

Creating this environment can feel risky, but I would argue that playing it safe is the greater risk. You don't want your best people to strain against professional developmental constraints as they try and evolve like I did in my wine and spirits job all those years ago. After all, if they are as good as they think and the leaders led them to believe, then why shouldn't they expect them to see opportunity that allows them to be themselves at their fullest? When they wake up to the fact that they have more potential than your organization can provide opportunity for, they will do what I did:

leave you and the organization. They will live their entrepreneurial spirit and seize opportunities for themselves or for another company. Either way, there's a good chance they will become your competition.

Amusingly, I have gotten the blame as a consultant for compelling people to do exactly that. "You woke them up," more than a few have said. As if sleeping on the job is a good thing! Have I woken you up? I hope so.

The Fortune 500 company leaders I surveyed about what was most important to them to effectively serve their employees and customers got this one right: 69 percent said maximizing their potential, and 31 percent said professional development. But when it came to the next pair and the ultimate goal of evolving, operationalizing, and mastering the six characteristics of the innovation mentality, they got it completely wrong.

Resow with Significance

Substitution Word	Evolution Word
Success	Significance

Lead Characteristic: Work with a Generous Purpose

Supporting Characteristic: Lead to Leave a Legacy

The conversation was not going well. In fact, my first minutes with a Fortune 500 executive in financial services were about as painful as any I have ever experienced in the decade I have been doing interviews as part of my consultations. This was more than simple resistance to the innovation mentality or questioning the six characteristics. I've dealt with that before and welcome the skepticism as you know. This executive even told me he thought a lot of the work was good albeit "ubiquitous." The pain developed after I tried to bridge his resistance by asking him, "What gives your leadership distinction?"

No answer.

"You've been here 15 years and people know you, so something about you must be distinctive to them? What is it?"

Again, nothing.

I've gotten plenty of off answers to these questions before but never such persistent silence. Then I realized this leader couldn't answer the questions because he didn't know how. As we continued with the interview, I turned to another subject, and the executive finally had plenty to say: "I'm the one who does the heavy lifting and don't get credit for it. I am the one that does the thing that nobody else does. I'm the one that keeps sharing ideas on how to do things better or differently to grow, and whether people love or hate them, they think I'm too full of myself. So I go and do the things those people don't want to do to test the ideas and prove to them that my thoughts they see as self-serving and even crazy actually have a greater benefit to everyone. And when they buy into it? I let them 'steal' my ideas, because I'm the one that cares about everyone else and then I get screwed. I guess I am screwing myself."

Hearing that pained me in a deep way as I thought back to my experience at American Seafoods: This executive was not resisting the innovation mentality because he didn't understand it or want to embrace it; he was trying to live it. He was a giver in a land of takers. That's why when I asked what gave him distinction, he couldn't answer, and later when I asked him, "What do you solve for?" he couldn't quite explain it.

After a long pause, I told him I was going to share an insight about his personal brand value proposition that could transform his career: He was a capacity builder. And his response amazed me: "If I were to tell people that my intentions were to help them build their capacity, rather than trying to prove everybody wrong, then maybe my leadership has been misrepresented and misunderstood." Exactly! He didn't know how to communicate his intentions or his own career journey. Once he understood his years of frustration, he shared this single insight. No wonder he felt stuck, undervalued, even "screwed." Rather than revealing his intentions and vulnerability, he got angry and defensive. As a result, he obscured his own influence from himself and others. He erased his leadership identity *and* his significance.

You must believe in the power of *significance* to *leave a legacy*, not only through your actions but by *working with a generous purpose* to help others find theirs.

Simply put, if success is a byproduct of sowing, significance is a byproduct of resowing and the ultimate byproduct of evolution. People who define their success as simply being more successful than their parents, the previous generation, their friends and neighbors, or the competition are climbing a ladder that leads to more "stuff" and selfishness, not significance. It doesn't matter how generously they end their lives. I always return to the story of Andrew Carnegie who used his success in railroads and other businesses to become one of the biggest philanthropists of all time. A lot of significant things came from that philanthropy, from Carnegie-Mellon University to libraries. Unfortunately, Carnegie built his success as a brutal boss who famously mistreated his people. Is that the legacy you want?

Success is great, but the way we measure it too often fails to consider its significance to others and ourselves. Professor Robert M. Wachter of the University of California at San Francisco echoed this idea in a *New York Times* editorial "How Measurement Fails Doctors and Teachers": "Our businesslike efforts to measure and improve quality are now blocking the altruism, indeed the love that motivates people to enter the helping professions. While we are figuring out how to get better, we need to tread more lightly in assessing the work of the professionals who practice in our most human and sacred fields."

I couldn't have said it better about the importance of evolving from success to significance, except to add that while Wachter focused on doctors and lawyers, I know we can't limit this to any field, because we are all human—or at least need to be a little more so. We have raised an entire generation that wants to find significance in something more than salary. Millennials, like all the shift populations, are not willing to play by the old rules. And how is that a bad thing? How can this not be channeled into something that can contribute in bigger ways? They are the ones we are working to leave a legacy for after all.

We are sowing to succeed, not resowing to be significant. Success is a byproduct of sowing; significance is a byproduct of resowing.

Significance comes most to those who are surrounded by people who want their success to continue. That means embracing the promise of the culture that you have attempted to integrate into the organization and continuing to invest in it. Truth is, I *know* we want this significance—all of us. I have seen it the dozens upon dozens of times I have presented my "Success to Significance Survey." Based on work I have experienced as a member of Northwestern University's Kellogg Innovation Network (KIN) Global think tank, led by Professor Robert C. Wolcott, the survey is a mainstay in my high-level workshops, because of its elegance, simplicity, and power to fuel significance. Just give your top three answers to the following sentences:

1. I want to live in a world that . . .
2. I will be most inspired in an organization that . . .
3. I will be most proud to lead a team that . . .

Take a moment to write down your answers, then look at the following top-three responses from KIN Global's work with thousands of executives that follow. Based on my experience with top executives nationwide, I suspect you will find some overlap.

1. I want to live in a world that . . .
   - offers equal opportunity
   - seeks peace, prosperity, and unconditional love
   - embraces unique differences

2. I will be most inspired in an organization that . . .
   - exists for a greater purpose than pure profit
   - serves to eliminate poverty and makes the world a better place
   - has leaders who listen and have a clarity of purpose

3. I will be most proud to lead a team that . . .
   - helps each other become better
   - believes in their jobs and duties beyond the job
   - leaves a legacy and rewards positive social change

So many of us want similar goals—we just want to get there in our own way. Problem is our significance, like our personal brand value propositions and leadership identities, has become dependent on the company's brand. We no longer enable people to shape and influence the future of companies as individuals. As a result, those companies not only forget how to serve humans, but also they forget how to serve humanity. To reclaim significance requires those companies to do more than simply say they value individuals and giving back—to go beyond giving back to their communities with self-serving and well-publicized donations or manufactured collective service of company-wide giving programs or charitable initiatives. There is nothing wrong with everyone getting together to clean up the neighborhood, but that's manufactured giving defined by the company. What would individualized giving look like? Salesforce.org has a nice answer: They ask companies to join them in pledging 1 percent of all "important resources (product, time, and resources) to support integrating philanthropy into their business from an early stage . . . to improve communities around the world." The individual employees determine the direction of the giving to align with their goals. The company creates the mandate that aligns those individual goals with its own.

We can turn success into significance if we master the six characteristics of the innovation mentality.

Why can't more companies operationalize this? Because even when the company is not defining us, the sweet smell of success through sowing over and over again is captivating and can blind even the best of us to our significance. But this need not be a zero-sum game.

I remember when I got that first big order for Luna Rossa's products from Costco. The first thing I did was call my dad and without hesitating he said, "Son, you have to go celebrate."

"Dad, I can't, I have so much to do. I have to keep selling."

"Glenn," he replied. "There are times in life you have to step away and celebrate and reflect on what you have been able to achieve. In the end, a big part of life is experiencing happiness, and that is as fleeting as the success of that sale. You should look for things that bring you back to that feeling of happiness. Go find your people. Go celebrate with them, and then turn that celebration into significance, not just more sales."

My father *really did* say that to me. He said things like that all the time. But this was the first time I heard him. He wasn't telling me to buy a round of drinks and deliver a bunch of high-fives. Well, he wasn't saying *only* that (remember, this was a guy who helped invent Miller Lite). He was telling me that celebration is about more than closing a book on the past or acknowledging success of the team: It marks a new beginning for everyone, including you. It's about the love. So is the innovation mentality, and its ultimate step is sharing your significance to grow it in others.

It's not *your* significance; it's *theirs.* By sharing the significance of the opportunities you've seized with others, we multiply success for all.

If you were to leave your company today, what would be the legacy you leave behind? It's time to stop thinking (and reading) about these words and evolve—to operationalize them and make the mosaic we all want a reality. That's all that leader who erased his significance wanted: to be discovered by his peers and valued, and know they had his back and best interests at heart. Let generosity rule as we empower individuals to define this reality. Let's get beyond diversity.

To honor my father and the country that gave my family a future, I can't think of any legacy I'd be prouder to leave.

CHAPTER 9

WHAT WAS I WAITING FOR?

Before the second day of a two-day thought leadership session for a Fortune 500 retail company's senior executives, a participant said to me, "Glenn, my mind hurts."

I smiled, and she continued. "I couldn't sleep last night after the first day. I was watching a cooking show last night, and the person on screen was talking about the six characteristics. Well, the chef didn't know it or call it that. But I could hear it in the manner in which he was expressing himself to create a new meal with a different approach. I realized this morning that you are decoding me to think in the same way and differently than the ways the companies I've worked for wanted me to think. They just wanted me to do (sow). I realize why I have felt my career is incomplete. I know why I get so upset when the self-promoter gets promoted. I know why I am not advancing myself: I made the decision to give up a long time ago and just sow. I have wasted years in my career because I let go of my beliefs—beliefs I see now that represent the six characteristics. At their core they are not new. They just require courage to live them."

"So, what are you thinking? How will you make what you are seeing now a reality?" I asked.

"Well, the associated behaviors made them so much easier to understand but even easier to live them—naturally. That's what I think I did last night. Because of you, I will never be able to watch a cooking show or a movie or read the newspaper as I once did. I can see all of the characteristics so clearly and hope to also see them in the colleagues that I viewed as problems—now as opportunities previously unseen."

As we spoke, it dawned on me that we were not alone. A group of her colleagues had gathered around and leaned in as she spoke, silent but nodding. They heard what I did as this executive spoke and had started to develop the mindset to understand what she had: The six characteristics can, will, and must impact your lens—your line of sight. Without it, you will not hear or see characteristics in other people or what you read and watch, let alone yourself. For nearly a decade, I've had a front-row seat to the harsh realities that run deep within organizations representing the most respected brands in the world. These concerns have been escalating for years. It's what I call the things that people are thinking about, but do not dare to say. It's time to say it: To truly operationalize them and the innovation mentality, you must evolve your perception and thinking and be vulnerable and courageous enough to open yourself up to it all.

After the session, I thought about this moment and my own sense of vulnerability in writing this book and about how I evolved during my journey to awaken to this thinking. When I finished the first draft, I realized it had been 12 months since I asked myself, What do I and my business solve for? With the noise of the 2016 presidential election playing in the background, I resolved to answer the question and lifted myself up in an act of true reciprocity with my readers. So, I read the book start to finish, asked the question, and . . . quickly realized that what I am asking you to do in this book is *hard*—really intense and difficult—even for the guy who created it! This is a journey of learning how to be uncomfortable, vulnerable, and courageous to see, sow, grow, and share—welcoming differences and knowing how to confidently turn businesses, yourself, and indeed America around. Committing to live the six characteristics doesn't just guide me or leaders like the one at that thought-leadership session on how to more effectively lead their employees and organizations. It transforms us to rediscover and reclaim our identities in order to evolve with significance, and then continue that evolution by resowing what we have learned into new possibilities.

The answer to what my business and I solve for will not surprise you, of course. It is basically a good summary of what you have just read and learned how to do:

- *Drive growth through the Cultural Demographic Shift.* The influence of the Cultural Demographic Shift is telling us that growth strategies are becoming less about the business defining the individual and more about the individual defining the business. Leadership must prepare for this shift by moving individuality to the center of the organization's growth strategy. Leaders must implement authentic solutions that strengthen intellectual capital and know-how around the distinct needs of those individuals within workforce and consumer populations to influence growth strategies faster and more efficiently. That's when sustainable growth/ROI happens.
- *Understand leadership identity to maximize organizational and marketplace growth.* Understanding and strengthening your leadership identity is the first step in embracing and operationalizing an innovation mentality and leading through the Cultural Demographic Shift. Without strong leadership identities, businesses fail to maximize the full potential of the workplace and marketplace. Leaders must develop and manage their leadership identities—the unique distinguishing factors they are known for and that can be consistently expected of them to fuel more intimate, high-performance workplace environments and seize opportunities previously unseen.
- *Strengthen corporate culture and organizational teams.* Departments have operated as silos for too long. They must come together or businesses will continue to solve for the wrong things and lose their identities. Organizations must drive engagement in the workplace

and growth in the marketplace by moving away from traditional models that promote top-down, hierarchical, departmental, siloed, one-size-fits-all approaches. They must activate departments throughout the entire organization and strengthen competencies in which employees and consumers are at the center of their growth strategies.

- *Identify and close opportunity gaps.* Opportunity gaps are created when leaders and organizations are not innovative enough, because they don't know what they're solving for. They lack the mindset of the innovation mentality to see, sow, grow, and share to evolve. But without strategy change is merely substitution not evolution. Evolution requires their organizations to embrace new ideas and ideals. Only then will they stop widening opportunity gaps by ignoring diversity of thought and mismanaging competitive threats and unforeseen trends. Only then will they stop losing talent, market share, and shareholder value by solving for the wrong things.

So what are you waiting for? My clients around the country are already starting the work to embrace a new type of thinking that helps them evolve and stay ahead of the rapid changes in the workplace and marketplace. They want to break free from old ways of doing things that slow down growth and make it difficult to create distinct competitive advantages. This is what an innovation mentality solves for in the workplace and marketplace to enable evolution in any business and industry and drive growth.

Are you ready to own all this in your leadership and business? If you have the courage to commit to the innovation mentality; have the will to unleash your passionate pursuits; are ready to believe in yourself and your people, and see, sow, grow, and share opportunities previously unseen; and can break free from the substitutional thinking of the past . . . then the possibilities are truly endless. It's time for you to become a natural explorer of what is in front of you and reclaim the innovation mentality America has lost.

APPENDIX

A PRIMER ON WHAT THE SIX CHARACTERISTICS SOLVE

Almost every company has a mission or vision statement or a set of values that define that mission. Before reading the following list, identify the most important words in yours and write them down. Then, figure out *the lead, support, and any other characteristic that solves for it.* Once you do that, take a look at the list that follows and see what I think the lead characteristic is.

1. *See Opportunity in Everything*
   - Addressing blind spots
   - Alignment
   - Ambiguity
   - Broaden perspectives
   - Build on positive momentum
   - Close-mindedness
   - Education
   - Enable thinking

- Exploration
- Fill gaps
- Guiding principles
- Lack of innovation
- Maximizing potential
- Myopic vision
- Nothing left off the table
- Overcoming skepticism
- Overcoming perceived obstacles
- Possibilities
- Shared beliefs
- Significance: the "why"

2. *Anticipate the Unexpected*
   - Avoiding blind spots
   - Excelling in environment of uncertainty
   - Expectation
   - Linear thinking
   - Minimizing disruption
   - Need for momentum
   - Preparedness
   - Proactive understanding
   - Resetting the strategy
   - Risk management
   - Risk mitigation
   - Security shield
   - Short sightedness
   - Situational awareness
   - Threats from competition
   - Unintended consequences

3. *Unleash Your Passionate Pursuits*
   - Complacency
   - Embracing change
   - Exploration
   - Fear of change

- Lack of intimacy
- Need for momentum
- Overcoming fear of failure
- Persistence
- Resiliency
- Solve constraint
- Status quo
- Taking ownership
- Turnaround

4. *Live with an Entrepreneurial Spirit*
   - Aligning expertise
   - Alignment
   - Beginning of the culture play
   - Breaking down silos
   - Clarity
   - Definition of "resources"
   - Eliminate mediocrity
   - Embrace diversity of thought
   - Execution/can do
   - Figuring out a way to evolve
   - Growing with people
   - Long-term success
   - Maximizing potential
   - Operationalizing change
   - Poor resource alignment
   - Poor relationships
   - Resource utilization
   - Solving for meaningful disconnects
   - Strengthens engagement
5. *Work with a Generous Purpose*
   - Cohesion/unity
   - Create engagement
   - Development of people
   - Expectation

- Genuine interest in people
- Need or influence
- Lack of common purpose
- Lack of intimacy
- Lack of loyalty
- Leading by example
- Mentorship
- Potential/growth
- Reduces negative aspects of individualism
- Selfishness
- Shared beliefs over corporate values
- Significance: the "why"
- Social responsibility
- Survive to thrive
- Territorialism

6. *Lead to Leave a Legacy*
   - Alignment
   - Building a great culture
   - Continuity
   - Culture inefficiency
   - Expectation
   - External perception
   - Fragmentation
   - Greater good
   - How deep is your footprint?
   - Need for influence
   - Lack of empathy
   - Long-term growth
   - Purpose-driven culture
   - Shortsightedness and short-term focus
   - Significance: the "why"
   - Sustainability
   - Teamwork

ACKNOWLEDGMENTS

Annette Llopis: Your love, devotion, and patience have fueled my courage to make a difference in this world. You breathe strength into my soul. I love you.

Annabella Llopis: You are the miracle of my life. Your spirit drives me to create a better pathway for your future. I love you.

Frank Llopis: Your wisdom from heaven continues to influence and inspire my dreams and ambitions. I love and miss you, Dad.

Jenny Llopis: Your motherly love and Cuban idioms drive me to be the best son, father, brother, husband. I love you, Mom.

Eric Llopis: Thank you for having my back and pushing me to reach my full potential. Love you, bro.

Jim Eber: Without your genius, the content doesn't tell the entire story nor do I complete my sentences with the intended purpose and significance. You will always be my "with," and I am honored and grateful.

Michael O'Neill: Your masterful ways always make the content stronger. Your teaching me the power of word sequence will always be appreciated.

Guilherme Oliveira: Thank you for pushing the organization to think bigger and better. You're beyond your years in wisdom, and I am excited about your future.

Sandy Sickler: Thank you for being an important part of the journey and providing our clients clarity and understanding of our mission.

Jen Dorsey, Vanessa Campos, and Karen Billipp: I could not imagine a better team behind the book than Entrepreneur Press. Thank you for valuing our words and ideas.

Steve Handley: Since childhood you've been the one I can always count on. Thank you for your loyalty.

Walter Fawcett: You always inspire me to think bigger. Thank you for your unconditional support.

Adlai Wertman: I will forever be grateful that you always have my best interests at heart. You've never let me down, and I appreciate your wisdom.

Jim Beran: Your wisdom has fueled me during the toughest times of my journey. Thank you for always being there for me.

Roland Schertenleib: Thank you for your artistry, strategic thinking, and design brilliance in elevating the organization's brand.

Lou Mercado: Thank you for valuing diversity of thought. Your ability to work with a generous purpose is a testament to your leadership and ability to focus on the advancement of others.

Clay and Terry Corwin: Thank you for your special friendship and constant reminders of the fundamentals. It's why Lion's Heart will continue to change lives of young leaders.

Marisa Salcines: Thank you for your commitment to strengthening the message of the immigrant perspective.

Steve Schooler: Thank you for always believing and having faith in the journey.

Alberto Benito-Canales: Thank you for dedication and tireless commitment strengthening our client engagement.

Mark DeBellis: Thank you for your mentorship and always taking the time to guide me.

Brad Lea: Thank you for pushing me to keep charging and inspiring others to do the same. You are the original rhino.

Rich Melcombe: Your uncommon ways provided clarity and common sense. Thank you for pushing me to see more.

John Nackel: Thank you for guiding me to see the impact of operationalizing the CDS in the health-care industry and for the wisdom to understand that saving lives and ROI are not mutually exclusive.

Lee Lubin: You are one of the smartest people I know, and our bond is unbreakable. Thank you for protecting my intellectual capital and business interests for over 20 years.

Mike Fernandez: You have represented such an important part of my journey in such a short period of time and I am tremendously grateful.

Magic Johnson and all the leaders who attended my "Preparing U.S. Leadership for the Seismic Cultural Demographic Shift" summit: Your stories and thoughts were powerful, insightful, and inspiring.

And finally thank you to my clients for believing in and supporting *The Innovation Mentality*. Without your trust and willingness to take a leap of faith to evolve this book could not be.

ABOUT THE AUTHOR

Glenn Llopis (pronounced 'yō-pēs) is the Chairman of the Glenn Llopis Group—a nationally recognized thought-leadership, human capital, and business strategy consulting firm.

Glenn is best known as the "Opportunity Expert" because of his expertise in identifying and solving for business opportunity gaps that others don't see. Through his work both independently and through the Glenn Llopis Group, he guides leaders and organizations to embrace a new type of thinking that helps them evolve and stay ahead of the rapid changes in the workplace and marketplace. Glenn shows those leaders and organizations how to break free from old ways of doing things that slow down growth and make it difficult to create distinct competitive advantages. This is what an innovation mentality solves for in the workplace and marketplace to enable evolution in any business and industry: driving growth through the Cultural Demographic Shift™, leadership identity (maximizing organizational and marketplace growth), strengthening corporate cultures and organizational teams, and identifying and closing opportunity gaps.

A UCLA graduate, Glenn fast-tracked at the Gallo Wine Company and Sunkist Juice Beverages where he became the youngest executive in the company's 100-year history. Leading the successful turnaround of Sunkist's juice beverage division opened the door for his next endeavor—at only 30 years old—as a senior executive at American Seafoods Company. The result was an increase in market share, new brand introductions, and a full-scale transformation of the company. Glenn then went on to form his own successful food business before transitioning into his current role as a consultant, executive coach, and keynote speaker to Fortune 500 companies. In 1997, Glenn founded the Center for Hispanic Leadership (CHL) Academy, which creates competitive advantage for Fortune 500 companies through their development and advancement of top Hispanic talent.

In addition to *The Innovation Mentality*, Glenn is the best-selling author of the book, *Earning Serendipity* (2009) and contributing writer to *Forbes*, *Huffington Post*, *Entrepreneur*, and *The Harvard Business Review*. In 2014, he was recognized as a top 20 influential writer at Forbes and a top 100 leadership speaker and business thinker by *Inc. Magazine*.

Glenn is a member of the Kellogg Innovation Network, serves on the advisory board of the Brittingham Social Enterprise Lab at the Marshall School of Business at the University of Southern California, and is a board member at Lion's Heart, a teen volunteering and leadership nonprofit organization. He is also a mentor for Junior Achievement and a member of the exclusive Renaissance Weekend think-tank. Glenn is frequently featured as a business leadership expert on CNN, Fox News, Bloomberg, Univision, ABC, NBC, and CBS. He lives in California with his family.

You can connect to Glenn through www.theinnovationmentality.com and www.glennllopisgroup.com.

INDEX

D

E

I Want to Hear from You!

Join Us at

www.innovationmentality.com

Now that you've finished the book, let's continue the conversation and evolve together starting at the official *Innovation Mentality* landing page. This is more than just an open invitation to evolve together: My goal is to explore the breadth and depth of what *The Innovation Mentality* can solve for in you and your organization. My commitment is to respond to and discuss your questions and personal stories about how you and your organization connected to *The Innovation Mentality*. I will also provide links to exercises to help your organization, its leaders, and you create even greater clarity and understanding to apply what we have covered in the book. This application is the key to pulling everyone further into the ecosystem of the six characteristics and influencing evolutionary thinking.

Until then, I encourage you and your organization to be courageous and vulnerable—allow your leadership identity to blossom so you both can see what others don't, do what others won't, and keep pushing until prudence says quit.